T0224481

Communications in Computer and Information Science 861

Commenced Publication in 2007
Founding and Former Series Editors:
Phoebe Chen, Alfredo Cuzzocrea, Xiaoyong Du, Orhun Kara, Ting Liu,
Krishna M. Sivalingam, Dominik Ślęzak, Takashi Washio, and Xiaokang Yang

More information about this series at http://www.springer.com/series/7899

Zheng Li · He Jiang · Ge Li ·
Minghui Zhou · Ming Li (Eds.)

Software Engineering and Methodology for Emerging Domains

16th National Conference, NASAC 2017
Harbin, China, November 4–5, 2017
and 17th National Conference, NASAC 2018
Shenzhen, China, November 23–25, 2018
Revised Selected Papers

 Springer

Editors
Zheng Li ⓘ
Beijing University of Chemical Technology
Beijing, China

He Jiang ⓘ
Beijing Institute of Technology
Beijing, China

Ge Li
Peking University
Beijing, China

Minghui Zhou
Peking University
Beijing, China

Ming Li
Nanjing University
Nanjing, China

ISSN 1865-0929   ISSN 1865-0937 (electronic)
Communications in Computer and Information Science
ISBN 978-981-15-0309-2   ISBN 978-981-15-0310-8 (eBook)
https://doi.org/10.1007/978-981-15-0310-8

This Springer imprint is published by the registered company Springer Nature Singapore Pte Ltd.
The registered company address is: 152 Beach Road, #21-01/04 Gateway East, Singapore 189721, Singapore

Preface

The National Software Application Conference (NASAC) is the annual conference of the CCF Technical Committees of Software Engineering and System Software.

NASAC 2017, the 16th event in the series, had a special theme on "Intelligent Software Engineering," which focused on the application of Artificial Intelligence (AI) techniques to Software Engineering (SE) problems. The work is typified by recent advances in SBSE, but also by long established work in probabilistic reasoning and machine learning for SE. As a result of this area, the SE community has adopted, adapted, and exploited many of the practical algorithms, methods, and techniques that have emerged from the AI community. In the other aspect, software repositories are growing exponentially, and new datacenters hosting tens of thousands of open source software projects are being developed around the world. SE has truly entered the era of big data, which demands further more AI techniques.

NASAC 2018, the 17th event in the series, had a special theme on "Software Mining," since software systems have been playing important roles in business, scientific research, and our everyday lives. It is critical to improve both software productivity and quality, which are major challenges to SE researchers and practitioners. In recent years, software mining has emerged as a promising means to address these challenges. It has been successfully applied to discover knowledge from software artifacts (e.g., specifications, source code, documentations, execution logs, and bug reports) to improve software quality and development process (e.g., to obtain the insights for the causes leading to poor software quality, to help software engineers locate and identify problems quickly, and to help the managers optimize the resources for better productivity). Software mining has attracted much attention in both SE and data mining communities.

Both NASAC 2017 and NASAC 2018 called for high-quality submissions describing original and significant work. The submissions must not have been previously published or considered for publication elsewhere.

NASAC 2017 received 11 submissions (English track only, Chinese track not counted). After a thorough reviewing process, four papers were selected for presentation as full papers. We further called for submissions with the same theme, and received six submissions. Two more full papers were accepted after reviewing.

NASAC 2018 received 20 submissions and all of these submissions went through a rigorous reviewing process. Most submissions received three reviews. The track chairs examined all the reviews to further guarantee the reliability and integrity of the reviewing process. Finally, five papers were accepted.

The high-quality program would not have been possible without the authors who chose NASAC 2017 and 2018 as a venue for their publications. We are also very grateful to the Program Committee members and Organizing Committee members, who put a tremendous amount of effort into soliciting and selecting research papers with a balance of high quality and new ideas. Last but not least, we also want to thank all authors for their contributions and support.

We hope that you enjoy reading and benefit from the proceedings of NASAC 2017 and 2018.

August 2019

Zheng Li
He Jiang
Ge Li
Minghui Zhou
Ming Li

Organization

NASAC 2017 (16th National Software Application Conference) was organized by the CCF Technical Committees of Software Engineering and System Software and hosted by Harbin Institute of Technology. The conference comprises both an English Track and a Chinese Track. The following lists only the program chairs and Program Committee for the English Track.

Organizing Committee

English Track Program Chairs

Zheng Li	Beijing University of Chemical Technology, China
He Jiang	Dalian University of Technology, China
Ge Li	Peking University, China

English Track Program Members

Xiaoying Bai	Tsinghua University, China
Yan Cai	Chinese Academy of Sciences, China
Yuting Chen	Shanghai Jiao Tong University, China
Lin Chen	Nanjing University, China
Wei Dong	National University of Defence Technology, China
Dunwei Gong	China University of Mining and Technology, China
Dan Hao	Peking University, China
Jiang He	Dalian University of Technology, China
Yue Jia	University College London, UK
Bo Jiang	Beihang University, China
Ge Li	Peking University, China
Yang Liu	Nanyang Technological University, Singapore
Changhai Nie	Nanjing University, China
Xin Peng	Fudan University, China
Ju Qian	Nanjing University of Aeronautics and Astronautics, China
Xiaokang Qiu	Purdue University, USA
Chang-Ai Sun	University of Science and Technology Beijing, China
Jun Sun	Singapore University of Technology and Design, Singapore
Xin Xia	University of British Columbia, Canada
Xiaoyuan Xie	Wuhan University, China

Chang Xu	Nanjing University, China
Jifeng Xuan	Wuhan University, China
Jun Yan	Chinese Academy of Sciences, China
Zijiang Yang	Western Michigan University, USA
Hongyu Zhang	Microsoft Research Asia, China
Jian Zhang	Chinese Academy of Sciences, China
Lu Zhang	Peking University, China
Tao Zhang	Harbin Engineering University, China
Jianjun Zhao	Kyushu University, Japan

NASAC 2018 (17th National Software Application Conference) was organized by the CCF Technical Committees of Software Engineering and System Software and hosted by Shenzhen University. The conference comprises both an English Track and a Chinese Track. The following lists only the program chairs and Program Committee for the English Track.

Track Chairs

Minghui Zhou	Peking University, China
Ming Li	Nanjing University, China

Program Committee

Yan Cai	Institute of Software, Chinese Academy of Sciences, China
Jeff Huang	Texas A&M University, USA
Liguo Huang	Southern Methodist University
Xuan Huo	Nanjing University, China
He Jiang	Dalian University of Technology, China
Jing Jiang	Beihang University, China
Zheng Li	Beijing University of Chemical Technology, China
Lin Liu	Tsinghua University, China
David Lo	Singapore Management University, Singapore
Xinjun Mao	National University of Defense Technology, China
Xin Peng	Fudan University, China
Xiaokang Qiu	Purdue University, USA
Tao Wang	National University of Defense Technology, China
Xin Xia	Monash University, Australia
Xiaoyuan Xie	Wuhan University, China
Chang Xu	Nanjing University, China
Jifeng Xuan	Wuhan University, China
Hongyu Zhang	The University of Newcastle, Australia
Yuming Zhou	Nanjing University, China
Jiaxin Zhu	Institute of Software, Chinese Academy of Sciences, China

Organizers

Organized by

China Computer Federation (CCF), China

Hosted by
CCF Technical Committees of Software Engineering and System Software, and

Harbin Institute of Technology   Shenzhen University

Contents

Intelligent Software Engineering (NASAC 2017 English Track/CSBSE 2017)

Learning to Generate Comments for API-Based Code Snippets

Yangyang Lu[1,2], Zelong Zhao[1,2], Ge Li[1,2(✉)], and Zhi Jin[1,2(✉)]

[1] Key Lab of High-Confidence Software Technology (Peking University),
Ministry of Education, Beijing 100871, China
{luyy,zhaozl,lige,zhijin}@pku.edu.cn
[2] School of Electronics Engineering and Computer Science,
Peking University, Beijing 100871, China

Abstract. Comments play an important role in software developments. They can not only improve the readability and maintainability of source code, but also provide significant resource for software reuse. However, it is common that lots of code in software projects lacks of comments. Automatic comment generation is proposed to address this issue. In this paper, we present an end-to-end approach to generate comments for API-based code snippets automatically. It takes API sequences as the core semantic representations of method-level API-based code snippets and generates comments from API sequences with sequence-to-sequence neural models. In our evaluation, we extract 217K pairs of code snippets and comments from Java projects to construct the dataset. Finally, our approach gains 36.48% BLEU-4 score and 9.90% accuracy on the test set. We also do case studies on generated comments, which presents that our approach generates reasonable and effective comments for API-based code snippets.

Keywords: API sequences · Comment generation ·
Deep neural networks

1 Introduction

Code comments are an important part of software projects. Previous research has shown that adding comments to code snippets could help developers understand the functionality of code more effectively, and improve the readability and maintainability of software projects [21,22,26]. Furthermore, comments are usually viewed as significant resource for software reuse tasks, such as code retrieval and bug report generation [14,18]. However, writing comments is a labor-intensive operation which is often delayed or ignored by developers [12,19]. Therefore, the lack of code comments is a common problem in software development.

To address the absence problem of comments, lots of work has been done to generate code comments automatically. Early research uses rule-based approaches [1,5,10,20,27], which usually define heuristic rules to extract the

© Springer Nature Singapore Pte Ltd. 2019
Z. Li et al. (Eds.): NASAC 2017/2018, CCIS 861, pp. 3–14, 2019.
https://doi.org/10.1007/978-981-15-0310-8_1

content from code snippets and combine them with predefined templates to gain comments. They often require additional domain knowledge and can only generate restricted comments with templates. Then researchers proposed keyword-based approaches [8,13] which leverage latent semantic analysis techniques to extract keywords from code snippets. But the final outputs of these approaches are actually key-word lists rather than common comment sentences. After that, retrieval-based approaches [24,25] leverage existed code snippets and comments in Q&A web-sites and open source projects, then use code clone and information retrieval to retrieve comments of code snippets that implementing similar functions as final comments. However, they heavily rely on the efficiency and accuracy of code clone detection.

To avoid the above issues of previous approaches, language model based approaches are proposed. They learn language models from corpora of code snippets and corresponding comments by probabilistic models [15] or deep neural networks [2,3,11], then predict comments word by word based on the learnt language models. On this basis, machine translation models are further introduced into automatic comment generation recently, which take comment generation as a translation task from code snippets to comment sentences. Related preliminary work [9,16] has been done to generate pseudo-code from code snippets. They show that end-to-end comment generation approaches of machine translation ideas are feasible and effective.

In this paper, we focus on the task of comment generation for API-based code snippets. With the growth of software projects' scale, more and more developers rely on API libraries to implement expected requirements [23]. Generating comments for API-based code snippets could help developers understand, modify and reuse existed code resource, which is beneficial to development activities relied on API libraries.

We propose an end-to-end approach to generate comments for API-based code snippets, which extracts method-level API sequences and applies machine translation neural networks. Research work on API reuse [18,28], like API usage recommendation, treats API sequences as abstract functionality representations of method-level API-based code snippets. Our approach follows this assumption and generates comments for API-based code snippets by translating API sequences to comment sentences with deep neural networks. We leverage open source Java projects data from Github, extract pairs of method-level API sequences and comments as training and test datasets, and learn end-to-end neural networks of comment generation for API-based code snippets. The evaluation result of 36.48% BLEU-4 score and the case study on 24K generated comments show the effectiveness of our approach. To the best of our knowledge, our work is the first to generate comments for API-based code snippets with extracted API sequences via end-to-end neural networks.

The rest of this paper is organized as follows: Sect. 2 illustrates our approach of comment generation for API-based code snippets with API sequences. Section 3 introduces the dataset information, quantitative evaluation results and qualitative case studies. Section 4 gives the conclusion and discusses future work.

2   Approach

2.1   Overview

In this paper, we extract API sequences from API-based code snippets and train generative translation models to encode functional semantics implicated in API sequences and translate them for predicting corresponding comments word by word. Thus our approach contains two stages: the offline training stage and online test stage.

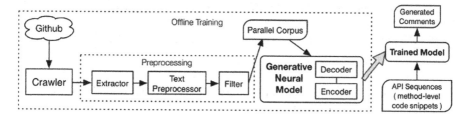

Fig. 1. Overview of our approach.

Figure 1 shows the overview of our approach. The offline training stage is composed of corpus crawling, data preprocessing and model training. We first crawl Java software projects updated before April 2016 from Github[1] and keep source code files from projects of which stars are at top-5K ranking. Then we use AST toolkits to extract API sequences and comments from method-level code snippets of crawled projects. After text preprocessing on comments and filtering operations based on statistical information of corpus, we finally get the parallel corpus of API sequences and comments (Details are presented in Sect. 3.1). Table 1 shows a pair of API sequence and comment extracted from a method-level API-based code snippet. It can be seen that the extracted API sequence keeps the core functional semantics of this code snippet.

With the parallel corpus of API sequences and comments, we build and train generative neural models based on the idea of machine translation. Figure 1 shows the basic components - an encoder and a decoder. The encoder accepts API sequences as inputs and learn to understand their implicated semantics. The decoder predicts comments word by word based on context information provided by the encoder. With the trained encoder and decoder, comments can be generated word by word from API sequences of API-based code snippets in the online test stage.

2.2   Models of Generating Comments from API Sequences

In this paper, we treat comment generation from API-based code snippets as a translation task from API sequences to comment sentences, and leverage two sequence-to-sequence neural networks to generate comments from API

---

[1] https://github.com.

Table 1. An Example of The Extracted API Sequence and Comment

```
1  /**
2   * Returns the screen/display size
3   *
4   * @param context
5   * @return
6   */
7   public static Point getDisplaySize(Context context) {
8       WindowManager wm = (WindowManager) context.getSystemService(Context.WINDOW_SERVICE);
9       Display display = wm.getDefaultDisplay();
10      Point size = new Point();
11      display.getSize(size);
12      int width = size.x;
13      int height = size.y;
14      return new Point(width, height);
15  }
```

$android.content.Context.getSystemService \rightarrow$
$android.view.WindowManager.getDefaultDisplay \rightarrow android.graphics.Point.new \rightarrow$
$android.view.Display.getSize \rightarrow android.graphics.Point.new$
▷ returns the screen display size

sequences. Sequence-to-sequence neural networks remove the aligning process in traditional statistical machine translation models and implement the end-to-end translation.

We first apply the sequence-to-sequence neural network in the literature [7] on comment generation from API sequences (annotated as "seq2seq"). As shown in Fig. 2(a), the seq2seq model consists of two recurrent neural networks as the encoder and decoder separately. Given an API sequence $(x_1, x_2, ..., x_m)$, the encoder accepts it as the input and encodes the whole sequence into a fix-sized context vector c. The decoder accepts c and predicts the comment output $(y_1, y_2, ..., y_n)$ word by word from the empty symbol "⟨ GO ⟩" to the terminal symbol "⟨ EOS ⟩". The prediction objective is to maximize the conditional probability $P(y_1, y_2, ..., y_n | x_1, x_2, ..., x_m)$. According to the predicting process in seq2seq, it can be computed as follows:

$$P(y_1, y_2, ..., y_n | x_1, x_2, ..., x_m) = \prod_{t=1}^{n} p(y_t | y_1, y_2, ..., y_{t-1}) \tag{1}$$

To train the seq2seq model on the whole corpus D, the objective function is to maximize the average log-likelihood of generating the correct comment S_{com} from the API sequence S_{api}:

$$J = \frac{1}{|D|} \sum_{(S_{api}, S_{com}) \in D} \log p(S_{com} | S_{api}) \tag{2}$$

Furthermore, we find that words in comments show latent alignment relations with API methods in the API sequences. For example, "display" aligns to the API method "android.view.WindowManager.getDefaultDisplay" and "size" to "android.view.Display.getSize" in Table 1. Besides, we find that API sequences in the corpus may be long (detailed in Sect. 3.1). Existed experimental study on machine translation using seq2seq models shows that evaluation results will decrease with the growth of input length when the length of the test set is larger

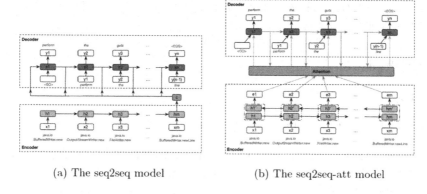

(a) The seq2seq model   (b) The seq2seq-att model

Fig. 2. Comment generation from API sequences.

than the length of the training set [6]. To capture the latent alignment relations between API sequences and comments and improve the encoding effect on long sequences, we further introduce the attention-based sequence-to-sequence model in the literature [4] into our task (annotated as "seq2seq-at").

As shown in Fig. 2(b), the seq2seq-att model adds an "Attention" module between the encoder and the decoder. The encoder transfers the input API sequence $(x_1, x_2, ..., x_m)$ into an intermediate sequence $(e_1, e_2, ..., e_m)$ rather than a context vector in the seq2seq model. When the decoder predicts the word at i-th position of the comment, the corresponding hidden state s_i is computed by the previous hidden state s_{i-1}, the previous predicted word y_{i-1} and a specific context vector c_i as follows:

$$s_i = f(s_{i-1}, y_{i-1}, c_i) \tag{3}$$

The specific context vector c_i is gained from the attention module based on the intermediate sequence $(e_1, e_2, ..., e_m)$ of the encoder and the predicted sequence of the decoder. The process can be described by the following equations.

$$c_i = \sum_{j=1}^{m} \alpha_{ij} e_j \tag{4}$$

$$\alpha_{ij} = \frac{\exp(v_{ij})}{\sum_{k=1}^{m} \exp(v_{ik})} \tag{5}$$

$$v_{ij} = a(s_{i-1}, e_j) \tag{6}$$

In the above equations, the function a plays the role of aligning API methods in the API sequence and words in the comment. The weight α_{ij} can be seen as the probability of translating the comment word y_j from the API method x_i. The attention module is usually implemented with a multilayer perceptron so that the whole seq2seq-att model could be trained by stochastic gradient descent.

Finally, the objective function of the seq2seq-att model is the same as the one of seq2seq model (Eq. 2).

3 Evaluation

3.1 Dataset

We build our dataset of parallel API sequences and comments according to the following steps:

First we crawl open source Java projects until April 2016 from Github. Based on the star ranking of projects, we keep source code files of the top-5K projects as the preliminary dataset.

Then we use Eclipse JDT to parse method-level code snippets into AST trees and extract API sequences and corresponding comments. First sentences under "JavaDoc Comment" nodes of AST trees are used as comments. We ignore method code without comments. As for API sequences, we mainly extract APIs in JDK and Android libraries. Because we do statistics on projects' tags and API library frequency with "import" statements, then find that most crawled projects are related to mobile developement and API libraries of high frequencies are JDK and Android. Eclipse JDT could extract JDK APIs from code snippets directly from AST trees, but fail on Android APIs. Thus we combine "import" statements and the package list of Android library to identify Android method calls in AST trees. Then API sequences of JDK and Android APIs are extracted as the order of method calls in code snippets.

As for extracted comments, we filter JavaDoc marks such as "@link" and "@code", remove HTML tags, split sentences into word sequences by whitespaces, decompose words in the CamelCase format and finally do the lowercase transformation.

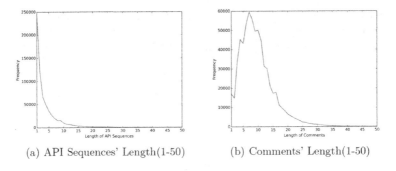

(a) API Sequences' Length(1-50)   (b) Comments' Length(1-50)

Fig. 3. Distribution of length on API sequences and comments.

After that, we do statistics on the length of API sequences and comments. The longest length of API sequences and comments is 6, 325 and 389 respectively, and the average lengths are 4.42 and 9.81 respectively. The distributions of their lengths are shown in Fig. 3. So we set the length scopes of API sequences and comments both as [3,20], then we remove samples with too long or too short lengths from the dataset.

Finally, we get 217, 156 pairwise samples of API sequences and comments after the length filtering operation. The 217K samples are split as the ratio of 8 : 1 : 1 for training, validation and test. According to the training set, we get the vocabularies of API methods and words in comments, of which the size is 24, 511 and 22, 491 respectively. We cut 24K API methods and 22K words of high frequencies as the final vocabularies.

3.2 Experimental Settings

We implement the two generative models by tensorflow 1.0.1[2]. All the encoders and decoders use LSTM as hidden layers. The unit number of LSTM is 512. We make experiments of 2 and 3 layers for each model. The iterative number of training epochs is set to 50 for all the experiments. We train the models on servers with NVIDIA GeForce GTX 1080 GPU and 16 GB DDR4 memory. It takes about 7 to 8 h to train each model. The attention-based models need more training time than models without attention under the same epoch number.

3.3 Results

Here we use two metrics, BLEU and Accuracy, to evaluate generated comments in the test set.

BLEU is the specific metric proposed for machine translation [17], which reflects how close the generated translation are in words and length to human-expected references. The computation of BLEU is fast and independent of specific languages. BLEU is effected by the n-gram overlap ratio and a penalty weight of length differences between candidate translations and reference translations. Here we use the nltk 3.2.1[3] toolkit to compute BLEU scores under 1-gram to 4-gram (annotated as BLEU-1 to BLEU-4).

We also want to know how many comments could be generated correctly, that is the same as the original sentences. Then accuracy is used to evaluate this aspect, computed by the ratio of correctly generated comments in the whole test set.

To the best of our knowledge, we are the first to generate comments for API-based snippets with API sequences. Currently we haven't found appropriate baselines from previous work. So we first compare results between groups of different experimental settings. Table 2 shows the BLEU and accuracy scores.

It can been seen that the attention mechanism could improve the scores of both BLEU and accuracy under the same number of hidden units and layers. The growth of hidden layers is also beneficial to the results. Then we take the

---

[2] https://www.tensorflow.org.
[3] https://www.versioneye.com/python/nltk/3.2.1.

Table 2. Comment Generation Results: BLEU and Accuracy(%)

Model	Settings	BLEU-1	BLEU-2	BLEU-3	BLEU-4	Accuracy
seq2seq	2 * 512	20.75	25.64	30.01	34.90	8.13
seq2seq	3 * 512	22.45	27.18	31.44	36.21	8.86
seq2seq-att	2 * 512	20.88	25.83	30.22	34.41	9.19
seq2seq-att	3 * 512	22.68	27.54	31.57	36.48	9.90

BLEU scores in natural language machine translation [4,7] as an indirect reference. The 34.90% $\sim$ 36.48% BLEU-4 scores have achieved the numerical level of current machine translation tasks, which shows the feasibility and effectiveness of generating comments from API sequences with our approach.

What's more, we do case studies on generated comments of the test set. We split generated results into three groups: (1) totally correct, that is as same as the original comments; (2) with high BLEU scores: results of which BLEU-1 scores are higher than 50%, that is sharing more than half of words with original comments; (3) with low BLEU scores: results left after filtering by (1) and (2). Table 3 shows partial cases of the above three groups. For each case, the lines present the API sequence, the original comment and the generated comment (in bold). By analyzing cases of generated results, we can find the that:

– Our approach could generate exactly correct comments from API sequences of different lengths (Case 1–2), which validates the capability of our approach to encode API sequences and decode comments.
– As for the results of high BLEU scores, they are different from original comments mainly in three aspects: word absence, word redundancy and word substitution.

Case 3 shows an example of word absence. The generated comment loses the word "negative". After observing the corresponding API sequence, we can find that the generated comment captures the correct functionality. The word "negative" is not reflected by the API sequence. We find that missing words are usually attributive nouns or adjectives. We think the reason of word absence is the semantic abstraction of API sequences, which may lose some words related to specific variables.

Case 4 shows an example of word redundancy, which predict "views" twice. When the decoder is confused about prediction, it seems to prefer words of high frequency or words related to the generated history part and predict existed words repeatedly. The reason may relate to the low co-occurrence of some words in the corpus, which makes it hard to capture their semantic relationship by our approach.

Case 4 also shows an example of word substitution. The word "puts" is replaced by its synonym "inserts" in the generated comment. Interestingly, we find that our approach may replace words in original comments with antonyms. In Case 5 , the word "close" is replaced by "open" and "hide" by "show" since API methods in its corresponding API sequence could also

Table 3. Generation comment from API sequences in the test set

Correct Results
① *android.graphics.Rect.new* → *android.graphics.Paint.descent* → *android.graphics.Paint.ascent*
▷ determines the height of this view
▷ **determines the height of this view**
② *android.content.res.Resources.getDisplayMetrics* → *java.lang.OutOfMemoryError.new* → *android.graphics.Bitmap.setDensity* → *android.graphics.Canvas.new* → *android.graphics.Canvas.setBitmap* → *android.graphics.Canvas.new* → *android.graphics.Bitmap.eraseColor* → *android.graphics.Canvas.save* → *android.graphics.Canvas.scale* → *android.graphics.Canvas.translate* → *android.graphics.Canvas.restoreToCount* → *android.graphics.Canvas.setBitmap*
▷ create snapshot of the view into bitmap
▷ **create snapshot of the view into bitmap**
Results of High BLEU Scores
③ *java.math.BigInteger.new* → *java.math.BigInteger.new* → *java.math.BigInteger.add* → *java.math.BigInteger.toByteArray* → *java.math.BigInteger.signum*
▷ add two negative numbers of different length
▷ **add two numbers of different length**
④ *android.view.View.getLayoutParams* → *java.util.ArrayList.add* → *android.view.View.dispatchStartTemporaryDetach* → *android.view.View.hasTransientState* → *android.util.LongSparseArray.new* → *android.util.SparseArray.new* → *java.util.ArrayList.add* → *java.util.ArrayList.add*
▷ puts view into the list of scrap views
▷ **inserts view into the list of views views**
⑤ *android.support.v4.widget.ViewDragHelper.smoothSlideViewTo* → *android.support.v4.widget.ViewDragHelper.abort* → *android.view.View.layout* → *android.view.View.layout*
▷ close the panel to hide the secondary view
▷ **open the panel to show the secondary view**
⑥ *java.lang.Class.getClassLoader* → *java.lang.Class.getName* → *java.lang.String.replaceAll* → *java.lang.ClassLoader.getResources* → *java.util.Enumeration.hasMoreElements* → *java.util.Enumeration.nextElement* → *java.net.URL.getProtocol* → *java.lang.String.equals* → *java.net.URL.getPath* → *java.lang.String.startsWith* → *java.lang.String.length* → *java.lang.String.substring* → *java.lang.String.replaceAll* → *java.net.URLDecoder.decode* → *java.lang.String.replaceAll*
▷ finds the path to jar that contains the class provided if any
▷ **find jar that contains class of the same name if any**
Results of Low BLEU Scores
⑦ *java.lang.Object.getClass* → *java.lang.Class.getDeclaredField* → *java.lang.reflect.AccessibleObject.setAccessible* → *java.lang.reflect.Field.get* → *java.lang.Throwable.getLocalizedMessage* → *java.io.IOException.new* → *java.lang.Throwable.getLocalizedMessage*
▷ given sql router connection retrieve the encapsulated connection
▷ **extracts the jdbc jdbc connection output stream of the mysql server**
⑧ *android.graphics.Picture.new* → *android.graphics.Picture.beginRecording* → *android.graphics.Picture.endRecording*
▷ renders this svg document to picture object
▷ **creates new picture file using given file**
⑨ *java.lang.IllegalArgumentException.new* → *android.graphics.Bitmap.compress* → *java.io.OutputStream.flush* → *java.io.OutputStream.close*
▷ writes the tags from this exif interface object into jpeg compressed bitmap removing prior exif tags
▷ **adds bitmap to the compressed stream**

be used to implement the opposite operations. Furthermore, our approach could generate comments with similar meaning of original comments by paraphrasing (Case 6). The above phenomenons present that our approach could understand semantics of API sequences mostly, learn the language model of comments and predict the comment effectively.
- The results of low BLEU scores could be divided into meaningless sentences and ones with clear semantics. The former mainly contains empty sentences and results with too many repetitive words. We think the problems may come from continuously repetitive APIs of API sequences, out-of-vocabulary words in original comments or the mismatching relations of semantics between API sequences and comments.

Then in the latter ones, most of them are irrelevant to original comments in the functional semantics. There are also some interesting results that hold relevant semantics but gain low BLEU scores. They may describe similar functionality of the original comments but with different words and order (Case 7-8). Furthermore, they may present more general meaning than original comments, but match the corresponding API sequences, since API sequences hold abstract semantics of the code snippets.

4   Conclusion

In this paper, we propose an end-to-end approach to generate comments for API-based code snippets automatically. It leverages API sequences to represent the core semantics of code snippets and generates comments from API sequences with sequence-to-sequence neural networks. Our approach trains generative neural models by parallel API sequences and comments extracted from open source Java projects. The experiments achieve 36.48% BLEU-4 score (machine translation metric) and 9.90% accuracy (exactly correct generation). Further case studies on results of correct, high and low BLEU scores show the feasibility and effectiveness of our approach. To the best of our knowledge, we are the first to generate comments for API-based code snippets from API sequences in a way of translation. To improve the results of comment generation for API-based code snippet-s, the following aspects can be explored in future work: (1) Make fine-grained filtering on the corpus, such as refining comments with POS tagging and removing continuously repetitive APIs in API sequences; (2) Leverage information of AST trees. We discard the structural information and other identifiers here. If we could combine them with current API sequences and use a recursive neural network in the encoder, comment generation results may be improved with more context.

References

1. Abid, N.J., Dragan, N., Collard, M.L., Maletic, J.I.: Using stereotypes in the automatic generation of natural language summaries for C++ methods. In: 2015 IEEE International Conference on Software Maintenance and Evolution (ICSME), pp. 561–565. IEEE (2015)

2. Allamanis, M., Barr, E.T., Bird, C., Sutton, C.: Suggesting accurate method and class names. In: Proceedings of the 2015 10th Joint Meeting on Foundations of Software Engineering, pp. 38–49. ACM (2015)
3. Allamanis, M., Peng, H., Sutton, C.: A convolutional attention network for extreme summarization of source code. In: International Conference on Machine Learning, pp. 2091–2100 (2016)
4. Bahdanau, D., Cho, K., Bengio, Y.: Neural machine translation by jointly learning to align and translate. arXiv preprint arXiv:1409.0473 (2014)
5. Buse, R.P., Weimer, W.R.: Automatic documentation inference for exceptions. In: Proceedings of the 2008 International Symposium on Software Testing and Analysis, pp. 273–282. Citeseer (2008)
6. Cho, K., Van Merriënboer, B., Bahdanau, D., Bengio, Y.: On the properties of neural machine translation: encoder-decoder approaches. arXiv preprint arXiv:1409.1259 (2014)
7. Cho, K., et al.: Learning phrase representations using RNN encoder-decoder for statistical machine translation. arXiv preprint arXiv:1406.1078 (2014)
8. Haiduc, S., Aponte, J., Marcus, A.: Supporting program comprehension with source code summarization. In: Proceedings of the 32nd ACM/IEEE International Conference on Software Engineering, vol. 2, pp. 223–226. ACM (2010)
9. Haije, T., Intelligentie, B.O.K., Gavves, E., Heuer, H.: Automatic comment generation using a neural translation model. Inf. Softw. Technol. **55**(3), 258–268 (2016)
10. Hill, E., Pollock, L., Vijay-Shanker, K.: Automatically capturing source code context of NL-queries for software maintenance and reuse. In: Proceedings of the 31st International Conference on Software Engineering, pp. 232–242. IEEE Computer Society (2009)
11. Iyer, S., Konstas, I., Cheung, A., Zettlemoyer, L.: Summarizing source code using a neural attention model. In: Proceedings of the 54th Annual Meeting of the Association for Computational Linguistics. Long Papers, vol. 1, pp. 2073–2083 (2016)
12. Kajko-Mattsson, M.: A survey of documentation practice within corrective maintenance. Empirical Softw. Eng. **10**(1), 31–55 (2005)
13. McBurney, P.W., McMillan, C.: Automatic documentation generation via source code summarization of method context. In: Proceedings of the 22nd International Conference on Program Comprehension, pp. 279–290. ACM (2014)
14. Montandon, J.E., Borges, H., Felix, D., Valente, M.T.: Documenting APIs with examples: lessons learned with the apiminer platform. In: 2013 20th Working Conference on Reverse Engineering (WCRE), pp. 401–408. IEEE (2013)
15. Movshovitz-Attias, D., Cohen, W.W.: Natural language models for predicting programming comments. In: Proceedings of the 51st Annual Meeting of the Association for Computational Linguistics. Short Papers, vol. 2, vol. 2, pp. 35–40 (2013)
16. Oda, Y., et al.: Learning to generate pseudo-code from source code using statistical machine translation (t). In: 2015 30th IEEE/ACM International Conference on Automated Software Engineering (ASE), pp. 574–584. IEEE (2015)
17. Papineni, K., Roukos, S., Ward, T., Zhu, W.J.: Bleu: a method for automatic evaluation of machine translation. In: Proceedings of the 40th annual meeting on association for computational linguistics, pp. 311–318. Association for Computational Linguistics (2002)
18. Raghothaman, M., Wei, Y., Hamadi, Y.: Swim: synthesizing what i mean-code search and idiomatic snippet synthesis. In: 2016 IEEE/ACM 38th International Conference on Software Engineering (ICSE), pp. 357–367. IEEE (2016)

19. de Souza, S.C.B., Anquetil, N., de Oliveira, K.M.: A study of the documentation essential to software maintenance. In: Proceedings of the 23rd Annual International Conference on Design of Communication: Documenting & Designing for Pervasive Information, pp. 68–75. ACM (2005)

20. Sridhara, G., Hill, E., Muppaneni, D., Pollock, L., Vijay-Shanker, K.: Towards automatically generating summary comments for java methods. In: Proceedings of the IEEE/ACM International Conference on Automated Software Engineering, pp. 43–52. ACM (2010)

21. Takang, A.A., Grubb, P.A., Macredie, R.D.: The effects of comments and identifier names on program comprehensibility: an experimental investigation. J. Prog. Lang. 4(3), 143–167 (1996)

22. Tenny, T.: Program readability: procedures versus comments. IEEE Trans. Software Eng. 14(9), 1271–1279 (1988)

23. Thung, F., Lo, D., Lawall, J.: Automated library recommendation. In: 2013 20th Working Conference on Reverse Engineering (WCRE), pp. 182–191. IEEE (2013)

24. Wong, E., Liu, T., Tan, L.: Clocom: mining existing source code for automatic comment generation. In: 2015 IEEE 22nd International Conference on Software Analysis, Evolution, and Reengineering (SANER), pp. 380–389. IEEE (2015)

25. Wong, E., Yang, J., Tan, L.: Autocomment: mining question and answer sites for automatic comment generation. In: 2013 28th IEEE/ACM International Conference on Automated Software Engineering (ASE), pp. 562–567. IEEE (2013)

26. Woodfield, S.N., Dunsmore, H.E., Shen, V.Y.: The effect of modularization and comments on program comprehension. In: Proceedings of the 5th International Conference on Software Engineering, pp. 215–223. IEEE Press (1981)

27. Zhang, S., Zhang, C., Ernst, M.D.: Automated documentation inference to explain failed tests. In: 2011 26th IEEE/ACM International Conference on Automated Software Engineering (ASE 2011), pp. 63–72. IEEE (2011)

28. Zhong, H., Xie, T., Zhang, L., Pei, J., Mei, H.: MAPO: mining and recommending API usage patterns. In: Drossopoulou, S. (ed.) ECOOP 2009. LNCS, vol. 5653, pp. 318–343. Springer, Heidelberg (2009). https://doi.org/10.1007/978-3-642-03013-0_15

Test Oracle Prediction for Mutation Based Fault Localization

Zheng Li⬛, Yonghao Wu, Haifeng Wang, and Yong Liu(✉)⬛

College of Information Science and Technology, Beijing University of Chemical Technology, Beijing, People's Republic of China
lyong@mail.buct.edu.cn

Abstract. In the process of software debugging, it is very critical and difficult to identify the locations of faults in an effective and accurate manner. Mutation-based fault localization (MBFL) is one of the most effective automated fault localization techniques that have been recently proposed, and it requires the execution results (passed or failed) of test cases to locate faults. One problem preventing MBFL from becoming a practical testing technique is the large amount of human effort involved, i.e., the test oracle problem, which refers to the process of checking an original program's output of each test case. To mitigate the impact of this problem, we use mutant coverage information and learning algorithms to predict the oracle of the test cases in this paper. Empirical results show that the proposed method can reduce 80% of the human cost required to check the test oracles and achieve almost the same fault localization accuracy as compared to the original MBFL.

Keywords: Software debugging · Mutation-based fault localization · Test oracle prediction

1 Introduction

Software debugging is an important part of software development, including software checking, fault locating, and bug fixing. Various studies have shown that it is expensive to inspect and locate faults in software systems [6,17,22,37]. To reduce the time consumption and resource costs required in fault finding, many researchers have studied automated software fault localization techniques [2] over the past few decades, and various fault localization techniques have been proposed.

Coverage-based fault localization (CBFL) is one of the most popular fault localization techniques [20,24,30,36,44]. CBFL is a dynamic fault localization method that executes test cases on the program under test, and collects the coverage information, which includes call sequences [7], branches, du-pairs [28], and statement frequency [42]. CBFL calculates the degree of suspiciousness of each program element being faulty based on the frequency spectrum of the test cases, and element with a higher degree of suspiciousness is more likely to be faulty.

© Springer Nature Singapore Pte Ltd. 2019
Z. Li et al. (Eds.): NASAC 2017/2018, CCIS 861, pp. 15–34, 2019.
https://doi.org/10.1007/978-981-15-0310-8_2

Therefore, CBFL can provide information on the probability of each element as a faulty element, and assist developers at examining the elements one by one according to the probability from high to low. CBFL has been recognized as an effective and helpful technique, and can diminish the developers' debugging effort. However, CBFL has a limitation in terms of an impractical fault localization accuracy where all statements share the same spectrum and same ranking.

Mutation-based fault localization (MBFL) is another fault localization technique [21,35], which uses the information of test cases executed on mutants to calculate the degree of suspiciousness of the program elements. MBFL consists of three steps: executing the program under test, generating and executing mutants, and calculating the fault suspiciousness of each statement to generate a check list. A mutant is a program that is seeded with an artificial defect by using mutation operators. The mutation operator refers to a series of mapping programs that automatically generate mutants. A mutant is killed if the outputs of the program under test and this mutant are different, and the mutant is not killed if the two outputs are the same. An empirical study shows that the fault localization accuracy of MBFL is higher than that of CBFL, even in multiple-faulty program scenarios [35].

Although the accuracy of MBFL has been significantly improved compared with CBFL, there still are two major challenges to MBFL. One is the huge execution time required by a large amount of test cases and mutants, and the other is the human cost required to check whether each test case is passed or failed.

The execution information of the test cases on each mutant is required for MBFL to finish fault localization. Because the numbers of test cases and mutants are large for large-sized programs, the execution cost of MBFL is very high. Various techniques have been proposed to reduce the cost of a mutation execution, including mutant reduction methods [25,29,46] and mutation execution dynamic optimization method [13,26]. Empirical studies showed that these techniques can save many mutation executions and maintain almost the same fault localization accuracy as the original MBFL.

The other problem of MBFL is caused by the test oracle problem, because MBFL requires the execution results of the test cases to calculate the suspiciousness of each statement. Checking the execution results of all test cases will incur a large time cost [31]. In general, the output is passed or failed for each test case must be obtained by software testing engineers, and thus determining the output for a large number of test cases can result in a significant amount of human labor. For the current study, a method for predicting the test oracle based on the code coverage [45] was proposed; however, the prediction accuracy of this method is low and the fault localization precision is affected compared to the original fault localization techniques with test oracles.

To reduce the human cost of MBFL caused by test oracle, this paper employs mutant coverage information and learning-based algorithms to predict the execution results of test cases. The motivation of the study described in this paper includes the following: Compared with the code coverage, because each statement can generate a few mutants, mutant coverage can provide more information, and mutant coverage information can be generated during the MBFL process because MBFL is a type of mutation-testing based fault-localization technique; in addition, learning-based techniques can use the labels of partial test cases and construct a binary-classification model to classify other test cases as passed or failed. To validate the effectiveness of the method proposed in this paper, we conducted an empirical study on 31 single-fault versions and 114 multiple-fault versions from three subject programs, the results of which show that the proposed method can save about 80% of human time, and can achieve almost the same fault localization precision as the original MBFL.

The main contributions of this paper can be summarized as follows:

- This paper uses the mutant coverage to construct a coverage vector of test cases. Compared with statement coverage, mutant coverage can provide more information to precisely predict the test oracle. Empirical results show that the classification accuracy of mutant coverage is much better than statement coverage when using the same classification algorithm.
- This paper employs various learning-based algorithms to classify test cases as passed or failed, and the empirical results show that a neural-network based algorithm can provide the best classification accuracy.
- This paper constructs a framework of MBFL using a predicted test oracle, and the experimental results show that the fault localization accuracy is almost the same as the original MBFL with the test oracle.

The remainder of this paper is organized as follows. Section 2 introduces the background and related studies, including the test oracle problem, mutation-based fault localization, and learning-based algorithms. Section 3 describes the framework of mutation-based fault localization with predicted test oracle. The experimental design and results analysis are presented in Sects. 4 and 5, respectively. Section 6 discusses the threats of this paper. Finally, Sect. 7 provides some concluding remarks and areas of future work.

2 Background and Related Work

In this section, we describe the background and related studies on test oracle and MBFL, provide an example illustrating how MBFL operates, and introduce neural networks and other learning-based algorithms.

2.1 Test Oracle

In the field of software engineering and software testing, a test oracle is a mechanism used to determine whether a test case has passed or failed. To determine the test oracle of a given test case, the output of the test case is compared with the output the program should achieve, which is always found through human effort.

The term "test oracle" was first proposed by Howden [18], and Elaine Weyuker conducted additional work on different types of test oracles [1], which have been widely studied and applied [4,23].

However, there is a human oracle problem with regard to a test oracle [47], which can result in huge labor costs, namely, the output of each test case needs to be manually checked. When the number of test cases and the input data reach a certain scale, a significant human cost will be incurred, which is a problem that is not limited to fault localization techniques.

Current studies have attempted to reduce the cost of test oracle or use other less expensive methods to replace test oracle, and such studies can reduce the cost of software testing. Jingxuan Tu et al. applied metamorphic testing to code-coverage based failure proximity without test oracle [10]. Zhang et al. proposed an approach based on test classification to enable the use of unlabeled test cases in localizing faults [49]. Alessandro et al. proposed a static and dynamic source-code analysis method to generate test oracle [3]. The purpose of these studies is to reduce labor costs, thereby avoiding the human oracle problem.

In this study, we tried to reduce the cost of test oracle by using learning-based methods to improve the efficiency of MBFL.

2.2   Mutation Based Fault Localization

With MBFL, the test case suite achieves similar results on a faulty program and mutant, and reflects the similarity of behavior between the two [12,25]. The results of each test case executed on the program under testing can be recorded as R, and the value of R may be P or F. A value of P indicates that the output of such test cases executed on a faulty program is the same as expected, and an F indicates that the output of the test case executed on a faulty program does not match the expected result. The execution result of the same set of test cases on a mutant and on the program under testing refers to whether the test case kills the mutant. Here, K means the test case killed the corresponding mutant, where the output of the test case executed on the mutant differs from that on the program under testing. In addition, N indicates that the test case did not kill the corresponding mutant, where the output of test case executed on the mutant is the same as that on the program under testing. The following four parameters of each mutant can be generated according to the above rules: a_{kp}, which is the number of passed test cases that killed the mutant; a_{np}, which indicates the number of passed test cases that did not kill the mutant; a_{kf}, indicating the number of failed test cases that killed the mutant; and a_{nf}, which shows the number of failed test cases that did not kill the mutant. The suspiciousness of each mutant can be calculated by formulas using these four parameters, and the commonly used MBFL suspiciousness formulas are shown in Table 1. Recent studies have suggested that the accuracy of fault localization can be improved using MBFL, which is combined with a mutation analysis and fault localization approaches [33–35].

Table 2 shows an illustrative example of MBFL with three transformed suspiciousness formulas shown in Table 1. The program *mid* shown in this example has 13 statements with a test suite t of six test cases $t1, ..., t6$, and the third statement is a faulty statement, which should be $if(y < z)$. The bottom row refers to the execution results of all test cases, namely P (passed) and F (failed). In Table 2, 1 is used to indicate that the mutant has been killed by the corresponding test case. The Suspiciousness column notes the suspiciousness value of each mutant calculated using the *Ochiai* [39], *Jaccard* [19], and *OP2* [30] formulas, as shown in Table 2. The suspiciousness value of each statement, which is shown in bold face, is the maximum suspiciousness value of all mutants generated by this statement.

Table 1. Commonly used MBFL suspiciousness formula

Name	Method
Ochiai	$Sus(s) = \dfrac{a_{kf}}{\sqrt{(a_{kf}+a_{nf})*(a_{kf}+a_{kp})}}$
Jaccard	$Sus(s) = \dfrac{a_{kf}}{a_{kf}+a_{nf}+a_{kp}}$
Op2	$Sus(s) = a_{kf} - \dfrac{akp}{a_{kf}+a_{nf}+1}$

2.3   Neural Network and Machine Learning Algorithms

Figure 1 shows the neural network model, and the original goal of the artificial neural network approach was to solve a problem in the same way as the human brain [27,32]. Over time, attention became focused on matching specific intelligence, leading to biological deviations. Artificial neural networks have been used for a variety of areas, including computer vision, speech recognition, machine translation, social network filtering, board and video games, and medical diagnostics [9,41,43].

Learning is an important part of neural network research, and its adaptability is realized through learning. According to changes in the environment, the weights are adjusted to improve the system's behavior. The learning rule of a neural network is to use the steepest descent method to continuously adjust the weights and thresholds of the network through back propagation, and to finally minimize the global error coefficient.

In this paper, a neural network algorithm is used as a classifier to predict test oracle. First, we need to manually derive the output of a small number of test cases as passed or failed, and use this part of test case as the training data to train the neural network. After training is completed, the neural network can be used to determine whether the output of all remaining test cases as passed or failed. The neural network used in this paper has an ReLU activation function, and a momentum factor of 0.99. The training samples was randomly selected in this study.

Table 2. Example of relative information from calculating suspiciousness using MBFL

	program	mutants	test suite						Suspiciousness		
			t1	t2	t3	t4	t5	t6	Jaccard	Ochiai	Op2
	mid(int x,int y,int z){		3,3,5	1,2,3	3,2,1	5,5,5	5,3,4	2,1,4			
1	int m,										
2	m = z,										
3	if(y < z − 1)//fault	M1:< → <=		1			1		1.00	1.00	2.00
		M2:< → >	1		1			1	0.00	0.00	0.00
		M3:< → >=	1	1	1		1	1	0.40	0.63	1.40
		M4:< → ==	1	1			1	1	0.50	0.71	1.60
		M5:< → !=			1				0.00	0.00	0.00
		M6:< → true		1	1		1		0.67	0.82	1.80
		M7:< → false	1					1	0.00	0.00	0.00
4	if(x<y)	M8:< → <=							0.00	0.00	0.00
		M9:< → >						1	0.00	0.00	0.00
		M10:< → >=						1	0.00	0.00	0.00
		M11:< → ==							0.00	0.00	0.00
		M12:< → !=						1	0.00	0.00	0.00
		M13:< → true						1	0.00	0.00	0.00
		M14:< → false							0.00	0.00	0.00
5	m = y,										
6	else if(x<z)	M15:< → <=							0.00	0.00	0.00
		M16:< → >	1					1	0.00	0.00	0.00
		M17:< → >=	1					1	0.00	0.00	0.00
		M18:< → ==	1					1	0.00	0.00	0.00
		M19:< → !=							0.00	0.00	0.00
		M20:< → true							0.00	0.00	0.00
		M21:< → false	1					1	0.00	0.00	0.00
7	m = x,										
8	else										
9	if(x>y)	M22:> → <=							0.00	0.00	0.00
		M23:> → >		1	1		1		0.67	0.82	1.80
		M24:> → >=		1	1		1		0.67	0.82	1.80
		M25:> → ==			1		1		0.33	0.50	0.80
		M26:> → !=		1					0.50	0.71	1.00
		M27:> → true		1					0.50	0.71	1.00
		M28:> → false			1		1		0.33	0.50	0.80
10	m = y,										
11	else if(x>z)	M29:> → <=							0.00	0.00	0.00
		M30:> → >		1					0.50	0.71	1.00
		M31:> → >=		1					0.50	0.71	1.00
		M32:> → ==							0.00	0.00	0.00
		M33:> → !=		1					0.50	0.71	1.00
		M34:> → true		1					0.50	0.71	1.00
		M35:> → false							0.00	0.00	0.00
12	m = x,										
13	return m,										
	}		P	F	P	P	F	P			

To verify the effectiveness of neural network algorithm, we also compared the experimental results between neural network and other classical machine-learning algorithms, including Bayesian [5,15], support vector machine (SVM) [16], and k-nearest neighbor (KNN) [14] algorithms.

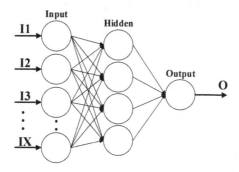

Fig. 1. Model of neural network algorithm

3   MBFL with Predicted Test Oracle

The framework of MBFL with predicted test oracle used in this paper is shown in Fig. 2, and can be divided into four steps: execute the program under testing, test oracle prediction, generate and execute mutants, and finally, calculate the suspiciousness value of mutants and statements.

(1) Executing the program under test: The main task of this step is to use the test suite to execute the program under test, obtain the output data and coverage information of all test cases. The output data refer to the results printed out after the program is executed for each test case.

(2) Generating and executing mutants: The main task of this step is to generate and execute the mutants. First, the mutation operator is used to seed artificial defects on selected statements; we then execute the test suite on all mutants to obtain the results, that is, the information regarding whether the mutant is killed by the corresponding test case.

(3) Test oracle prediction: The main task of this step is to predict the test oracle for all test cases. First, we select a small portion of test cases and manually determine their output data as failed or passed. The execution results of these test cases and the mutant coverage vector of each test case are used as training data to train the neural network. The remaining test cases are then used as test samples, and the neural network model is used to predict the results of these test samples.

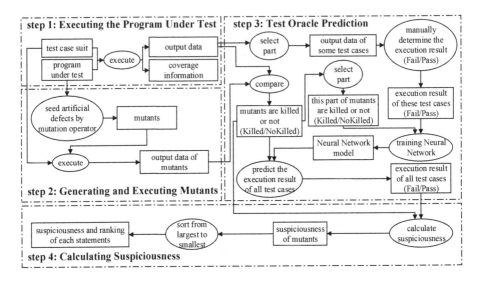

Fig. 2. Framework of MBFL with predicted test oracle

The mutant coverage vector of each test case refers to the information regarding whether the test case kills all mutants. For example, we use the program in Table 2 as the program under testing, and test case $t1$ as the training sample. We already know that the execution result of $t1$ is passed. We use the information that the mutants were killed by test case $t1$ as input to train the neural network, and use the result of test case $t1$ as the expected output. The number of input nodes is equal to the number of mutants, and there are 35 mutants in the program in Table 2, and thus $X = 35$ in Fig. 1. Because only mutants numbered 2, 3, 4, 7, 16, 17, 18, and 21 are killed by test case $t1$, when training the neural network using $I2$, $I3$, $I4$, $I7$, $I16$, $I17$, $I18$, and $I121$ the value is 1, and the value of the remaining input nodes is 0. Because the execution result of test case $t1$ is passed, the value of the true output O is 0.

Afterward, the predicted data are propagated forward, that is, after the data are input from the input layer, the predicted value is obtained through a calculation of the hidden layer and output layer, and the predicted value is the output result of the output layer. The weight of the update is reversely propagated, and the error between the predicted output and the real output of the model is calculated according to the real output of the sample. The error is then propagated back to each hidden layer. The error of each layer is calculated, and then according to the error of each layer, the weight is updated. When the error between the predicted output and the real output reaches the allowable range, we finish the neural network training and obtain the neural network model.

Finally, we use the trained neural network model to predict the output of all other test cases.

For instance, the mutants numbered 1, 2, 3, 5, 6, 23, 24, 25, and 28 in Table 2 are killed by test case $t3$. Then, the value of $I1$, $I2$, $I3$, $I5$, $I6$, $I23$, $I24$, $I25$, and $I28$ in the node is 1, and the remaining input nodes have a value of zero. Afterward, the prediction data are spread forward, and the prediction data are the prediction output result of test case $t3$. In the ideal case, the prediction result should be the same as the result of the $t3$ execution in Table 2, which is 0.

(4) Calculating the suspiciousness: The main task of this step is to calculate the suspiciousness of each statement in the program under test. For the method using MBFL, the results of the execution of the test cases and the results of the execution of the mutants are first used to calculate the suspiciousness of all mutants based on the formulas in Table 1. Afterward, the suspiciousness value of each statement is set to maximum among its generated mutants.

4   Experiment Design

4.1   Research Questions

The empirical study is conducted with two main goals. The first is to evaluate the precision of test oracle prediction. The second is to evaluate the fault localization accuracy of MBFL with predicted test oracle. Specifically, this paper aims to answer the following research questions:

RQ1: Compared with the statement coverage based test case information, how does the mutant coverage based test case information perform in terms of the prediction of test oracle with the same neural network algorithm?

RQ2: Among neural network, Bayes, SVM, and KNN, which classification algorithm is the best at predicting test oracle?

RQ3: Compared with original MBFL, how good is the fault localization of MBFL with the predicted test oracle?

RQ1 and **RQ2** concern the accuracies of different methods with regard to their test oracle predictions, and **RQ3** compares the fault localization between MBFL with predicted test oracle and original MBFL with all test oracles.

All experiments were performed on an HP server with 24 Intel Xeon(R) E5-2620 cores and 16 GB of memory.

4.2   Subject Programs

To address the above research questions, three subject programs with 114 versions were selected from the Software artifact Infrastructure Repository (SIR) [10] as benchmarks. The first two programs come from Siemens Suite, and the last program, sed, is a real-world program. They are all open-source C programs with faulty versions and corresponding test suites. Table 3 shows the detailed information on all subject programs, including the number of single-fault and multiple-fault versions, the line of code, the number of test cases, and the fault type of each subject program.

Table 3. Subject programs

Programs	#Faulty versions		#LOC	#Tests	Fault type
	Single-fault	Multiple-fault			
tot_info	10	35	412	1052	Seeded
tcas	12	28	173	1608	Seeded
sed	9	50	12062	360	Real/Seeded

In this study, the GNU gcov [48] tool was employed to collect coverage information of test cases. For every statement, the mutation analysis tool Proteum/IM [8], which is a well-known tool and is widely used in mutation testing studies, is leveraged to generate mutants.

4.3 Evaluation Metrics

Evaluation Metrics for Test Oracle Prediction. In this paper, the test oracle prediction problem is constructed as a binary classification problem, and commonly used evaluation metrics of the binary classification problem include *Precision, Recall, F-measure,* and *FalsePositive* (FP) *rate*. These metrics are calculated based on the confusion matrix shown in Table 4. For the test oracle prediction problem, *TruePositive* (TP) indicates the number of passed test cases correctly predicted as passed, *FalsePositive*(FP) denotes the number of passed test cases incorrectly predicted as failed, *FalseNegative* (FN) indicates the number of failed test cases incorrectly predicted as passed, and *TrueNegatives* (TN) is the number of failed test cases correctly predicted as failed. All of these above evaluation metrics range from zero to 1, and higher values of *Precision, Recall,* and *F-measure,* and lower values of the *FPrate* indicate a better prediction technology.

Table 4. Confusion matrix and evaluation metrics for binary classification algorithm

	True Class		
	P	N	
Hypothesized Class Y	True Positives	False Positives	$Precision = \frac{TP}{TP+FP}$
N	False Negatives	True Negatives	$Recall = \frac{TP}{TP+FN}$ $F\text{-}measure = \frac{2*Precision*Recall}{Precision+Recall}$ $FPrate = \frac{FP}{N}$
Column Totals:	P	N	

Evaluation Metrics for Fault Localization. In this paper, a widely used method, *EXAMscore,* is employed to evaluate the fault localization precision of MBFL. The $EXAM score$ uses the percentage of located faults by examining certain percentage statements, and a higher $EXAM score$ indicates a better fault localization technique [38]. The $EXAM score$ is defined through the following formula:

$$EXAM\ score = \frac{\%\ of\ located\ faults}{\%\ of\ examined\ code}$$

T-Test for Evaluating Data Differences. A t-test is a statistical hypothesis test that follows a Student t-distribution under the null hypothesis [11,40]. A t-test can be used to determine if two sets of data are significantly different from each other. In our study, we calculate the P-value to test the differences in fault localization accuracy between different MBFL techniques.

5   Experiment Results and Analyses

5.1   Comparison Between Mutant Coverage and Statement Coverage

In this study, we leverage mutant coverage to construct test case information for test oracle prediction. To validate its effectiveness, an empirical comparison of test oracle prediction accuracy between two types of test case information, namely, mutant coverage and statement coverage, is conducted on all subject program versions shown in Table 3.

We selected 20%, 40%, 60%, and 80% of the cases as training set and the remaining cases as the predicted set, and employed the same classification algorithm, neural network, to predict the test oracle. We calculated the value of metrics under these different configurations, and visually compare these two types of test case information through the violin plots shown in Figs. 3 and 4. In the violin plot, the X-axis represents different proportions of a training set using different techniques, and the Y-axis indicates the *Precision, Recall, F-measure,* and *FPrate*. "MC20%" or "SC20%" indicate the results of the mutant coverage or statement coverage test case information, respectively, with 20% of the training test cases. Each block in the violin plot indicates the distribution of one evaluation metric and the corresponding formula. The breadth of the block represents the data density of the corresponding value of the Y-axis for all subject program versions.

Because the subject programs shown in Table 3 contain single-fault and multiple-fault versions, and the number of faults certainly has an impact on test oracle prediction results. In this study, we made the same comparison under single-fault and multiple-fault versions separately. Specifically, Figs. 3 and 4 show a comparison of the *Precision, Recall, F-measure,* and *FPrate* in single-fault and multiple-fault scenarios.

As shown in Fig. 3(a), the distribution of the *Precision* of the mutant coverage is centered at approximately 1.0, and has a much higher *Precision* in all training sets. Similarly, the mutant coverage has a much higher *Recall* and

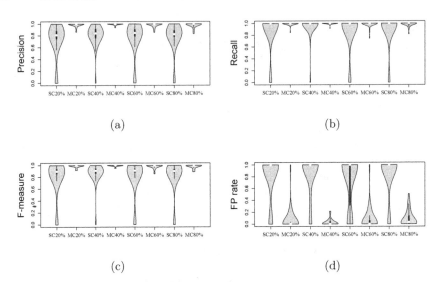

Fig. 3. Comparison of test oracle prediction results for single-fault versions

F-measure, as shown in Figs. 3(b) and (c). The experimental results show that the mutant coverage is 28.65% more precise than the statement coverage, and the mutant coverage has increased by 10.19% and 19.91% in *Recall* and *F-measure* on average, respectively.

As shown in Fig. 3(d), The record mutant coverage has a much lower *FPrate* than the statement coverage in different training sets, with a decrease of 91.43% over the statement coverage on average.

Simultaneously, we studied in multiple-fault cases, the results of which are shown in Fig. 4.

Figures 4(a)–(d) show a comparison of the two types combining neural network algorithm with regard to *Precision*, *Recall*, *F-measure*, and *FPrate* in the multiple-fault cases, respectively.

Compared with single-fault situation, although the statement coverage and mutant coverage have a more scattered distribution, the mutant coverage also has a higher *Precision* relatively with an improvement of 137.54%, as shown in Fig. 4(a). In addition, in the case of multiple faults, the mutant coverage is 55.33% and 99.57% higher in *Recall* and *F-measure* on average. In addition, it is 68.97% lower in *FPrate*.

In conclusion, we can claim that mutant coverage with the neural network algorithm can be much better than statement coverage, and the former has a much better prediction effect with different proportions of training sets.

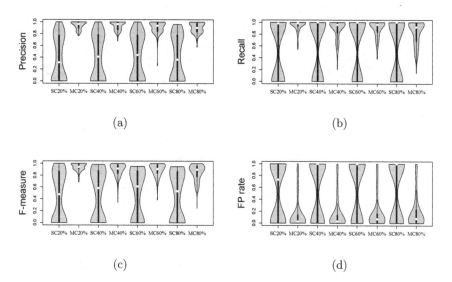

Fig. 4. Comparison of CBFL and MBFL with regard to *Precision, Recall, F-measure,* and *FPrate* in the case of multiple faults

5.2 Comparison Between Different Learning Algorithms

In this section, we mainly compare the neural network algorithm and machine-learning algorithm by calculating the *Precision, Recall, F-measure,* and *FPrate* separately under the MBFL technique. Meanwhile, we selected 20%, 40%, 60%, and 80% of the test cases as the training set. The comparison is shown in 8 line charts, where the X-axis represents the different program versions, and the Y-axis indicates the *Precision, Recall, F-measure,* and *FPrate*. We studied both single-fault and multiple-fault cases, and Fig. 5 shows the case of a single fault.

Figures 5(a)–(p) show a comparison of the machine-learning and neural network algorithms with regard to the *Precision, Recall, F-measure,* and *FPrate* in a single fault case, respectively.

From Fig. 5(a), we can see that the Bayes algorithm is visually higher than the other three lines with regard to the *Precision* metric, and we can draw the same conclusion from Figs. 5(c) and (d). In Fig. 5(b), the neural network (NN) algorithm is better than the others. The results shown in Figs. 5(e), (g), and (h) indicate that the Bayes algorithm has a lower *Recall* in the 20%, 60%, and 80% training test cases. In addition, the Bayes algorithm has a higher *F-measure* and lower *FPrate*, whereas the SVM shows the worst performance in Fig. 5(i)–(p). In this case, the Bayes algorithm has a better performance than the other three algorithms in a single fault case.

The results of multiple-fault comparisons are shown in Fig. 6.

Figures 6(a)–(p) show a comparison of the machine-learning and neural network algorithms with regard to the *Precision, Recall, F-measure,* and *FPrate* in the multiple-fault case, respectively.

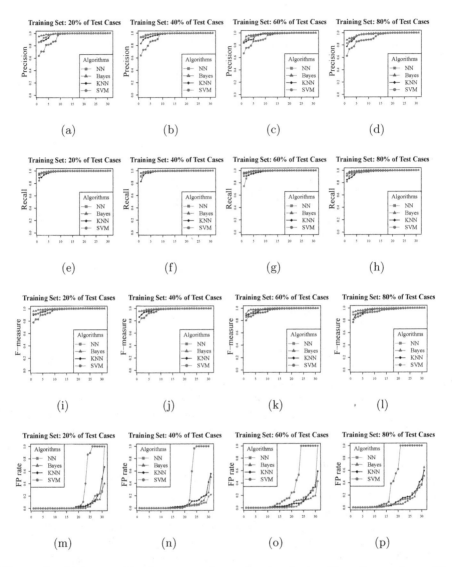

Fig. 5. Combining machine-learning and neural network algorithms for versions with a single fault

We can see from Figs. 6(a)–(l) that the neural network algorithm achieves a higher *Precision, Recall*, and *F-measure* in different proportions of the training test cases. Similarly, from Figs. 6(m)–(p), the Bayes algorithm achieves the lowest *FPrate*. Therefore, we can conclude that the neural network algorithm achieves a better prediction in a multiple-fault situation.

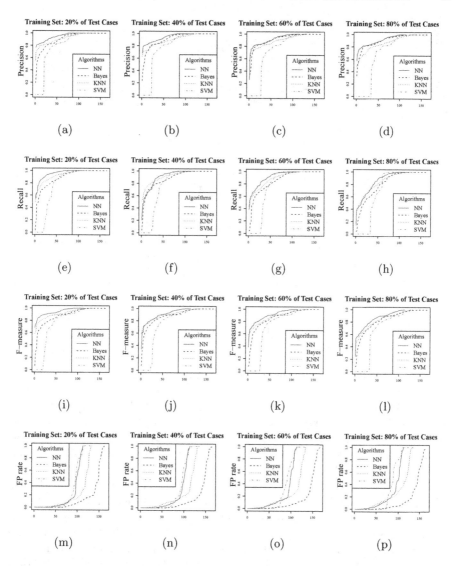

Fig. 6. Combining machine-learning and neural network algorithms for versions with multiple faults

In summary, we can conclude that the Bayes algorithm is suitable for test oracle prediction in a single-fault case, and the neural network algorithm is suitable for a multiple-fault case.

5.3   Performance of MBFL with and Without Test Oracle Prediction

In this section, we compare the performance of MBFL with and without using the neural network algorithm for fault localization prediction by choosing 20% of the

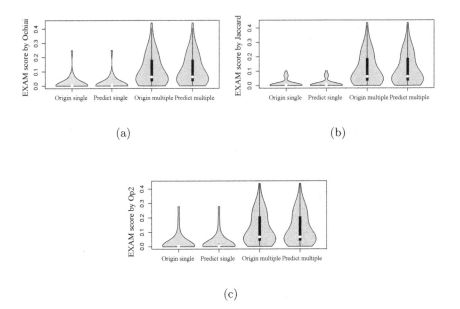

(a)   (b)

(c)

Fig. 7. Performance of MBFL with and without use of neural network algorithm

test cases as training sets and the rest for the prediction. Single and multiple fault cases were studied to predict the rank of a faulty statement, and we calculated the $EXAMscore$ of the faulty statements using three MBFL formulas ($Jaccard$, $Ochiai$, and $Op2$). The results are shown graphically through the violin plots, where the X-axis represents the MBFL without (Origin) and with (Predict) the use of the neural network algorithm in single and multiple-fault cases, and Y-axis represents the $EXAMscore$.

Figures 7(a)–(c) show a comparison of the MBFL technique, $Jaccard$, $Ochiai$, and $Op2$, with and without the use of the neural network algorithm, respectively.

The results in Fig. 7 show the distribution of $EXAMscore$ with the different MBFL formulas, which indicates that there no significant difference was found with regard to the effect of the MBFL between with and without combining the neural network algorithm. Therefore, the test oracle prediction can be used in MBFL to reduce the significant expense of a mutation execution.

To further investigate the differences between MBFL without (Origin) and with (Predict) the use of the neural network algorithm, a statistical analysis was conducted. Table 5 summarizes the results of an independent sample t-test on the $EXAMscore$ of MBFL with and without the use of the neural network algorithm. These results are based on the three MBFL formulas. Suppose that the $EXAMscore$ using the neural network algorithm is A, and the $EXAMscore$ without the use of the neural network algorithm is B, for H_0, the data distribution of A is the same across B, whereas for H_1, the data distribution of A is not the same across B. Table 5 shows the different degrees of significance

Table 5. Statistical comparison (P-values)of MBFL with and without neural network algorithm

Programs	Fault type	Jaccard	Ochiai	Op2
sed	Single fault	0.993	0.990	0.956
	Multiple faults	0.974	0.949	0.968
tcas	Single fault	1.000	1.000	1.000
	Multiple faults	0.990	0.981	0.960
tot_info	Single fault	0.969	0.969	0.975
	Multiple faults	0.970	0.977	0.957
all	Single fault	0.975	0.980	0.955
	Multiple faults	0.968	0.958	0.991

between Origin and Predict. It can be seen that there is no statistically significant difference between Origin and Predict in the different program versions at a statistically significant level, namely, $\alpha = 0.05$.

In conclusion, we determined that MBFL combining neural network algorithm did not achieve similar performance in fault localization, and we achieved almost the same fault localization effect by reducing 80% of the cost of the human oracle.

6   Threats to Validity

This paper uses the following threat of validity: The number of experiments and the number of versions used in the experiment were limited. Experimental selection of the program was also limited. For the experiment, a representative procedure that is widely used in the field of fault localization was chosen. However, there are many unknowns in reality debugging, and thus our experiments cannot cover or apply to all situations in reality. Therefore, the focus of future work will be to use more large real-world programs.

Although MBFL is a highly accurate fault localization technique, it can be costly because traditional methods require a manual output expected by each test case.

7   Conclusion and Future Work

This paper presented a neural-network based prediction method that uses the execution path of a few test cases and their tag information to train the output tags of most of the remaining test cases. Based on the experiments and a comparison, mutant coverage using the neural network algorithm can be much better than statement coverage. Further, this paper compared a neural network algorithm with a machine-learning algorithm for test oracle prediction, the results of which show that MBFL combining the neural network algorithm achieves better test oracle prediction than when combined with other algorithms for a multiple-fault case. Finally, we achieved almost the same prediction and fault localization accuracies when using the neural network algorithm with MBFL, with an 80% test oracle reduction compared with MBFL without using the algorithm.

As future work, we intend to use more complex and larger experimental procedures. We also intend to use more real-world and larger programs to render our results more universal as well as realistic.

Acknowledgment. The work describes in this paper is supported by the National Natural Science Foundation of China under Grant No.61872026, 61672085 and 61702029.

References

1. Weyuker, E.J.: The oracle assumption of program testing. In: 13th International Conference on System Sciences, pp. 44–49 (1980)
2. Agrawal, H., Horgan, J.R., London, S., Wong, W.E.: Fault localization using execution slices and dataflow tests. In: International Symposium on Software Reliability Engineering. Proceedings, pp. 143–151 (1995)
3. Arantes, A.O., de Santiago, V.A., Vijaykumar, N.L.: On proposing a test oracle generator based on static and dynamic source code analysis. In: 2015 IEEE International Conference on Software Quality, Reliability and Security-Companion (QRS-C), pp. 144–152. IEEE (2015)
4. Barr, E.T., Harman, M., Mcminn, P., Shahbaz, M., Yoo, S.: The oracle problem in software testing: a survey. IEEE Trans. Software Eng. **41**(5), 507–525 (2015)
5. Cheeseman, P., Stutz, J.: Bayesian classification (autoclass): theory and results. In: Fayyad, U.M., et al. (eds.) Advances in Knowledge Discovery and Data Mining AAAI, pp. 153–180 (1996)
6. Chen, X., Chen, J.H., Ju, X.L., Gu, Q.: Survey of test case prioritization techniques for regression testing. J. Software **24**(8), 1695–1712 (2013)
7. Dallmeier, V., Lindig, C., Zeller, A.: Lightweight bug localization with ample (2005)
8. Delamaro, M.E., Maldonado, J.C., Vincenzi, A.M.R.: Proteum/IM 2.0: an integrated mutation testing environment. In: Wong, W.E. (ed.) Mutation Testing for the New Century, pp. 91–101. Springer, Boston (2001). https://doi.org/10.1007/978-1-4757-5939-6_17
9. Devlin, J., Zbib, R., Huang, Z., Lamar, T., Schwartz, R., Makhoul, J.: Fast and robust neural network joint models for statistical machine translation. In: Meeting of the Association for Computational Linguistics, pp. 1370–1380 (2014)
10. Do, H., Elbaum, S., Rothermel, G.: Supporting controlled experimentation with testing techniques: an infrastructure and its potential impact. Empirical Software Eng. **10**(4), 405–435 (2005)
11. Efron, B.: Student's t test under symmetry conditions. Publ. Am. Stat. Assoc. **64**(328), 1278–1302 (1969)
12. Gong, P., Geng, C.Y., Guo, J.X., Zhao, R.L.: Dynamic mutation execution strategy for mutation-based fault localization. Comput. Sci. **43**(2), 199–203 (2016)
13. Gong, P., Zhao, R., Li, Z.: Faster mutation-based fault localization with a novel mutation execution strategy. In: IEEE Eighth International Conference on Software Testing, Verification and Validation Workshops, pp. 1–10 (2015)

14. Guo, G., Wang, H., Bell, D., Bi, Y., Greer, K.: KNN model-based approach in classification. In: Meersman, R., Tari, Z., Schmidt, D.C. (eds.) OTM 2003. LNCS, vol. 2888, pp. 986–996. Springer, Heidelberg (2003). https://doi.org/10.1007/978-3-540-39964-3_62

15. Habib, M.T., Shuvo, S.B., Uddin, M.S., Ahmed, F.: Automated textile defect classification by bayesian classifier based on statistical features. In: International Workshop on Computational Intelligence, pp. 101–105 (2017)

16. Hao, P.Y., Chiang, J.H., Tu, Y.K.: Hierarchically svm classification based on support vector clustering method and its application to document categorization. Expert Syst. Appl. **33**(3), 627–635 (2007)

17. Harrold, M.J., Gupta, R., Soffa, M.L.: A methodology for controlling the size of a test suite. ACM Trans. Software Eng. Methodol. (TOSEM) **2**(3), 270–285 (1993)

18. Howden, W.E.: Theoretical and empirical studies of program testing. IEEE Trans. Softw. Eng **4**(4), 305–311 (1978)

19. Jaccard, P.: Etude de la distribution florale dans une portion des alpes et du jura. Bulletin De La Societe Vaudoise Des Sciences Naturelles **37**(142), 547–579 (1901)

20. Jones, J.A.: Empirical evaluation of the tarantula automatic fault-localization technique. In: IEEE/ACM International Conference on Automated Software Engineering, pp. 273–282 (2005)

21. Kooli, M., Kaddachi, F., Natale, G.D., Bosio, A., Benoit, P., Torres, L.: Computing reliability: on the differences between software testing and software fault injection techniques. Microprocess. Microsyst. **50**, 102–112 (2017)

22. Leon, D., Podgurski, A.: A comparison of coverage-based and distribution-based techniques for filtering and prioritizing test cases. In: International Symposium on Software Reliability Engineering, p. 442 (2003)

23. Li, N., Offutt, J.: Test oracle strategies for model-based testing. IEEE Trans. Softw. Eng. **PP**(99), 1 (2017)

24. Liu, X., Liu, Y., Li, Z., Zhao, R.: Fault classification oriented spectrum based fault localization. In: IEEE Computer Software and Applications Conference, pp. 256–261 (2017)

25. Liu, Y., Li, Z., Wang, L., Hu, Z., Zhao, R.: Statement-oriented mutant reduction strategy for mutation based fault localization. In: IEEE International Conference on Software Quality, Reliability and Security (2017)

26. Liu, Y., Li, Z., Zhao, R., Gong, P.: An optimal mutation execution strategy for cost reduction of mutation-based fault localization. Inf. Sci. **422**(January 2018), 572–596 (2017)

27. Major, T.C., Conrad, J.M.: The effects of pre-filtering and individualizing components for electroencephalography neural network classification. In: Southeastcon, pp. 1–6 (2017)

28. Masri, W.: Fault localization based on information flow coverage. Software Testing Verification Reliab. **20**(2), 121–147 (2010)

29. Masri, W., Abouassi, R., Elghali, M., Alfatairi, N.: An empirical study of the factors that reduce the effectiveness of coverage-based fault localization. Environ. Health Perspect. **114**(11), 142–143 (2009)

30. Naish, L., Lee, H.J., Ramamohanarao, K.: A model for spectra-based software diagnosis. ACM Tran. Software Eng. Methodol. (TOSEM) **20**(3), 1–32 (2011)

31. Noor, T.B., Hemmati, H.: Studying test case failure prediction for test case prioritization. In: The International Conference, pp. 2–11 (2017)

32. Palmer-Brown, D., Jayne, C.: Hypercube neural network algorithm for classification. In: Iliadis, L., Jayne, C. (eds.) AIAI/EANN -2011. IAICT, vol. 363, pp. 41–51. Springer, Heidelberg (2011). https://doi.org/10.1007/978-3-642-23957-1_5

33. Papadakis, M., Traon, Y.L.: Using mutants to locate unknown faults. In: IEEE Fifth International Conference on Software Testing, Verification and Validation, pp. 691–700 (2012)
34. Papadakis, M., Traon, Y.L.: Effective fault localization via mutation analysis: a selective mutation approach. In: ACM Symposium on Applied Computing, pp. 1293–1300 (2014)
35. Papadakis, M., Traon, Y.L.: Metallaxis-FL: Mutation-Based Fault Localization. Wiley, Chichester (2015)
36. Perez, A., Rui, A., Deursen, A.V.: A test-suite diagnosability metric for spectrum-based fault localization approaches. In: International Conference on Software Engineering, pp. 654–664 (2017)
37. Pressman, R.S.: Software engineering: a practitioner's approach, 2nd edn. (1992)
38. Renieres, M., Reiss, S.P.: Fault localization with nearest neighbor queries. In: IEEE International Conference on Automated Software Engineering. Proceedings, pp. 30–39 (2003)
39. Rui, A., Zoeteweij, P., Gemund, A.J.C.V.: An evaluation of similarity coefficients for software fault localization. In: Pacific Rim International Symposium on Dependable Computing, pp. 39–46 (2006)
40. Ruxton, G.D.: The unequal variance T test is an underused alternative to student's T test and the mann whitney U test. Behav. Ecol. **17**(4), 688–690 (2006)
41. Seki, H., Yamamoto, K., Nakagawa, S.: A deep neural network integrated with filterbank learning for speech recognition. In: IEEE International Conference on Acoustics, Speech and Signal Processing, pp. 5480–5484 (2017)
42. Shu, T., Ye, T., Ding, Z., Xia, J.: Fault localization based on statement frequency. Inf. Sci. **360**(C), 43–56 (2016)
43. Storbeck, F., Daan, B.: Fish species recognition using computer vision and a neural network. Fish. Res. **51**(1), 11–15 (2001)
44. Tip, F.: A Survey of Program Slicing Techniques. CWI (Centre for Mathematics and Computer Science) (1994)
45. Tu, J., Xie, X., Xu, B.: Code coverage-based failure proximity without test oracles. In: Computer Software and Applications Conference, pp. 133–142 (2016)
46. Wang, X., Jiang, S., Gao, P., Xiaolin, J.U., Wang, R., Zhang, Y.: Cost-effective testing based fault localization with distance based test-suite reduction. Sci. China **60**(9), 092112 (2017)
47. Weyuker, E.J.: On testing non-testable programs. Comput. J. **25**(4), 465–470 (1982)
48. Yang, Q., Li, J.J., Weiss, D.M.: A survey of coverage-based testing tools. Comput. J. **52**(5), 589–597 (2009)
49. Zhang, X.Y., Zheng, Z., Cai, K.Y.: Exploring the usefulness of unlabelled test cases in software fault localization. J. Syst. Softw. **136**, 278–290 (2018)

Parallel Evolutionary Algorithm in Scheduling Work Packages to Minimize Duration of Software Project Management

Jinghui Hu[1,2], Xu Wang[3], Jian Ren[3(✉)], and Chao Liu[3]

[1] AVIC Manufacturing Technology Institute, Beijing 100024, China
[2] Aeronautical Key Laboratory for Digital Manufacturing Technology,
Beijing 100024, China
[3] State Key Laboratory of Software Development Environment,
School of Computer Science and Engineering, Beihang University,
Beijing 100191, China
renjian@buaa.edu.cn

Abstract. Software project management problem mainly includes resources allocation and work packages scheduling. This paper presents an approach to Search Based Software Project Management based on parallel implementation of evolutionary algorithm on GPU. We redesigned evolutionary algorithm to cater for the purpose of parallel programming. Our approach aims to parallelize the genetic operators including: crossover, mutation and evaluation in the evolution process to achieve faster execution. To evaluate our approach, we conducted a "proof of concept" empirical study, using data from three real-world software projects. Both sequential and parallel version of a conventional single objective evolutionary algorithm are implemented. The sequential version is based on common programming approach using C++, and the parallel version is based on GPGPU programming approach using CUDA. Results indicate that even a relatively cheap graphic card (GeForce GTX 970) can speed up the optimization process significantly. We believe that deploy parallel evolutionary algorithm based on GPU may fit many applications for other software project management problems, since software projects often have complex inter-related work packages and resources, and are typically characterized by large scale problems which optimization process ought to be accelerated by parallelism.

Keywords: Software project management · Evolutionary algorithm · NVidia CUDA · Parallel computing · GPGPU

1 Introduction

In an actual development process of software project, the project manager's responsibility is to properly schedule the tasks of software project development,

© Springer Nature Singapore Pte Ltd. 2019
Z. Li et al. (Eds.): NASAC 2017/2018, CCIS 861, pp. 35–51, 2019.
https://doi.org/10.1007/978-981-15-0310-8_3

supervise the programming work of the software engineer and arrange the whole development progress of the software to ensure that the software can be delivered before the deadline [1]. Therefore, the project management problem is not only a very fundamental problem in software engineering, but also a very difficult problem in the actual work for the project manager.

In fact, software project management is an art of staff management and task scheduling in software engineering. It requires an overall understanding of the lifecycle of software development, such as planning tasks, staff organization and so on. Through a survey on the practice of software project management [2–5], we found that the different task management designed by the project manager, such as the arrangement order of the work packages in a project, or the different resource allocation in the same human resources team, will have a great impact on the project's overall duration. Excellent project managers can shorten the overall duration by arranging the order of tasks, making full use of the team's resources or allocating human resources properly. However, at the beginning of a software project, the project managers need to spend a lot of time on the discussion that what kind of difficulties will be faced in the process of development and the detail of resources allocation in software engineering phase [6], such as requirements analysis, system design, system development, system testing etc.

However, an automatic method to properly arrange the entire software project management process is still lacking. We target at two typical difficulties preventing automatic techniques to be realized into a real world project: (1) the complexity of the problem model causes difficulties when a project manager is formalizing the problem he/she is facing, (2) the execution time of the optimization process is quite often unbearable comparing to the result it yields.

In this paper, we introduce a framework to deploy a conventional evolutionary algorithm to solve the work package scheduling problem as a single objective optimization problem. And by catering the most computation intensive portion of algorithm to run on a parallel manner, this framework speeds up the execution of optimization process significantly. With an empirical study on three real world software project data, we show how this framework can ease above mentioned two typical problems that most of the existing optimization techniques to project management are facing. We claim that heuristics provides mangers with intuitive features towards "simple-to-deploy", and parallel computation running on GPU provides faster execution time.

The main purpose of this paper is to push forward the automated software project management powered by the search-based approach, which is an important component of search-based software engineering (SBSE) and also a future development trend of software engineering project management in the era of big data and parallel computing.

The rest of this paper is organized as follows. First, we give a brief background of evolutionary algorithm and software project management problem in Sects. 2 and 3. Then we introduce the design of algorithm implemented in a parallel manner in Sect. 4. Section 5 presents the results of empirical study. In Sect. 6, we provide a brief overview of related work before concluding in Sect. 7.

2   Evolutionary Algorithm

2.1   Meta-heuristic Algorithms

In the development process of computer science, the design of program algorithm provides much power to promote the advancement of computer science and technology. We know that in solving the similar kind of problem, the computational efficiency of different algorithms is completely different.

Algorithm has become the soul to solve practical problems using computer. In addition to the classical algorithm that can be used to calculate a certain problem at a given time, a class of algorithms is found with different performance. The nature of this algorithm is that no performance guaranteed can be given in theory but is often possible to give the solution of the problem efficiently in practice. This class of algorithms is called meta-heuristic algorithm.

Unlike the traditional algorithm, the meta-heuristic algorithm tries to provide one or more disaggregation in one calculation, and the corresponding optimal solution can be found in the process of searching. The meta-heuristic algorithm can often find a good solution, but there is no way to prove that it will not get a worse solution, or cannot even find solution. The evolutionary algorithm used in this paper usually gives an approximate optimal solution within a given time, but can not to ensure that this solution is best at a given time.

In reality, there are some extreme situations in the process of implementing the heuristic algorithm, that is, some solutions that the meta-heuristic algorithms need are difficult to find or they cannot be found at all. The heuristic algorithm is often used to solve some Non-Deterministic Polynomial complete problems (NPC) because the calculative requirement of NPC is very large so some deterministic algorithms cannot be used to find the optimal solution. However, the meta-heuristic algorithm can get a good answer in a reasonable time when dealing with NPC, so the meta-heuristic algorithm is also a hot field for academic community.

The thought of the meta-heuristic algorithm has been formed for a long time and since its formation, the research on it has not been interrupted. As a result, there are many ways to achieve it. In recent decades, the research of meta-heuristic algorithm has developed rapidly, and there have been many more mature and specific subalgorithms. In the 1970s, Professor Holland [7] proposed genetic algorithm. Genetic algorithm simulates the evolutionary method of biological population to find the optimal solution of some problems, which opens up a new upsurge in research on meta-heuristic algorithm. Ever since the 1980s, a number of new meta-heuristic algorithms emerged [8], such as Simulated Annealing Algorithm, Artificial Neural Network, Tabu Search and etc.

2.2   Evolutionary Algorithm

Evolutionary algorithm [9] origins from Darwin's theory of evolution and Mendel's theory of genetic gene. Its essence is an efficient global search algorithm that imitates the biological evolution of nature. In the process of searching for the optimal solution, it can automatically acquire and accumulate the more optimal individual in the large population, and control search process adaptively. It can converge to the better solution oriented according to the natural law of the strong stronger and the weak weaker. As is known to all, the difficulty of software project management problem is to find the right order of the work package under the precondition of satisfying the constraint of the resource. However, there are numberless constitute of the work package. Traversal is the easiest approach but it requires too much computing resources and results to lower effectiveness. So we need an approach which consumes less time with a perfect solution.

The core of the evolutionary algorithm is the design of encoding of candidate solutions and the fitness function. The evolutionary algorithm first encodes the solutions according to the different requirements of problem. Each individual in the population represents a solution to the problem. At the same time, for each solution of the problem, we also need to design the fitness function. The fitness value of different solutions is used to measure the adaptability of different individuals. Individuals with high adaptability are more likely to survive in the evolution process of population. After encoding, there are four steps including initialized population, crossover, mutation and selection. The specific operation of initialized population is to generate the first generation of population randomly; The cross is to product new offspring population by the individual hybridization between parents then the mutation is to mutate certain genes in the individuals and mutated individuals will be involved in population hybridization to maintain the species diversity of the population. As a result, the operation above will bring some novel solutions; Finally, the selection is to choose better individuals in the whole population according to the natural law of winning. In a word, the evolutionary algorithm obtains the optimal solution by the evolution of the population.

3   Project Management Problem

3.1   Project Plan

The core of project management problem is work package scheduling and resource allocation. Figure 1 is a Gantt chart of typical software project management, which illustrates work package arrangement of a real industry software engineering. Generally, all the important phases in software engineering, such as project planning, requirements analysis, design, development, testing, deployment etc., are inseparable from the allocation of work packages. These work packages have a mutually restrictive relationship. Some work packages must be started when other work packages are completed. For instance, the analysis of software requirements is often to take place after the completion of project planning while some work packages can be done at the same time, and there is no impact on each other, such as software development and software testing can often be synchronized. The goal of project manager is using the shortest possible time to complete all work packages within the software project duration.

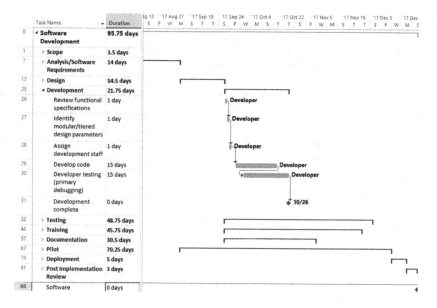

Fig. 1. Software project plan in a Microsoft Project file (.mpp)

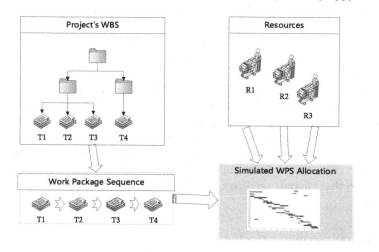

Fig. 2. Project plan of software development

In the process of project management, the work packages in the project are allocated by simulation. See Fig. 2, Firstly, the whole project is decomposed into several work packages by *work breakdown structure*, and those work packages are arranged into a corresponding *work package sequence*. Secondly, according to the dependencies of the work packages and the restriction of resource, each kinds of resources is allocated to the corresponding work package by *first-come-first-served* algorithm. Finally, the project's overall duration is yielded from the simulation.

3.2 Definition and Assumptions

The goal of this paper is to find an optimal solution or near optimal solution for the project management problem described as follows:

For a software project with N work packages and M kinds of resources, there is a directed acyclic dependencies between these work packages, and each resource can only be assigned to the specified work package. It is necessary to arrange the order of the work package reasonably and make the overall construction duration as short as possible under the condition of satisfying the work package dependency and the resource allocation restriction.

There are three assumptions for our project management problem.

Assumption I: The software project plan can be decomposed into a set of work packages containing N elements $T = \{t_1, t_2, ..., t_N\}$. Each work package in set T is indivisible (i.e., The work package cannot be split to other work package in the schedule), the set of work packages have a pre-estimated workload, the composition of the workload is the collection $E = \{e_1, e_2, ..., e_N\}$. The function $TE : T \rightarrow E$, the mean of this function is that for a given work package t_i, produces an estimated workload $e_i = TE(t_i)$ for a work package t_i, where e_i is the estimated workload of t_i.

Assumption II: The work packages in the software project can be processed with M kinds of resources, which constitute a resource set $R = \{r_1, r_2, ..., r_M\}$, for each project's work package set T and the resource set R, There exists a function $TR : T \times R \rightarrow \{0, 1\}$, for the given work package t_i and the resource r_j, $TR(t_i, r_j) = 1$ means the resource r_j can be allocated to the work package t_i, while $TR(t_i, r_j) = 0$ means cannot.

Assumption III: All work packages in the set T of the software project plan have dependencies. These dependencies form a set $Dep = \{t_i \rightarrow t_j \mid t_i, t_j \in T, t_j$ depends on $t_i\}$. As the assumption of this paper, $t_i \rightarrow t_j$ means that t_j depends on t_i, that is the work package t_j must be arranged after the work package t_i, and satisfy the formula $t_j.start \leq t_i.end$ (where $t.start$ and $t.end$ respectively indicate the start time and the end time of the work package t). And assume that there is no direct or indirect "loop" dependency between work packages.

3.3 The Objective of Problem

The objective of project management is to find an optimal work package sequence under the three assumptions above. The notation of work package sequence (WPS) is as follows:

$$S = \{(t_{p_1}, r_{q_1})... \rightarrow (t_{p_j}, r_{q_j}) \rightarrow ...(t_{p_N}, r_{q_N}) \mid t_{p_i} \in T, \overset{\bullet}{r}_{q_j} \in R\} \qquad (1)$$

where every (t_p, r_q) means resource r_q is allocated to work package t_p. The WPS needs to meet the following two restrictions:

1. $\nexists i < j, t_j \rightarrow t_i \in Dep$. (The WPS must satisfy the dependencies)
2. $\nexists i, k, TR(t_i, r_k) = 0$. (All work packages must have at least one resource)

For the work package arrangement sequence S, each work package t is given $t.start$ (the start time) and $t.end$ (the end time). The total cost duration function of the project is defined as $f(S) = max\{t.end \mid t \in T\}$. That is, the overall duration represents the maximum value of the end time of all work packages in a work package arrangement sequence S, which also means when the last work package of the project is completed, the entire project ends. The objective function is defined as following:

$$\textbf{Objective: } min(f(S)) = min(max\{t.end \mid t \in T\}) \qquad (2)$$

The objective of the project management problem is to find a work package sequence S to arrange the whole project under the condition of satisfying the restriction of dependencies and resources, so that the overall duration is minimized.

4 Design of Algorithm

This section introduces the two important steps in using the evolutionary algorithm. One is to choose the representation of the problem's solution, the other is to define a appropriate fitness function.

4.1 The Representation of Solution

For the above-mentioned problem, the representation of solution is defined as follows. This paper uses *work package sequence* (hereinafter referred to as *WPS*) to represent a solution of project management problem. The representation of such a solution is actually a priority arrangement sequence of the work packages in the whole project, and the number of solutions for a project containing the N work packages is $N!$, which is large enough to do random search.

$$T_1 \rightarrow T_5 \rightarrow T_6 \rightarrow T_4 \rightarrow T_8 \rightarrow T_3 \rightarrow T_9 \rightarrow T_2 \rightarrow T_7 \qquad (3)$$

For example, Eq. (3) is solution, the solution represents the work package sequence in the priority of T_1, T_5, T_6, T_4, T_8, T_3, T_9, T_2, T_7, while arranging the work packages. This representation is beneficial and intuitive to programming.

4.2 Fitness Evaluation

The above-mentioned representation of solution make each individual encoded as *WPS*. The fitness value of *WPS* is the project's overall duration, which is calculated by simulating the assignment of work packages in the set of package sequence, see Eq. (1).

The Algorithm 1 illustrates how to calculate corresponding project overall duration. Firstly, according to first-come-first-served rule, the front work packages in a *WPS* have high priority to get resources, the back work packages has low priority. Secondly, the TR function defines which work package can get which resources, if two work packages that require the same resources, the higher priority one will use the resources firstly, the lower priority one will use the resources after the higher one releases the resources. Finally, the project's overall duration is the last end time after all work packages are allocated the resources. As we can see from the Algorithm 1, to calculate the overall duration, the algorithm must traverse all N work packages and M kinds of resources, so the average complexity of fitness evolution is $O(N \times M)$.

Algorithm 1. Fitness Evaluation Algorithm

---

input: WPS, R, TE, TR
output: *duration*
  for i **from** 1 **to** $WPS.length$ **do**
    $t \leftarrow WPS[i]$
    $effort \leftarrow TE(i)$
    for r **in** R **do**
      $r.occupy \leftarrow 0$
    end for
    for r **in** R **do**
      if $TR(t, r) = true$ **then**
        $t.start \leftarrow r.occupy$
        $t.end \leftarrow r.occupy + effort$
        $r.occupy \leftarrow t.end$
        break
      end if
    end for
  end for
  $duration \leftarrow 0$
  for t **in** WPS **do**
    if $t.end > duration$ **then**
      $duration \leftarrow t.end$
    end if
  end for

4.3   Genetic Operators

There are two main types of operators in evolutionary algorithms: *crossover* and *mutation.* **Crossover** In evolutionary algorithms, crossover is a genetic operator used to vary the programming of a chromosome or chromosomes from one generation to the next. In this paper, we use a two-point crossover, that is, two points are selected randomly on the parent organism strings. Everything between the two points is swapped between the parent organisms, rendering two child organisms then exchange corresponding part of chromosomes to get offspring individual. **Mutation** In evolutionary algorithms, Mutation is a genetic operator used to maintain genetic diversity from one generation of a population of genetic algorithm chromosomes to the next. In this paper, we use two-point exchange mutation, that is, two points is selected randomly on individual organisms strings, and then exchange the two points.

4.4   Parallel Evolutionary Algorithm

Figure 3 summarizes the basic process of the evolutionary algorithm. Figure 3(a) is common sequential evolutionary algorithm, the algorithm has several steps, such as initialization, crossover, mutation, and selection. Candidate solutions to the optimization problem play the role of individuals in a population, and the fitness function determines the convergence of the solutions. Evolution of the population then takes place after the repeated application of the above operators. Figure 3(b) illustrates a parallel evolutionary algorithm. The parallel one follows most steps in sequential one, but put the top time-consuming work on GPU. The steps of crossover, mutation and evolution runs in different cores in GPU so that the speed of calculation can be improved a lot.

4.5   Runtime Environment

The hardware environment of algorithm implementation is as follows: the run-time processor that executes the sequential evolutionary algorithm is the Intel i7 series CPU (abbreviated as CPU). The runtime processor of the parallel evolutionary algorithm is the NVidia GeForce GTX 970 (abbreviated as GPU). The major difference between CPU and GPU is that they have different number of computation cores. Normally, the computation speed of a GPU core is lower than a CPU core. But GPU has far more than the number of CPU cores. In this paper, The CPU we used has 8 cores and the GPU has 1664 cores.

The software environment that runs application is as follows: the sequential programs runs on Microsoft Visual Studio 2012 C++ Compiler environment, the

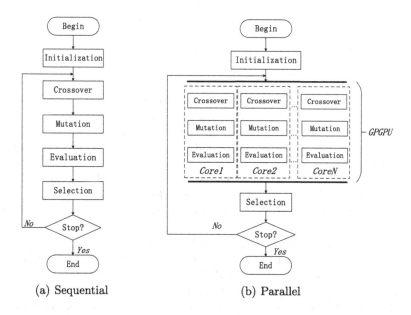

(a) Sequential   (b) Parallel

Fig. 3. Sequential and parallel evolutionary algorithm

parallel one runs on CUDA 7.0.28 Runtime environment. Both sequential and parallel application is evaluated in the same computer.

5   Experimental Results

To assess the evolutionary algorithm proposed in this paper, two separated evaluation experiments are made for the effectiveness of evolutionary algorithm and the efficiency of parallel evolutionary algorithm in project management problem. The purpose of the experiment is to address the following two research questions:

RQ1: Does the evolutionary algorithm effectively optimize project management problem, and get an optimized solution?

RQ2: Is the parallel evolutionary algorithm able to improve the efficiency in the project management problem?

5.1   Industrial Project Data

Three industrial project plans have been used in the experimental studies for this paper, which are named as *A-Input*, *B-DBUpgrade* and *C-SmartPrice*. These data come from real world projects and have fundamental details, such as work packages, resources and dependencies. Table 1 shows the number of each project.

Table 1. Three project's parameters

	# work packages	# resources	# dependencies
A-Input	33	4	33
B-DBUpgrade	106	8	105
C-SmartPrice	74	14	73

A-Input is a simulated small-scale project planning. it is a team work plan for finishing class assignments. *B-DBUpgrade* is a real software development plan, which's goal is to upgrade the Oracle database from the *9g* version to the *10g* version. *B-DBUpgrade* is Oracle's non-public version of the project planning. There were different layers of the organisation involved including DBAs, BSAs, developers and users. Furthermore, the project also included the training of the staff for the new features of the system. *C-SmartPrice* consists of a supply chain enhancement of medium size affecting mostly the website as well as a few internal applications [10].

Figure 4 illustrates the relationship between work packages and resources. In each sub-figure, the rectangle represents a work package in the project plan, the content in the rectangle is the work packages' ID and duration; the arrows between work packages suggest dependencies, notice that some redundant dependencies is removed; the folders in the bottom are some certain types of resources that can be allocated to work packages.

5.2 Effectiveness Experiment for Algorithm

In order to answer **RQ1**, this section designs an effectiveness experiment for evolutionary algorithm. The basic configuration used in the experiment is that 100 individuals runs in 50 generations. For each generation in the evolutionary algorithm, we evaluate each individuals' fitness value in the whole population, and then plot the statistical data into a boxplot diagram.

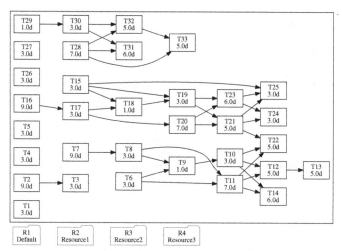

(a) *A-Input*, 33 work packages, 4 resources and 33 dependencies

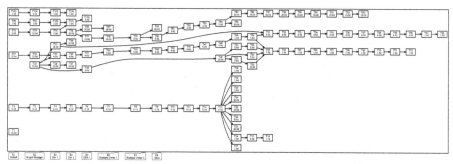

(b) *B-DBUpgrade*: 106 work packages, 8 resources and 105 dependencies

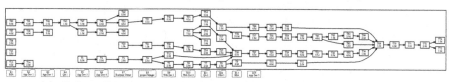

(c) *C-SmartPrice:*, 74 work packages, 14 resources and 73 dependencies

Fig. 4. Three Projects' *work packages, resources* and *dependencies*

The boxplot diagram shows the five kinds of statistical data of all individuals' fitness value in each generation. The data are the minimum, the lower quartile, the median, the upper quartile and the maximum values of the whole population. Figure 5 shows the results of the above-mentioned three industrial projects. In each sub-figure, the tick labels on the horizontal axis indicate the total number of internal generations that have been carried out, and also indicates the point

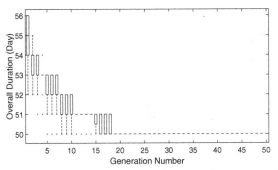

(a) *A-Input*'s solution converges on *19th* generation

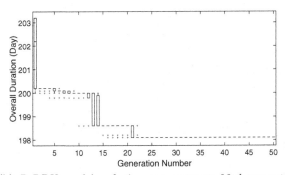

(b) *B-DBUpgrade*'s solution converges on *22rd* generation

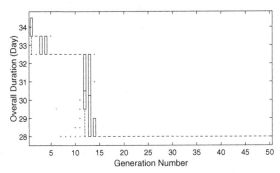

(c) *C-SmartPrice*'s solution converges on *15th* generation

Fig. 5. Statistics of fitness value in each generation

at which the algorithm updated the population used for fitness computation. At each point on the horizontal axis, the entire population is depicted using a boxplot to give both a sense of the values obtained for completion time as the evolution progresses and the distribution of the fitness values in the population. From the trend of three projects in the figures, it can be seen that the population is diversified when the population is initialized and as the number of generation increase, all the fitness value begins to decrease, and finally converges to an optimized result.

The convergence of solutions is quite fast and stable. Figure 5(a) shows the solution of *A-Input* converges on 19th generation. Figure 5(b) shows the solution of *B-DBUpgrade* converges on 22rd generation. Figure 5(c) shows the solution of *C-SmartPrice* converges on 15th generation. Those results show us evolutionary algorithm will find an optimized overall duration for specific project plan.

Through the above analysis results of experimental data, we can accurately answer **RQ1**. In the project management problems, the evolutionary algorithm does have a good optimization and improvement.

5.3   Efficiency Experiment for Algorithm

In order to answer **RQ2**, this section conducts an efficiency experiment that compares the efficiency between the parallel evolutionary algorithm and the sequential one.

Table 2. The comparison of sequential and parallel implementation

Time (ms)	A-Input		B-DBUpgrade		C-SmartPrice	
	CPU	GPU	CPU	GPU	CPU	GPU
1	7991.8	4102.5	45225.1	21217.5	29642.9	14844.3
2	8431.8	4279.7	44832.1	21377.9	28733.7	14543.6
3	7504.1	3947.9	44934.9	21227.2	28657.9	15003.4
4	7442.1	4642.5	44197.1	21340.3	29489.5	14882.8
5	7376.9	4263.8	45233.7	22448.2	29379.5	14921.5
6	7385.4	4188.6	45197.5	20956.1	28687.9	14723.3
7	8238.8	4540.2	45305.4	21777.2	29786.3	13978.8
8	7470.7	4226.4	45322.8	21147.1	31231.7	14811.1
9	7604.8	3778.2	45040.7	21004.7	28319.7	14292.0
10	7451.9	4712.4	45970.6	21500.9	28322.1	14429.7
Avg.	7689.8	4268.2	45126.0	21399.7	29225.1	14643.1

The initial configuration of the two algorithms is the identical, which the number of population is 1000 and the number of generation is 100. Each generation runs several steps including crossover, mutation and selection etc. A timer is set to record the total executing time of the experiments. The timer starts after loading initial data and ends after the result is calculated. This operation allows us to count the real executing time both in the sequential environment and the parallel environment under the same criteria. The efficiency experiments are repeated 10 times. Table 2 shows the comparison of sequential and parallel implementation executing time on all three industrial projects. By the comparison of average executing time of 10 times results, the average executing time of *A-Input* on CPU is 1.80 times than GPU, the average executing time of *B-DBUpgrade* on CPU is 2.10 times than GPU and the average executing time of *C-SmartPrice* on CPU is 2.00 times than GPU.

In summary, the executing time of sequential algorithm on CPU is roughly twice as long as the parallel algorithm on GPU. So it can be a good answer to **RQ2** that parallel evolutionary algorithm can improve the efficiency on computing the project management problems.

6   Related Works

In 1993, Chang et al. [2] first proposed the project management problem. The view of Chang is that software project management net (SPM-Net) can be used to schedule tasks and manage the resources of software development. In his article, Chang's project management problem is based on the simulative data, the reason leading to this is the real industrial data of software project management is very scanty. In 2007, Alba and Chicano [3] optimized the search algorithms for project management, and solve the project management problem using genetic algorithm. Their goal is using a search-based approach to reduce the final completion duration of a project. In 2009, Ren et al. [4] first applied co-evolutionary algorithms to solve project management problem. Recently, Sarro et al. [11] proposed a multi-objective decision support approach to help balance project risks and duration against overtime, so that software engineers can better plan overtime. At present, the search space of the work package based on the project management is more and more huge, the sequential algorithm is not so effective to solve such problems. Thus, finding a parallel algorithm has become a hot topic on research [6].

In recent years, search-based project management problem has become an important branch of search-based software engineering, and has become a new field of research. At the same time, the number of papers related to search-based project management problem is also rising, which makes many researchers willing to engage in search-based project management problem, so in turn provides a new platform for practice and innovation of the search-based project management problem [5]. In 2011, Thomas [12] proposed an approach to describe software project problems with a set of multi-objective criteria for portfolio managers using the COCOMO II model and introduce a multi-objective evolutionary approach. In 2014, Samanta [13] gone through a very brief idea on Genetic Algorithm and implemented the algorithm using MATLAB. The search-based algorithm is a compute-intensive method, which means the computer's CPU will be used usually consumed a lot. Therefore, the traditional sequential computing model cannot meet the requirement of increasing calculation speed. In 2007,

Alba and Chicano [14] began using search-based methods to improve the optimal solution of problems, and for the first time using a parallel code model to test the efficiency of search-based methods. In 2013, Jing [15] began solving software project scheduling problems with ant colony optimization. In recent years, more search-based software engineering methods (such as simulated annealing, climbing algorithms, evolutionary algorithms, tabu search, etc.) have been used to solve project management problem, and these methods are usually able to get good convergence solution on project management problem.

As the development of the algorithm, how to speed up the calculation of the algorithm has become a hot spot in academic community. In 2012, Zhang et al. [16] apply GPGPU to simulation for complex scenes and later on they proposed a GPU-based parallel MOEAs [17]. CUDA is a generic parallel computing architecture developed by NVIDIA, which can be used to improve the performance of GPGPU [18] and also can be optimized by meta-heuristic algorithms [19,20]. In 2014, Jianmei [21] proposed five novel parallel algorithms for solving multi-objective combinatorial optimization problems exactly and efficient. Compared to our work, those algorithms are different in solved questions, but there is the same thought of parallelization to gain the faster speed. They apply the algorithm to the case of software-system designs and get great solution, which illustrate the great characteristic of parallelization in the domain of software engineering. In general, the parallel evolution algorithm can be implemented on the GPU platform using the CUDA [22]. With the development of the technology of parallelism, a general-purpose GPU (GPGPU) is used to improve the speed of calculation in software engineering.

Furthermore, a common project management tool which deal with the mathematical models have not been implemented, so it is difficult to apply the theory to the industrial project management process. In 2012, Stylianou [23] and Gerasimou first developed a tool for project management, which they named IntelliSPM. The tool uses Matlab and Java programming language and supports staffing arrangement and resource allocation optimization. In their work, Stylianou uses the fitness function to dynamic calculate the dependencies between work packages, so the real project's dependencies may be broken during the calculation. So in current software engineering practice, the tool supporting project management is still lacking.

7   Conclusions and Future Work

This paper introduces a framework to solve the work package scheduling problem as a single objective optimization problem. The framework accelerates the optimization process by parallelizing the evolving of solutions on a graphic card. We conducted a "proof of concept" empirical study using data from three industrial software projects, aimed at demonstrate the effectiveness and efficiency of proposed framework. Results show that the population converge around 20 generations and the parallel version of single objective evolutionary algorithm spend half of the execution time compared to the sequential version, even with only one relative cheap hardware. Therefore, we claim that heuristics provides manager with intuitive features towards "simple-to-deploy", and parallel computation running on GPU provides shorter execution time.

Future work aims at extending the study reported in this paper with further data sets and accelerating hardware with more cores, above all, at considering a more sophisticated project model, which accounts for further factors not considered in this study, such as group configuration of staff and the interaction among staffing and scheduling. As the development of the scale of the software project, there are more than one objectives in the problem define. So we will increase the complexity of the model of the software project management problem and improved our algorithm to solve multi-objective problem. Future work will also include developing a set of automation tools and techniques. We believe that a optimization tool can automatically parsing a Microsoft Project file (.mpp) can be made useful to provide optimized solutions to aid the managers in practice.

Acknowledgements. This work was supported by the National Natural Science Foundation of China (61602021) and the State Key Laboratory of Software Development Environment (SKLSDE-2017ZX-20).

References

1. Stellman, A., Greene, J.: Applied Software Project Management. O'Reilly, Sebastopol (2005)
2. Chang, C.K., Jiang, H., Di, Y., Zhu, D., Ge, Y.: Time-line based model for software project scheduling with genetic algorithms. Info. Softw. Tech. **50**, 1142–1154 (2008)
3. Alba, E., Francisco, C.J.: Software project management with GA. Inf. Sci. **177**, 2380–2401 (2007)
4. Ren, J., Harman, M., Penta, M.D.: Cooperative co-evolutionary optimization of software project staff assignments and job scheduling. In: GECCO, pp. 495–519 (2011)
5. Penta, M.D., Harman, M., Antoniol, G.: The use of search-based optimization techniques to schedule and staff software projects: an approach and an empirical study. Softw. Pract. Exp. **41**, 495–519 (2011)
6. Pentico, D.W.: Assignment problems: a golden anniversary survey. Eur. J. Oper. Res. **176**, 774–793 (2007)
7. Holland, J.H.: Adaptation in Natural and Artificial Systems: An Introductory Analysis with Applications to Biology, Control, and Artificial Intelligence. U Michigan Press, Oxford (1975)
8. Harman, M., McMinn, P., de Souza, J.T., Yoo, S.: Search based software engineering: techniques, taxonomy, tutorial. In: Meyer, B., Nordio, M. (eds.) LASER 2008-2010. LNCS, vol. 7007, pp. 1–59. Springer, Heidelberg (2012). https://doi.org/10.1007/978-3-642-25231-0_1
9. Deb, K., Pratap, A., Agarwal, S., Meyarivan, T.: A fast and elitist multiobjective genetic algorithm: NSGA-II. IEEE TEC **6**, 182–197 (2002)
10. Ren, J.: Search Based Software Project Management. University of London, pp. 1–178 (2013)
11. Sarro, F., Ferrucci, F., Harman, M., Manna, A., Ren, J.: Adaptive multi-objective evolutionary algorithms for overtime planning in software projects. TSE **43**(10), 898–917 (2017)

12. Thomas, K., Jiri, K., Stefan, B.: Software project portfolio optimization with advanced multiobjective evolutionary algorithms. Appl. Soft Comput. **11**(1), 1416–1426 (2011)
13. Samanta, S.: Genetic algorithm: an approach for optimization (Using MATLAB). Int. J. Latest Trends Eng. Technol. **3**, 261–267 (2014)
14. Pospichal, P., Jaros, J., Schwarz, J.: Parallel genetic algorithm on the CUDA architecture. In: Di Chio, C., et al. (eds.) EvoApplications 2010. LNCS, vol. 6024, pp. 442–451. Springer, Heidelberg (2010). https://doi.org/10.1007/978-3-642-12239-2_46
15. Jing, X., Xian-Ting, A., Yong, T.: Solving software project scheduling problems with ant colony optimization. Comput. OR **40**(1), 33–46 (2013)
16. Zhang, F., Li, Z., Wang, B., Xiang, M., Hong, W.: Hybrid general-purpose computation on GPU (GPGPU) and computer graphics synthetic aperture radar simulation for complex scenes. Int. J. Phys. Sci. **7**, 1224–1234 (2012)
17. Li, Z., Bian, Y., Zhao, R., Cheng, J.: A fine-grained parallel multi-objective test case prioritization on GPU. In: Ruhe, G., Zhang, Y. (eds.) SSBSE 2013. LNCS, vol. 8084, pp. 111–125. Springer, Heidelberg (2013). https://doi.org/10.1007/978-3-642-39742-4_10
18. Langdon, W. B., Lam, B. Y. H., Petke, J., Harman, M.: Improving CUDA DNA analysis software with genetic programming. In: GECCO 2015, pp. 1063–1070 (2015)
19. Langdon, W.B., Lam, B.H.Y., Modat, M., Petke, J., Harman, M.: Genetic improvement of GPU software. GPEM **18**(1), 5–44 (2017)
20. Langdon, W.B., Harman, M.: Optimizing existing software with genetic programming. IEEE Trans. Evol. Comput. **19**(1), 118–135 (2015)
21. Jianmei, G., et al.: Scaling exact multi-objective combinatorial optimization by parallelization. In: ASE 2014, pp. 409–420 (2014)
22. Vidal, P., Alba, E.: A multi-GPU implementation of a cellular genetic algorithm. In: 2010 IEEE World Congress on Computational Intelligence, pp. 1–7 (2010)
23. Stylianou, C., Gerasimou, S., Andreou, A.S.: A novel prototype tool for intelligent software project scheduling and staffing enhanced with personality factors. In: International Conference on Tools with Artificial Intelligence, pp. 277–284 (2012)

Multi-gene Genetic Programming Based Defect-Ranking Software Modules

Junxia Guo⬤, Yingying Duan, and Ying Shang$^{(\boxtimes)}$

College of Information Science and Technology,
Beijing University of Chemical Technology, Beijing, China
{gjxia,shangy}@mail.buct.edu.cn

Abstract. Most software defect prediction models aim at predicting the number of defects in a given software. However, it is very difficult to predict the precise number of defects in a module because of the presence of noise data. Another type of frequently used approach is ranking the software modules according to the relative number of defects, according to which software defect prediction can guide the testers to allocate the limited resources preferentially to modules with a greater number of defects. Owing to the redundant metrics in software defect data-sets, researchers always need to reduce the dimensions of the metrics before constructing defect prediction models. However a reduction in the number of dimensions may lead to some useful information being deleted too early, and consequently, the performance of the prediction model will decrease. In this paper, we propose an approach using multi-gene genetic programming (MGGP) to build a defect rank model. We compared the MGGP-based model with other optimized methods over 11 publicly available defect data-sets consisting of several software systems. The fault-percentile-average (FPA) is used to evaluate the performance of the MGGP and other methods. The results show that the models for different test objects that are built based on the MGGP approach perform better those based on other nonlinear prediction approaches when constructing the defect rank. In addition, the correlation between the software metrics will not affect the prediction performance. This means that, by using the MGGP method, we can use the original features to construct a prediction model without considering the influence of the correlation between the software module features.

Keywords: Software defect prediction ·
Multi-gene genetic programming · Defect rank model

1 Introduction

Software defect prediction has become one of the most active research areas in software engineering over the past few decades. The defects in software not only worsen the quality of the software but also increase the cost of software maintenance. The fixing of defects usually costs about 80% of the total budget of the software project [24]. The target of software defect prediction is to predict the defects in new software modules before the testing stage by mining historical software repositories and then utilizing the software characteristics to

© Springer Nature Singapore Pte Ltd. 2019
Z. Li et al. (Eds.): NASAC 2017/2018, CCIS 861, pp. 52–71, 2019.
https://doi.org/10.1007/978-981-15-0310-8_4

build prediction models. Using the prediction results of potential defect modules in a given software, testers can allocate assurance resources of limited quality in an efficient manner, and preferentially detect those modules that have more defects [14].

Many statistics and machine learning methods such as Logistic Regression (LR), Neural Network (NN), Naive Bayes (NB), Classification Trees (CT), Decision trees (DT), Ensemble learners (EL), Bagging, Boosting and Support Vector Machine (SVM) etc. have been proposed and applied to defect prediction for classification or regression task [7,19]. Most of the previous software defect prediction studies have adopted a defect proneness model, i.e., a binary class classification model, to classify the software modules into defect and non-defect modules [20,29,31]. Although this type of model has reported an excellent performance, it cannot identify the number of defects per module for the given software. A defect proneness model cannot provide sufficient guidance to the testers when they need to know an approximate number of defects per module.

More researchers have begun to focus on predicting the number of defects. There are mainly two kinds of models, defect count models and defect rank models. Defect count models estimate the exact number of defects for every module [21,28,30]. Some performance measures such as the average absolute errors (AAE), average relative errors (ARE), and root mean square error (RMSE), which reflect the degree of predicted values deviating from real values, are used to evaluate such prediction models. Thus, a smaller value indicates higher prediction accuracy. Defect rank models are different from defect count models, which do not focus on predicting the exact numbers of defects, but rather the relative number per module [21,32]. Therefore, testers can distribute test resources to software modules that have a relatively higher number of defects.

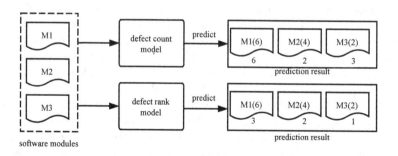

Fig. 1. Difference between a defect count model and a defect rank model.

Figure 1 depicts the difference between a defect count model and a defect rank model. Suppose the given software has three modules M1, M2, and M3. The actual numbers of defects corresponding to these three modules are 6, 4, and 2, and the prediction results obtained using the defect count model are 6, 2, and 3, respectively. The prediction results obtained using the defect rank model are 3, 2, and 1. It can be seen that the prediction accuracy (according to AAE and ARE) of the count model is higher than that of the rank model. However, the rank model gives a perfect module ranking because the software modules with larger numbers of defects will receive prior attention.

Hence, even if defect count models can provide more detailed information, it remains too difficult to predict the exact number of defects of a module. Yang et al. [27] pointed out that for the ranking task of software defect prediction, models with higher prediction accuracy (smaller AAE or ARE) might not provide a good ranking. Thus, they proposed an optimization prediction model, called the learning-to-rank (LTR) approach. This approach can provide better module ranking than prediction models obtained by minimizing the loss function based on each sample. However, issues found during their experiments still remain: (1) when the number of software metrics is large, the LTR linear model performs worse than the Random Forest (RF) model, and (2) the authors did not investigate the LTR nonlinear model to verify the generality of the approach.

The Genetic Programming (GP) algorithm, as a new type of nonlinear modeling method, does not need to predefine the function form of a model. It can automatically evolve the structure and parameters of the model. This provides the GP algorithm with strong flexibility in terms of modeling. The GP algorithm has been widely applied to various types of nonlinear prediction models. Garg et al. [11] compared a traditional regression analysis, an artificial neural network, and genetic programming in handling multi-collinearity problems (input variables having a strong correlation), and discovered that genetic programming is not affected by related input variables during treatment and is able to evolve more accurate prediction models. A multi-gene genetic programming approach has the capabilities of both standard genetic programming methods for modeling the structure selection and traditional regression methods for a parameter evaluation.

Based on the idea of found in the above approaches, in this paper, we consider to taking the advantages of the GP algorithm in handling the multi-collinearity problems into the prediction of the a relative number of defects in a given software system by using applying Multi-Gene Genetic Programming (MGGP). We construct defect prediction models using MGGP over 11 publicly available software defect data-sets and evaluate their performance and other methods based on the fault-percentile-average (FPA). Our results indicate that models based on MGGP can achieve more significant results than other types of models. In addition, we compare the optimized models and un-optimized models, and find that the optimized nonlinear models, by directly optimizing the ranking performance, are better than the un-optimized models i.e., the original nonlinear models with default parameters.

The main contributions of this paper are as follows.

(1) The MGGP algorithm is applied to construct software defect ranking models, and to design the details of the function sets, terminator sets, running control parameters, fitness functions, and termination rules.

(2) In this paper, we compare the experimental results of the MGGP prediction model constructed using all features of the defect data-set and partial features. It is found that the correlation between software features does not affect the prediction performance of the MGGP approach, which indicates that MGGP is robust even with redundant data.

The rest of this paper is organized as follows. Section 2 presents previous related studies and the background of this research. In Sect. 3, we describe the details of our MGGP-based defect prediction model. Section 4 details the software defect data-sets, metrics, and evaluation measures used. The experiments and results are presented in Sect. 5. We discuss the threats to the validity of our work in Sect. 6. Finally, Sect. 7 provides some concluding remarks and areas of future work.

2   Background

In this section, we firstly present the related work on software defect prediction. Then we describe essential background on MGGP.

Khoshgoftaar et al. [16] pointed out that models that have good prediction accuracy do not necessarily require good module-sorting through the adoption of two generalized linear regression models, namely, Poisson regression (PR) and zero-inflated Poisson regression (ZIPR). PR and ZIRP both have advantages in terms of the different cutoff points of the percentage of defects, which means there is no one model for all cutoff points that is better than any other model. Later, Khoshgoftaar et al. [15] defined a module-order model as a quantitative software quality model used to predict the rank-order of modules according to quality factors, such as the number of faults. Gao et al. [9] compared eight types of generalized linear regression models used to predict the numbers of faults in the software modules. The experimental results indicate that applying different measures can result in different conclusions.

Weyuker et al. [26] claimed that FPA is suitable for evaluating the performance of defect count models. Yang et al. [27] introduced a learning-to-rank approach to construct software defect prediction models by directly optimizing the ranking performance. Their empirical studies demonstrate the effectiveness of their approach for constructing defect prediction models in ranking tasks.

Afzal et al. [1] presented empirical results when using genetic programming for predicting the number of defects over three different industrial projects. They concluded that the GP evolved model achieves a statistically significant goodness of fit, as well as predictive accuracy. Rathore et al. [23] presented an approach to predicting the numbers of defects through genetic programming. They used the error rate, recall, and completeness for an evaluation on ten fault data-sets. Their results show that GP-based models can produce good accuracy and completeness in predicting the number of faults. Later, Rathore et al. [22] further presented an experimental study to evaluate and compare the capability of six fault prediction techniques, namely, genetic programming, multilayer perception, linear regression, decision tree regression, zero-inflated Poisson regression (ZIPR), and negative binomial regression (NBR), for the prediction of the number of defects. AAE and ARE were used to measure the performance of completeness, and applied a prediction for *level l* measures. They observed that the count models (NBR and ZIPR) generally underperformed the other models used.

The MGGP algorithm, developed based on the GP algorithm, was put forward by Hinchliffe and Hiden [13]. The GP algorithm is a type of biologically inspired machine-learning tool and is an extension of the genetic algorithm (GA) [18]. Unlike the GA, the individual encoding in the GP algorithm is usually denoted in a tree form, which makes the evolution process more flexible. Differing from a traditional regression analysis, which requires the user to specify the model structure, the GP algorithm can automatically evolve the structure and parameters of a mathematical model. Thus, it has been widely applied to various types of nonlinear modeling problems. However, it has yet to be applied to the construction of defect rank models.

Differing from the standard GP algorithm, an individual of MGGP contains one or more genes. Each gene is a standard GP tree. A mathematical model is obtained by combining all weighted genes [10]. MGGP can be expressed as Eq. 1, where g_i denotes the ith gene, n denotes the number of genes, α_0 denotes the bias terms, and α_i denotes the weight of the ith gene, which can be calculated based on the least squares.

$$y = \alpha_0 + \alpha_1 g_1 + \alpha_2 g_2 + \cdots + \alpha_n g_n \qquad (1)$$

When applying the MGGP algorithm to a practical problem, we need to consider the following five aspects [5]:

- Specify the set of functions
- Specify the set of terminals
- Specify the fitness function
- Specify the parameters for controlling the evolution process
- Specify the termination criterion and design the result of the evolution.

Among them, the set of functions correspond to the root nodes of the GP trees, which include the basic mathematical operators, such as plus, minus, multiply, divide, and boolean algebra operators. The set of terminals correspond to leaf nodes of GP trees, which generally include the input variables and random constants. In the evolution process, the genetic operations such as selection, crossover, and mutation are similar to those with the GA.

3   MGGP-Based Defect Prediction Model

Assume that there are m modules of the given software, and n metrics for defect prediction per module, which can be denoted as the matrix, $X = (x_{ij})_{m \times n}$, where $i = 1 \ldots m$, $j = 1 \ldots n$, and x_{ij} is the value of the jth metric on the ith software module. When counting the numbers of defects in the software modules, we can expand X into $X' = (x_{ij})_{m \times (n+1)}$, and thus $Y_i = (y_i)_{m \times 1}$ represents the real number of defects of the ith module. The goal of the software defect rank model is to predict the relative number of defects, which is denoted as $f(x)$. In this paper, a prediction model is constructed by analyzing the relationship between software metrics and the number of real defects in the training set.

The relationship between the number of defects and the software metrics can be described as follows:

$$f(x) = y = f(x_1, x_2, \ldots, x_n, C)(i = 1 \ldots n)$$

where y denotes the number of defects per module, x_i denotes the software metrics, C is a random constant, and f is the map relation of the number of defects and the corresponding software metrics. This is an individual expression that is linearly weighted by genes that do not exceed MaxGene, which is the maximum number of genes. Each gene is made up by the set of functions and set of terminals randomly. By controlling the maximum depth of the gene trees and the maximum number of genes, we can control the depth and length of the function f, which stands for the complexity of the MGGP prediction model. The details in using MGGP to construct a model are as follows:

1. **Input:** modules: $x_i = (x_{i1}, x_{i2}, \ldots, x_{in})$, where $i = 1 \ldots m$, which is the matrix of the defect numbers, and $X' = (x_{ij})_{m \times (n+1)}$, where $i = 1 \ldots m$, $j = 1 \ldots n$, which are the corresponding software metrics.
2. Set the parameters of MGGP, such as the population size, number of generations to run, maximum depth of the trees, maximum number of genes per individual, and termination threshold value. Define the functions of MGGP. More details are provided in Sect. 5.1.
3. Initialize the population. Generate genes randomly, and individuals through combining genes using the least squares. Calculate the individual fitness function values. Set the generation number to $t = 0$.
4. **Repeat** the following steps:
   (1) Combine no more than $Maxgene$ genes using the least squares to obtain the individual expression, and calculate the individual fitness.
   (2) Choose certain numbers of individuals and genes for a genetic operation according to the genetic probability.
   (3) Generate a new population through a genetic operation such as copy, crossover, or mutation.
   (4) $t{+}{+}$.
   Until $t < t_{max}$ (the maximum of iterations) *or*, the termination threshold value equals the preset fitness.
5. **Output:** the corresponding defect number of every module $f(x) = Y_i' = (y_i)_{m \times 1}$, where $i = 1 \ldots m$, and the best fitness value.

The details of the fitness function, i.e., the evaluation measure, are described in Sect. 4.3, and the parameters for MGGP are discussed in Sect. 5.1.

4 Experimental Methodology

In this section, we present a brief overview of the software defect data-sets used for the experimental study, using information of the software metrics. We also provide a description of the evaluation measure used in the experiments.

Figure 2 shows an overview of our experimental method. First, we divide all software defect data-sets into training data and testing data through a 10-fold cross-validation. We then set the parameters and define the functions of MGGP for each training data-set, and construct the MGGP training models. The trained MGGP model is then applied over the testing data. Finally, we evaluate and validate the results using the FPA measure.

4.1 Software Defect Data-Sets

We use two sets of publicly available data provided in paper [27] as experimental data-sets. One of the data-sets includes the information of five open-source software systems which is also used in paper [6]. The five software systems[1] are Eclipse JDT Core (eclipse), Eclipse PDE UI (pde), Equinox framework (equinox), Mylyn, and Apache Lucene (lucene). The other data-set is called Eclipse data-set[2] which is provided by Zimmermann et al. [32]. To avoid any ambiguity, we denote the latter Eclipse as Eclipse_II. Eclipse_II includes two kinds of data. One kind is based on files and another is based on packages. Each kind of data involves three releases. We denote them as Eclipse_II_File2.0 as Files2.0, Eclipse_II_File2.1 as Files2.1, Eclipse_II_File3.0 as Files3.0, Eclipse_II_Package2.0 as Package2.0, Eclipse_II_Package2.1 as Package2.1, Eclipse_II_Package3.0 as Package3.0 for convenience.

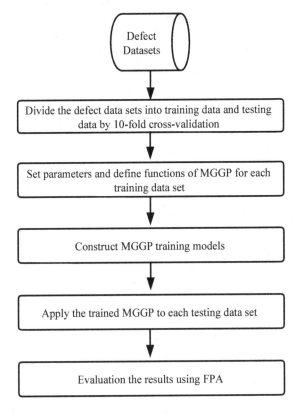

Fig. 2. The overview of our experimental method.

---

[1] http://bug.inf.usi.ch/.

[2] http://www.st.cs.uni-saarland.de/softevo/bug-data/eclipse/.

Table 1. Defect data-sets used in the experiments

Data-set name	Module number	Metric number	Faulty modules	% of faulty modules	Defect range	Total defects
eclipse	997	212	206	20.7%	[0, 9]	374
equinox	324	212	129	39.8%	[0, 13]	244
lucene	691	212	64	9.3%	[0, 9]	97
mylyn	1862	212	245	13.2%	[0, 12]	340
pde	1497	212	209	14.0%	[0, 28]	341
Eclipse_II_File2.0	6729	198	975	14.5%	[0, 31]	1692
Eclipse_II_File2.1	7888	198	854	10.8%	[0, 9]	1182
Eclipse_II_File3.0	10593	198	1568	14.8%	[0, 17]	2679
Eclipse_II_Package2.0	377	207	190	50.4%	[0, 88]	917
Eclipse_II_Package2.1	434	207	194	44.7%	[0, 71]	662
Eclipse_II_Package3.0	661	207	313	47.4%	[0, 65]	1534

The details of the data-sets are shown in Table 1. The column *Module Number* denotes the number of modules. The column *Metric Number* denotes the numbers of features of each data-set. The column *Faulty Modules* represents the number of modules whose defects are greater than zero. The column *Total Defects* represents the total number of defects of all modules in each data-set. The percentage of faulty (i.e., defective) modules varies by approximately 9%–55%, which makes the data-sets good candidates for the experimental study.

The data-sets have certain redundant metrics. For example, Wang et al. [25] and Menzies et al. [20] pointed out that a prediction model constructed using three metrics performs as good as one using all metrics. In fact, other features are calculated from the basic features extracted directly from the source code. As a result, the correlation between the same types of software features is high, and there are more redundant features. Thus we also select both three basic metrics and all metrics when conducting our experiments, and evaluate the results. The metric selection uses the information gain (InfoGain [20]) method. In information gain measures, the importance is based on how much information a feature can bring to the classification system. The more information it brings, the more important the feature is.

4.2   Software Metrics

The data in the first data-set, which is presented in paper [6], include six sets of metrics: process metrics, previous defects, source code metrics, entropy of changes, churn of source code metrics, and entropy of source code metrics. Eclipse_II includes two kinds of metrics: complexity metrics, and metrics based on the structure of abstract syntax trees. The former is collected at the file-level. The latter is collected at the package-level. The numbers of these data-set metrics can be found in Table 1.

4.3   Evaluation Measure

AAE and ARE are often used in existing software-defect ranking prediction models [17]. However, the purpose of a defect-ranking prediction model is to help testers allocate limited resources preferentially for those modules that have more defects. Usually, a few software modules contain most of the defects. Therefore, the Fault of Percentage (FP), the percentage of defects in the top m predicted modules, has become a commonly used evaluation measure. However, as Weyuker [26] pointed out, FP is sensitive to the value of m, which means a different m may provide completely different conclusions. Thus, Weyuker et al. proposed the Fault-Percentile-Average (FPA), which can overcome the shortcoming of FP being sensitive to the value of m.

Considering the k modules listed in increasing order of predicted number of defects as $f_1, f_2, f_3, \cdots, f_k$, and the actual number of defects of the k modules as $n_1, n_2, n_3, \cdots, n_k$, respectively, the top m predicted modules should have $\sum_{i=k-m+1}^{k} n_i$ defects. The proportion of actual defects in the top m predicted modules to all defects is

$$\frac{1}{n} \sum_{i=k-m+1}^{k} n_i,$$

where $n = n_1 + n_2 + \cdots + n_k$. The FPA is then defined as follows:

$$FPA = \frac{1}{k} \sum_{m=1}^{k} \frac{1}{n} \sum_{i=k-m+1}^{k} n_i$$

In practice, FPA is the average of the FPs when m takes different values. A higher FPA indicates a better ranking.

4.4   Wilcoxon Rank Sum Test

In statistics, a Wilcoxon rank-sum test [12] is also called a Mann-Whitney U test or Wilcoxon-Mann-Whitney test. This is a non-parametric test of a null hypothesis in which two sets of measurements are drawn from the same distribution. This test can be used to determine whether two independent samples were selected from a population having the same distribution[3].

In this study, to compare the difference in performance between the defect prediction techniques over the 11 data-sets, we apply a Wilcoxon rank-sum test using a 95% confidence level ($\alpha = 0.05$). We establish null hypothesis H0: the prediction results of the two defect prediction techniques come from the same distribution (there is no difference between them). Therefore, when the level of significance is 0.05, if the level of significance detected is greater than 0.05, the hypothesis is true and H0 is accepted; otherwise, the hypothesis is not true and H0 is rejected.

---

[3] https://en.wikipedia.org/wiki/MannWhitney_U_test.

5   Experiments and Results

In this section, we describe the parameters set for MGGP and other defect prediction models for comparison. We then present our research questions, along with our motivation, approach, and findings.

5.1   Set Parameters for MGGP

1. Function sets
   Because MGGP has an independent evolution, theoretically, sets of functions can contain a variety of functions. In addition to the basic mathematical operations, namely, $+, -, *, /$, and so on, we join the commonly used nonlinear functions such as *exp, log,* and *tanh*. Here, $/$ indicates protective division, *Exp* denotes an exponential function, *Log* is a natural logarithmic function, and *tanh* is a hyperbolic tangent function.
2. Terminal sets
   Generally, the terminal sets include input variables and random constants. In this paper, the input variables represent the specific values of the metrics.
3. Fitness function
   We use the FPA as a fitness function. If an individual's fitness value is bigger, the individual obtained is more optimal.
4. Parameters for controlling the evolution
   The population size, number of generations to run, maximum depth of the trees, maximum number of genes per individual, and parameters such as the crossover and mutation probabilities have a significant influence on the efficiency of the MGGP algorithm. In this paper, we adjust these parameters according to the experimental results, based on the experience value, in order to speed up the convergence of the algorithm.
5. Termination criterion
   The termination condition can be either the individual fitness value reaching the set threshold, or the number of MGGP iterations reaching the maximum number. For this study, we chose both situations as the termination criteria. After meeting any one of the two criteria, the MGGP stops.

5.2   Defect Prediction Models for Comparison

Bootstrap aggregating (Bagging) [3] is an ensemble learning technique. Bagging takes N times the Bootstrap sampling on the training data-set to obtain N training data subsets. Each subset uses the same algorithm to establish a decision tree. The final classification (or regression) result is the majority vote of the results of N decision trees (or average). Bagging can reduce the variance of the model and help avoid overfitting.

RF [4] consists of many Classification And Regression Tree (CART) decision trees. Each decision tree is based on a subset of training samples. During the training phase, features are filtered through node splitting of the decision tree.

The samples are subdivided until each training sample subset is correctly classified. During the test phase, sample classification is applied directly based on the trained features, which can increase the test speed (although slow the training speed). RF can handle a very large number of input attributes, and can be used for both classification and regression.

Gradient Boosting Regression (GBR) [8] constructs M weak classifiers first, and finally combines them into a strong classifier after many iterations. Each iteration is applied to improve the previous result and reduce the residual error of the previous generation model. A new combination model is established in the gradient direction with the residual error descent to ensure that the final result is the best.

Support Vector Regression (SVR) [2] is applied to find a regression plane such that all data of a set are closest to the plane, that is, to minimize the total deviation of all sample points from the hyperplane. At this time, the sample points are between the two boundary lines.

In this paper, we apply the idea of directly optimizing the ranking performance to existing nonlinear algorithms, including RF, bagging, GBR, and SVR. We denote the optimized methods as IRF, IBagging, IGBR, and ISVR, respectively, and compare these optimized methods with MGGP and LTR. These algorithms are carried out based on the Sklearn Python package. We adopt the GA algorithm to optimize the ranking performance.

5.3   Results

In this subsection, we show the research questions and experimental results in detail.

RQ1. How does our MGGP-based approach perform compared with other optimization methods?

Motivation. Yang et al. [27] indicated that the proposed LTR approach based on directly optimizing the ranking performance measure of the prediction models can provide better results than optimizing the individual-based loss functions. However, when the number of metrics is large, the LTR linear model performs even worse than nonlinear models, such as RF. In addition, there are many redundant metrics in the software data-sets. Although a dimensionality reduction improves the efficiency, it may cause information loss, which may affect the performance of the prediction model. In this paper, we apply the advantage of the MGGP algorithm in multi-collinearity system modeling and the forecasting field to the defect prediction field. An evaluation of its performance is necessary.

Approach. To answer this question, we compare the MGGP approach with five optimized methods (LTR, IRF, IBagging, IGBR, and ISVR), and investigate the performance of the MGGP-based model together with other optimized models. We conduct experiments on 11 data-sets when applying both all metrics, and three metrics selected using InfoGain. To prevent a sample error, we conduct 10-fold cross-validation of the experiments ten times. Therefore, the last records of the experimental results are the mean FPAs and the standard deviations of 10-fold cross-validation applied ten times. The results are shown in Tables 2 and 3. We provide the values of ideal FPA corresponding to each data-set in Table 2 for a convenient comparison. The ideal value is the result of the perfect ordering of the modules.

To compare the differences in performance between all models on the 11 data-sets, we apply the Wilcoxon rank-sum test at a significance of 0.05. The better results (significantly different by s) are shown in boldface.

Findings. Our MGGP-based prediction model achieves good results whatever using three or all metrics. In general, our MGGP-based prediction significantly outperforms the LTR and other optimization techniques for most of the data-sets. From Tables 2 and 3, we can see that the MGGP model performs significantly better (by s) than the other compared methods over eight out of the 11 data-sets (the ideal values are given as a reference). When using three metrics, MGGP performs better than LTR over all data-sets, better than ISVR over ten data-sets, better than IRF and IGBR over nine data-sets, and better than IBagging over eight data-sets. When using all metrics, MGGP performs better than LTR and ISVR over all data-sets, better than IGBR over ten data-sets, better than IBagging over eight data-sets, and better than IRF over nine data-sets, and is equal to IRF over one data-set (mylyn, whose p-value is 0.082 > 0.05). Therefore, regardless of using three or all metrics, we can conclude that MGGP can achieve better FPA results than the other compared methods over most of the data-sets. Nevertheless, compared with ideal models, further improvements are still needed. To summarize, the MGGP-based model is better than the other linear or nonlinear models. In addition, the MGGP approach performs better than the other existing methods in most cases.

To look at the difference in performance between the MGGP-based and other models more intuitively, the results are shown through box-plot diagrams of the FPA measures, as shown in Figs. 3 and 4. The x-axis indicates the defect prediction models, and the y-axis indicates the FPA values produced by the

Table 2. Means and Standard Deviations of FPA values over 11 defect data-sets with three metrics (with the exception of the LTR, the standard deviations of MGGP, IRF, IBagging, IGBR, and ISVR models times 0.01)

Data-set	MGGP	LTR	IRF	IBagging	IGBR	ISVR	Ideal
eclipse	**0.896 ± 0.65**	0.822 ± 0.047	0.886 ± 0.11	0.878 ± 0.35	0.885 ± 0.31	0.817 ± 0.37	0.934
equinox	0.858 ± 0.30	0.805 ± 0.039	0.754 ± 1.00	**0.867 ± 0.51**	0.791 ± 0.26	0.777 ± 0.31	0.875
lucene	**0.940 ± 1.57**	0.842 ± 0.063	0.878 ± 0.45	0.885 ± 0.37	0.876 ± 0.21	0.788 ± 0.36	0.968
mylyn	0.808 ± 0.61	0.735 ± 0.055	**0.821 ± 0.25**	**0.827 ± 0.48**	**0.823 ± 0.39**	0.633 ± 0.78	0.950
pde	0.823 ± 2.37	0.779 ± 0.051	**0.901 ± 0.20**	**0.916 ± 0.37**	**0.901 ± 0.33**	**0.874 ± 0.44**	0.953
Files2.0	**0.845 ± 0.45**	0.805 ± 0.021	0.825 ± 0.18	0.801 ± 0.50	0.824 ± 0.29	0.819 ± 0.73	0.952
Files2.1	**0.817 ± 0.52**	0.765 ± 0.022	0.631 ± 0.23	0.566 ± 0.60	0.627 ± 0.21	0.576 ± 0.43	0.959
Files3.0	**0.812 ± 0.50**	0.788 ± 0.016	0.774 ± 0.24	0.709 ± 0.43	0.766 ± 0.21	0.711 ± 0.82	0.951
Package2.0	**0.827 ± 0.64**	0.769 ± 0.063	0.764 ± 0.32	0.775 ± 1.88	0.681 ± 0.29	0.631 ± 0.64	0.886
Package2.1	**0.848 ± 0.60**	0.776 ± 0.062	0.743 ± 0.35	0.772 ± 0.63	0.709 ± 0.40	0.664 ± 0.65	0.887
Package3.0	**0.852 ± 0.55**	0.815 ± 0.031	0.756 ± 1.32	0.797 ± 0.43	0.779 ± 0.32	0.658 ± 0.50	0.894

defect prediction models over all data-sets. The box-plot includes six different parts, namely, the minimum, first quartile, median, third quartile, maximum, and outliers of the measures. The red line in the middle of the box represents the median of the measures.

Table 3. Means and Standard Deviations of FPA values over 11 defect data-sets with all metrics (with the exception of the LTR, the standard deviations of MGGP, IRF, IBagging, IGBR, and ISVR models times 0.01)

Data-set	MGGP	LTR	IRF	IBagging	IGBR	ISVR
eclipse	**0.908 ± 0.41**	0.823 ± 0.036	0.904 ± 0.15	0.898 ± 0.25	0.896 ± 0.35	0.796 ± 0.40
equinox	0.859 ± 0.42	0.802 ± 0.039	0.801 ± 0.97	**0.880 ± 0.33**	0.823 ± 0.29	0.688 ± 0.61
lucene	**0.950 ± 0.74**	0.816 ± 0.090	0.893 ± 0.42	0.888 ± 0.25	0.888 ± 0.26	0.739 ± 0.41
mylyn	0.881 ± 0.83	0.795 ± 0.037	0.874 ± 0.49	**0.901 ± 0.38**	0.867 ± 0.33	0.587 ± 0.29
pde	0.885 ± 1.13	0.763 ± 0.054	0.904 ± 0.32	0.922 ± 0.43	**0.914 ± 0.28**	0.858 ± 0.48
Files2.0	**0.866 ± 0.29**	0.825 ± 0.018	0.835 ± 0.22	0.816 ± 0.26	0.776 ± 0.35	0.789 ± 0.31
Files2.1	**0.820 ± 1.18**	0.779 ± 0.022	0.645 ± 0.37	0.585 ± 0.40	0.624 ± 0.40	0.545 ± 0.34
Files3.0	**0.815 ± 0.44**	0.795 ± 0.019	0.774 ± 0.26	0.727 ± 0.39	0.747 ± 0.30	0.689 ± 0.34
Package2.0	**0.860 ± 0.45**	0.785 ± 0.064	0.774 ± 0.33	0.832 ± 0.33	0.767 ± 0.29	0.641 ± 0.45
Package2.1	**0.846 ± 1.01**	0.772 ± 0.058	0.725 ± 0.20	0.760 ± 0.31	0.716 ± 0.25	0.628 ± 0.38
Package3.0	**0.859 ± 0.41**	0.814 ± 0.033	0.795 ± 0.26	0.792 ± 0.53	0.748 ± 0.30	0.641 ± 0.39

Figure 3 shows the box-plot results when using three metrics in the experiments. We can see that the ISVR model produces the lowest median value, and MGGP produces the highest. In addition, IBagging produces the lowest outlier value, ISVR produces the lowest minimum value, and MGGP produces the highest minimum value. For the maximum value, LTR produces the lowest maximum value, whereas IBagging produces the highest maximum value, and MGGP produces the highest outlier value.

Similarly, Fig. 4 shows the box-plot results of all data-sets with all metrics. We can see that the ISVR model produces the lowest median value, and MGGP produces the highest median value. ISVR produces the lowest minimum value. MGGP produces the highest minimum value. For the maximum value, LTR produces the lowest maximum value, whereas IBagging produces the highest maximum value, and MGGP produces the highest outlier value.

In general, we can conclude from Figs. 3 and 4 that when using either three metrics or all metrics together, MGGP performs better than the other optimized defect prediction models. In addition, LTR, IRF, IBagging, and IGBR achieve a moderate performance, and ISVR performs relatively poorly compared to the other defect prediction models.

Comparing the results of the MGGP-based model when applying all metrics and only three metrics, **we observed that the multi-collinearity of the metrics does not affect the performance of the MGGP-based defect prediction model.** The experimental results are shown in detail in Table 4, where the p-value is indicated in the corresponding brackets, and the s-significantly better results are in boldface. We can see that, when using all metrics, better results are obtained than when using three metrics over six of the data-sets, and comparable results are achieved over the other five data-sets.

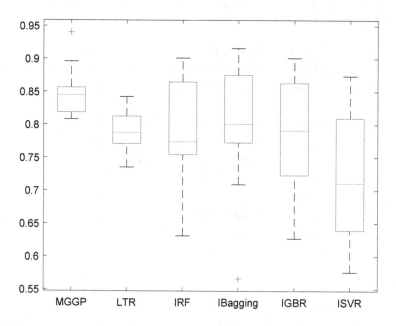

Fig. 3. Box-plot analysis for FPA values for all the data-sets with three metrics.

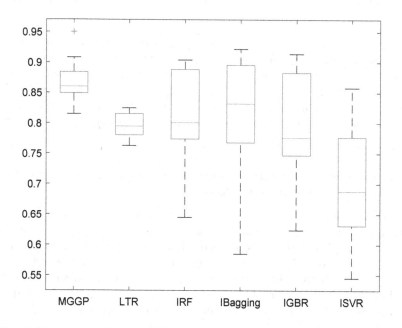

Fig. 4. Box-plot analysis for FPA values for all the data-sets with all metrics.

Table 4. Means and Standard Deviations of FPA results over 11 defect data-sets when applying all metrics and three metrics (the standard deviations times 0.01)

Data-set	MGGP all	MGGP three
eclipse	**0.908 ± 0.41**(.002)	0.898 ± 0.65
equinox	0.859 ± 0.42(.650)	0.858 ± 0.30
lucene	0.950 ± 0.74(.112)	0.940 ± 1.57
mylyn	**0.881 ± 0.83**(.0)	0.808 ± 0.61
pde	**0.885 ± 1.13**(.0)	0.823 ± 2.37
Files2.0	**0.866 ± 0.29**(.0)	0.845 ± 0.45
Files2.1	0.820 ± 1.18(.406)	0.817 ± 0.52
Files3.0	0.815 ± 0.44(.364)	0.812 ± 0.50
Package2.0	**0.860 ± 0.45**(.0)	0.827 ± 0.64
Package2.1	0.846 ± 1.01(.406)	0.848 ± 0.60
Package3.0	**0.859 ± 0.41**(.008)	0.852 ± 0.55

Hence, we can conclude that the MGGP-based model does not need to consider the multi-collinearity between the metrics in the context of software defect prediction. The correlation will not affect the prediction performance of the model, that is, the prediction model based on the MGGP method can directly employ the original features when constructing the software defect prediction model.

> **Answer to RQ1:** *Our MGGP-based prediction model performs better than the other optimized models over most of the defect data-sets regardless of whether three metrics or all metrics are applied. The multi-collinearity of the metrics does not affect the performance of the MGGP-based defect prediction model. Hence, applying the MGGP method to construct a defect prediction model is an appropriate direction.*

RQ2. Is the idea of directly optimizing the model performance measure effective for nonlinear models?

Motivation. Yang et al. [27] pointed out that directly optimizing the model performance measure is useful for constructing better software defect-ranking models. They applied this idea to just one simple linear regression model. However, they did not verify the idea for nonlinear models applied to a defect-ranking task. To explore whether this idea can be applied to a nonlinear software defect prediction model, we compared the performance of the original nonlinear prediction models with the improved models used in the experiments for RQ1.

Approach. We conduct the experiments using the original algorithms with default parameters implemented based on the Sklearn Python package. We apply

Table 5. Means and Standard Deviations of FPA values of original models over 11 defect data-sets using three metrics (the standard deviations times 0.01)

Data-set	RF	Bagging	GBR	SVR
eclipse	$\underline{0.805 \pm 0.65}$	$\underline{0.807 \pm 0.76}$	$\underline{0.802 \pm 0.29}$	$\underline{0.791 \pm 0.52}$
equinox	$\mathbf{0.786 \pm 0.42}$	$\underline{0.782 \pm 0.43}$	$\underline{0.778 \pm 0.09}$	$\underline{0.750 \pm 0.60}$
lucene	$\underline{0.743 \pm 1.39}$	$\underline{0.744 \pm 1.71}$	$\underline{0.744 \pm 0.25}$	$\mathbf{0.830 \pm 0.39}$
mylyn	$\underline{0.688 \pm 0.98}$	$\underline{0.687 \pm 0.98}$	$\underline{0.750 \pm 0.14}$	$\underline{0.580 \pm 0.36}$
pde	$\underline{0.737 \pm 0.84}$	$\underline{0.738 \pm 0.52}$	$\underline{0.764 \pm 0.05}$	$\underline{0.706 \pm 0.54}$
Files2.0	$\underline{0.741 \pm 0.34}$	$\underline{0.740 \pm 0.53}$	$\underline{0.809 \pm 0.05}$	$\underline{0.729 \pm 0.30}$
Files2.1	$\mathbf{0.667 \pm 0.66}$	$\mathbf{0.669 \pm 0.79}$	$\mathbf{0.781 \pm 0.04}$	$\mathbf{0.710 \pm 0.41}$
Files3.0	$\underline{0.691 \pm 0.48}$	$\underline{0.692 \pm 0.35}$	$\mathbf{0.787 \pm 0.06}$	$\underline{0.701 \pm 0.51}$
Package2.0	0.711 ± 0.61	$\underline{0.713 \pm 0.44}$	$\mathbf{0.722 \pm 0.06}$	$\underline{0.606 \pm 0.34}$
Package2.1	$\underline{0.725 \pm 0.90}$	$\underline{0.721 \pm 0.82}$	$\mathbf{0.729 \pm 0.06}$	$\underline{0.607 \pm 0.35}$
Package3.0	0.758 ± 0.36	$\underline{0.756 \pm 0.49}$	$\mathbf{0.784 \pm 0.05}$	$\underline{0.592 \pm 0.45}$

10-fold cross-validation ten times over the 11 data-sets using all metrics, and three metrics selected by InfoGain.

The Wilcoxon rank-sum test at a significance level of 0.05 was used to test whether the four optimized models are s-significantly different from the original models when using only three metrics or all metrics. The results are shown in Tables 5 and 6. If the FPA values are s-significantly different, the results that are better than those of the optimized models (Tables 2 and 3) are denoted in boldface. The worse results are underlined.

Findings. The optimized models based on the idea of directly optimizing the model performance measure perform better than the original models with the default parameters as a whole. As shown in Table 5, when using three metrics, RF with the default parameters achieves worse results than the optimized IRF over eight of the data-sets, comparable results over one data-set, and better results over only two data-sets. Bagging using the default parameters achieves worse results than optimized IBagging over ten data-sets, and better results over only one data-set. GBR with the default parameters achieves worse results than the optimized IGBR over six of the data-sets, and better results over the other five. Finally, the SVR with the default parameters achieves worse results than the optimized ISVR over nine of the data-sets, and better results over only two.

Table 6 shows the results when using all metrics. RF with the default parameters achieves worse results than optimized IRF over eight of the data-sets, comparable results over one data-set, and better results over only two data-sets. Bagging using the default parameters achieves worse results than optimized IBagging over ten of the data-sets, and better results over only one data-set. GBR with the default parameters achieves worse results than the optimized IGBR over

Table 6. Means and Standard Deviations of FPA values of original models over eleven defect data-sets with all metrics (the standard deviations of RF, Bagging, GBR, SVR models times 0.01)

Data-set	RF	Bagging	GBR	SVR
eclipse	0.843 ± 0.41	0.841 ± 0.49	0.835 ± 0.26	0.725 ± 0.45
equinox	0.794 ± 0.51	0.797 ± 0.47	0.798 ± 0.36	0.692 ± 0.28
lucene	0.799 ± 1.91	0.792 ± 2.20	0.762 ± 0.48	**0.748 ± 0.43**
mylyn	0.777 ± 0.66	0.780 ± 0.50	0.791 ± 0.11	**0.707 ± 0.40**
pde	0.769 ± 0.84	0.775 ± 0.84	0.805 ± 0.20	0.690 ± 0.34
Files2.0	0.769 ± 0.50	0.767 ± 0.64	**0.803 ± 0.39**	0.750 ± 0.33
Files2.1	**0.734 ± 0.92**	**0.730 ± 0.63**	**0.777 ± 0.17**	**0.721 ± 0.36**
Files3.0	0.721 ± 0.46	0.722 ± 0.54	**0.783 ± 0.05**	0.629 ± 0.34
Package2.0	0.753 ± 0.64	0.750 ± 0.66	0.741 ± 0.28	0.550 ± 0.54
Package2.1	**0.739 ± 0.75**	0.734 ± 1.00	**0.757 ± 0.15**	0.562 ± 0.49
Package3.0	0.772 ± 0.84	0.774 ± 0.39	**0.776 ± 0.05**	0.569 ± 0.60

six of the data-sets, and better results over the other five. The SVR with the default parameters achieves worse results than the optimized ISVR over seven of the data-sets, comparable results over one data-set, and better results over the remaining three.

Although the results of GBR shown in Tables 5 and 6 are average, we still believe that the idea of directly optimizing the model performance measure is more valuable for constructing better nonlinear defect ranking models.

> **Answer to RQ2:** *The idea of directly optimizing the model performance measure can be used in other nonlinear models, enhancing the prediction performance of the models as a whole. Therefore, this idea is more valuable for constructing better nonlinear defect ranking models.*

6   Threats to Validity

In this section, we discuss the threats to the validity of our study on software defect prediction.

6.1   Threats to Internal Validity

In this study, MGGP and other methods were used to construct software defect prediction models. These models require the appropriate parameters to be chosen for the model construction methods applied. We tried to optimize the parameters according to existing studies. However, the results may vary when using different data-sets or different numbers of metrics.

We choose the FPA as a performance evaluation measure for software defect-ranking models because it overcomes the shortcoming of the percentage of the defects found in the top m modules. However, when the goals of the software defect model change, the FPA measure might not be suitable. Thus, we should choose suitable measures to conduct further research on fitting different software defect prediction tasks.

6.2 Threats to External Validity

To compare our experiments with existing studies, the data-sets we used are from publicly available sources. There are many data-sets based on industrial software systems that are not publicly available. Owing to a wide difference between public and industrial development environments, when using different data-sets or different metrics, the results may differ.

7 Conclusions and Future Work

A software defect prediction model for a ranking task helps in allocating limited testing resources more efficiently, and preferentially detecting modules with more defects. The existence of multi-collinearity between software metrics may reduce the predictive performance of the model. Although a reduction in the dimensions of the data can improve the efficiency, such a reduction may cause some useful information to be prematurely deleted. In this study, we adopted the idea of MGGP to build defect-ranking models. In addition, we conducted a comprehensive evaluation and comparison of the proposed MGGP-based approach with other methods. We used 11 publicly available defect data-sets consisting of a wide range of real-world software projects to evaluate the performance difference between them. The results show that the MGGP-based models perform better in most of the defect data-sets regardless of using only three metrics or all metrics. Furthermore, we concluded that the optimized nonlinear models for directly optimizing the ranking performance work better than the original nonlinear models with default parameters as a whole.

The main findings of our study can be summarized as follows.

- **The MGGP-based model performs well in software defect-ranking prediction.** The experiments show that MGGP-based models can achieve a better performance than LTR and other optimized models. Thus, applying MGGP to defect-ranking prediction is valuable.
- **The optimized nonlinear model achieved by directly optimizing the ranking performance is better than the original nonlinear models with the default parameters.** This finding also verifies that researchers should adjust the parameters when conducting their experiments because doing so can achieve better results.
- **The multi-collinearity between software metrics does not influence the performance of the MGGP-based model, which means MGGP**

is more robust against noisy data for software defect prediction.
We believe that using the original defect data directly can help construct a
MGGP-based model that works well.

As future work, to validate the generality of the conclusions obtained in this
paper, we will further analyze the method on more data-sets. In addition, we will
apply more optimization algorithms to adjust the prediction models and make
them perform better for software defect-ranking prediction.

Acknowledgment. The work describes in this paper is supported by the National
Natural Science Foundation of China under Grant No. 61702029, 61872026 and
61672085.

References

1. Afzal, W., Torkar, R., Feldt, R.: Prediction of fault count data using genetic programming. In: Multitopic Conference, INMIC 2008. IEEE International, pp. 349–356 (2009)
2. Awad, M., Khanna, R.: Support vector regression. Neural Inf. Process. Lett. Rev. **11**(10), 203–224 (2007)
3. Breiman, L.: Bagging predictors. Mach. Learn. **24**(2), 123–140 (1996)
4. Breiman, L.: Random forests. Mach. Learn. **45**(1), 5–32 (2001)
5. Burke, E., Kendall, G.: Search methodologies: introductory tutorials in optimization and decision support techniques. Sci. Bus. **58**(3), 409–410 (2005)
6. D'Ambros, M., Lanza, M., Robbes, R.: Evaluating defect prediction approaches: a benchmark and an extensive comparison. Empir. Softw. Eng. **17**(4–5), 531–577 (2012)
7. Elish, K.O., Elish, M.O.: Predicting defect-prone software modules using support vector machines. J. Syst. Softw. **81**(5), 649–660 (2008)
8. Elith, J., Leathwick, J.R., Hastie, T.: A working guide to boosted regression trees. J. Anim. Ecol. **77**(4), 802–813 (2008)
9. Gao, K., Khoshgoftaar, T.M.: A comprehensive empirical study of count models for software fault prediction. IEEE Trans. Reliab. **56**(2), 223–236 (2007)
10. Garg, A.: Review of genetic programming in modeling of machining processes. In: Proceedings of International Conference on Modelling, Identification & Control, pp. 653–658 (2012)
11. Garg, A., Tai, K.: Comparison of regression analysis, artificial neural network and genetic programming in handling the multicollinearity problem. In: Proceedings of International Conference on Modelling, Identification & Control, pp. 353–358 (2012)
12. Haynes, W.: Wilcoxon rank sum test. In: Dubitzky, W., Wolkenhauer, O., Cho, K.H., Yokota, H. (eds.) Encyclopedia of Systems Biology, pp. 2354–2355. Springer, New York (2013). https://doi.org/10.1007/978-1-4419-9863-7
13. Hinchliffe, M., Hiden, H., Mckay, B., Willis, M., Tham, M., Barton, G.: Modelling chemical process systems using a multi-gene genetic programming algorithm. In: Genetic Programming (1996)
14. Jiang, Y., Cukic, B., Ma, Y.: Techniques for evaluating fault prediction models. Empir. Softw. Eng. **13**(5), 561–595 (2008)

15. Khoshgoftaar, T.M., Allen, E.B.: Ordering fault-prone software modules. Softw. Qual. J. **11**(1), 19–37 (2003)
16. Khoshgoftaar, T.M., Geleyn, E., Gao, K.: An empirical study of the impact of count models predictions on module-order models. In: Eighth IEEE Symposium on Software Metrics. Proceedings, pp. 161–172 (2002)
17. Khoshgoftaar, T.M., Seliya, N.: Fault prediction modeling for software quality estimation: comparing commonly used techniques. Empir. Softw. Eng. **8**(3), 255–283 (2003)
18. Koza, J.R.: Survey of genetic algorithms and genetic programming. In: Wescon/1995. Conference Record. Microelectronics Communications Technology Producing Quality Products Mobile and Portable Power Emerging Technologies, p. 589 (1995)
19. Malhotra, R.: A Systematic Review of Machine Learning Techniques for Software Fault Prediction. Elsevier Science Publishers B.V, Amsterdam (2015)
20. Menzies, T., Greenwald, J., Frank, A.: Data mining static code attributes to learn defect predictors. IEEE Trans. Softw. Eng. **33**(1), 2–13 (2006)
21. Nagappan, N., Ball, T.: Use of relative code churn measures to predict system defect density. In: International Conference on Software Engineering, pp. 284–292 (2005)
22. Rathore, S.S., Kumar, S.: An empirical study of some software fault prediction techniques for the number of faults prediction. Soft Comput. **21**(24), 1–18 (2017)
23. Rathore, S.S., Kumar, S.: Predicting number of faults in software system using genetic programming. In: International Conference on Soft Computing and Software Engineering, pp. 303–311 (2015)
24. Tassey, G.: The economic impacts of inadequate infrastructure for software testing. Natl. Inst. Stand. Technol. **15**(3), 125 (2002)
25. Wang, H., Khoshgoftaar, T.M., Seliya, N.: How many software metrics should be selected for defect prediction? In: Twenty-Fourth International Florida Artificial Intelligence Research Society Conference, Palm Beach, Florida, USA, 18–20 May 2011 (2005)
26. Weyuker, E.J., Ostrand, T.J., Bell, R.M.: Comparing the effectiveness of several modeling methods for fault prediction. Empir. Softw. Eng. **15**(3), 277–295 (2013)
27. Yang, X., Tang, K., Yao, X.: A learning-to-rank approach to software defect prediction. IEEE Trans. Reliab. **64**(1), 234–246 (2015)
28. Zhang, F., Hassan, A.E., Mcintosh, S., Zou, Y.: The use of summation to aggregate software metrics hinders the performance of defect prediction models. IEEE Trans. Softw. Eng. **43**(5), 476–491 (2017)
29. Zhang, F., Mockus, A., Keivanloo, I., Zou, Y.: Towards building a universal defect prediction model, pp. 182–191 (2014)
30. Zimmermann, T., Nagappan, N.: Predicting defects using network analysis on dependency graphs. In: ACM/IEEE International Conference on Software Engineering, pp. 531–540 (2008)
31. Zimmermann, T., Nagappan, N., Gall, H., Giger, E., Murphy, B.: Cross-project defect prediction: a large scale experiment on data vs. domain vs. process. In: Joint Meeting of the European Software Engineering Conference and the ACM SIGSOFT International Symposium on Foundations of Software Engineering, Amsterdam, the Netherlands, August, pp. 91–100 (2009)
32. Zimmermann, T., Premraj, R., Zeller, A.: Predicting defects for eclipse. In: International Workshop on Predictor MODELS in Software Engineering, Promise 2007: ICSE Workshops, p. 9 (2007)

Call Graph Based Android Malware Detection with CNN

Yuxuan Liu[1,2], Ge Li[1,2(✉)], and Zhi Jin[1,2(✉)]

[1] Key Lab of High Confidence Software Technologies,
Ministry of Education, Peking University, Beijing, China
{liuyuxuan,lige,zhijin}@pku.edu.cn
[2] Software Institute, Peking University, Beijing, China

Abstract. With the increasing shipment of Android malware, malicious APK detection becomes more important. Based on static analysis, we propose a new perspective to detect malicious behaviors. In particular, we extract the patterns of suspicious APIs which are invoked together. We call these patterns local features. We propose a convolutional neural network(CNN) model based on APK's call graph to extract local features. With the comparison of detection experiments, we demonstrate that the local features indeed help to detect malicious APKs and our model is effective in extracting local features.

Keywords: Android malware · Call graph · Neural networks

1 Introduction

Android malware detection is increasingly concernful in recent years. The worldwide shipment of Android smart phones has reached 1.7 billion in 2014, and 2.3 billion in 2015 [1]. As mobile phones become popular, the attacks on Android system also become more frequent. A report shows that Android comprises 11.25% of all the mobile malwares in 2010 but 79% in 2012 [2]. This trend is growing last few years. 1.19 million new Android malwares come out in 2013 and 1.55 million in 2014, and 440 thousand in the first three months in 2015, "which means that a new mobile malware strain for Android was discovered every 18 s" [3]. Huge amount of Android malwares bring not only disturbing advertisement but also real benefits loss, such as personal privacy leakage and huge property damage. An investigation in 2013 indicates that Android attackers can earn twelve thousand of dollars every month [4]. Besides, Android allows users to download applications from thirdparty markets as well as unidentified websites. Applications from unknown sources have higher possibility to contain malicious behaviors. Furthermore, Android applications request permissions during installation and Android system grants all the permissions by default. Although users have the authority to cancel some permissions, most of them just click agree without thinking about why the applications need the permissions. After the application

© Springer Nature Singapore Pte Ltd. 2019
Z. Li et al. (Eds.): NASAC 2017/2018, CCIS 861, pp. 72–82, 2019.
https://doi.org/10.1007/978-981-15-0310-8_5

is installed, there will be no more prompt about the use of permissions. These factors raise the risk of being attacked by Android malwares.

To protect users from malicious attacks and benefits loss, a lot of researches have been done on Android malware detection and Android APK analysis. APK is the short name of Android Package, which is downloaded onto mobile phones to install the application. According to an investigation in 2015, there are mainly four kinds of feature analysis to detect Android malware: static feature analysis, dynamic feature analysis, hybrid feature analysis, and application metadata feature analysis [11]. Hybrid feature is a combination of static features and dynamic features. However, only 10% of researches choose to use hybrid features, and only 3% choose application metadata. Thus static analysis and dynamic analysis are the mainline of Android malware detection.

This paper focuses on static analysis. Since APK detection is complex and the data set is abundant, researches always choose machine learning to help solve the problem. The mainline static analysis usually includes two steps: extract feature vectors and put the vectors into SVM [5,6]. Features usually contain requested permissions, filtered intents, suspicious calls and many security sensitive characteristics of the whole APK. Then, SVM will mine the malicious patterns and detect malware by the feature vector of an APK. However, they do not pay enough attention to local malicious features, which can sometimes determine whether an APK is malicious or benign. For example, intend to hide its malicious behaviors from users, some malware send premium messages during the early morning hours. If we extract the features of whole APK, we can just find it will get system time and send messages, which is quite normal for benign applications. Relatively, if we focus on the local features, we will find that the application calls get system time API and send messages API(Application Programming Interface) together, probably in a method, which is abnormal and can give us an alert that it may be a malicious behavior.

Analyzing APK file is a time-consuming work. To fetch the local features of an APK, we need to find a balance between information and the time it costs. Call graph is a proper choice. After we decompile the APK file, we can easily get the call graph of application by Soot. It takes about one minute to get the call graph on average, which is efficient in APK analysis. Besides, call graph contains the invoke relationship between methods and the APIs called by every method, from which we can extract local features. Convolutional neural networks is a suitable method to draw local information and it has significant effect in image progressing [12]. Thus we propose a convolutional neural network model based on the call graph of Android APK.

To evaluate our model, we carry several experiments on a data set of 1000 applications. Our model is 11.8% higher in recall and 6.9% higher in F-measure than the feature extracted from the whole APK angle. The result demonstrates that the local feature is effective for Android malware detection and indeed decrease the possibility of false labeling benign applications. It is worth mentioning that all the training and detecting process is automated without manual work.

There are mainly three contributions of this paper:

First, We propose a new angle to detect Android malwares in static APK analysis, which is to extract local features. Secondly, we give a convolutional neural networks model based on the call graph to extract the local features. Thirdly, we validate the effect of local features by several experiments.

In the rest of this paper, we first present the detailed convolutional neural network model in Sect. 2. Then we evaluate the model and illustrate the local feature's efficiency in Sect. 3. Afterwards we discuss some related works in Sect. 4 and make a conclusion in Sect. 5.

2   Approach

In this section, we will introduce our neural network model in detail. Figure 1 shows the architecture of the entire model from APK file to the output: APK file, method representation layer, convolution layer, pooling layer, hidden layer and output layer. We will present them in this order.

2.1   Method Representation Layer

After we decompile an APK file, we can easily extract its call graph by tool Soot. Each node on the call graph represents a method and every edge represents an invoke between methods. The call graph is a directed acyclic graph, which means we do not need to consider circle edges. There are usually a huge amount of methods in an APK. For some complicated applications, the total number can reach hundreds of thousands. Thus it's not sensible to feed all of the method nodes into neural networks, otherwise the model will be too slow and hard to train. So we must focus on some special methods which are suspicious for malware detection.

We choose a subset of "security sensitive methods" from [8] as suspicious methods:

1. Permission protected methods. Android have a permission management to prevent from applications' intrusion. If an application wants to invoke certain sensitive methods, for example take a picture, it need to get corresponding permission granted by users. These methods are highly suspicious for malware detection. Detailed information can be found in [9].
2. Source or sink methods. Source methods are those methods which may get sensitive data, like personal contacts. Sink methods are the methods which may leak the data out, for example send them through email. Rasthofer et al. specify those methods in [10].
3. Java reflection methods. Java reflection system is a dynamic system which enables executing java program to identify a class by its object, invoke an object's method, create an object of a class, and get the variables or methods of a class. These methods are also suspicious and may give us an alert at malware detection.

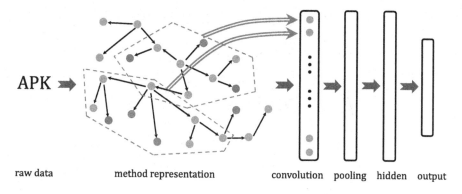

Fig. 1. The Architecture of convolutional neural network model(from APK to output).

There are 10029 suspicious methods in our final method set chosen from [8]. Since all suspicious methods are API calls, they will not invoke any other methods, which means they are all leaf nodes on the call graph. Fortunately, only 3% to 4% methods on the call graph are suspicious methods according to our statistics. In other words, this measure cuts down the scale of input greatly. So we can handle most of the APKs with the time and memory limit.

Like word to vector in the natural language model, we initialize the representations of suspicious methods randomly and optimize them through training process. We will discuss the dimension of representations in Sect. 3.

2.2 Convolution Layer

Local features are the patterns of the suspicious methods invoked together. From another view, we need to find the methods which invoke several suspicious methods. Invocation is divided into direct invocation and indirect invocation. For indirect invocation, we consider two-step invocation preliminarily. In other words, when we do convolution on a method, we only care about the suspicious methods called by it and by the methods it called. Convolution fits well in this situation. Like convolution on a picture, we can easily do the convolution on this call graph. Figure 2 gives an example of convolution. Suspicious methods are labeled blue and purple. As we do the convolution on the yellow node, we consider the three suspicious methods in the dotted line circle. Finally we get the brown node which contains the local features around the origin yellow one. Experiments in Sect. 3 shows the convolution helps to contract the local features efficiently in our model.

Another point is that we initialize the representation of suspicious methods. Every suspicious node in the call graph has its corresponding representation now. For the unsuspicious nodes, since they do not represent any suspicious information, we do not need to do convolution on them.

Besides, since a method may be more doubtful if it calls many suspicious methods indirectly. We have to distinguish the direct invocations and indirect

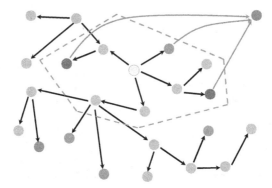

Fig. 2. Convolution on a node. We do the convolution on the yellow node and we get the brown node. The blue node in dotted line circle is a direct invocation, while the purple ones are indirect. (Color figure online)

invocations. So we use different weights for directly invoked suspicious methods and indirectly invoked suspicious methods:

$$y = \tanh \left(\sum_{i=1}^{n_1} W_{conv1} \cdot x_{der,i} + \sum_{j=1}^{n_2} W_{conv2} \cdot x_{ind,j} + b_{conv} \right)$$

where n_1 is the number of direct invocations to suspicious methods, n_2 is the number of indirect ones, x refers the representation of the suspicious methods, W_{conv} refers weights, and b_{conv} refers biases.

2.3 Pooling Layer, Hidden Layer and Output Layer

Pooling is a common and effective choice after convolution [12]. The are many kinds of pooling: sum pooling, average pooling, max pooling etc. In this paper, we test sum pooling and max pooling. Sum pooling gets a better performance. Thus the experiment result showed in Sect. 3 all use sum pooling. Hidden layer and output layer are ordinary neural network settings.

3 Evaluation

In this section, we specify our experiment in detail, including the data set, the tool implementation, the parameter settings, and the result analysis. With the comparison of the result given by the local feature model and the whole-APK feature model, we demonstrate the efficiency of local features, as well as the model we designed to contract them.

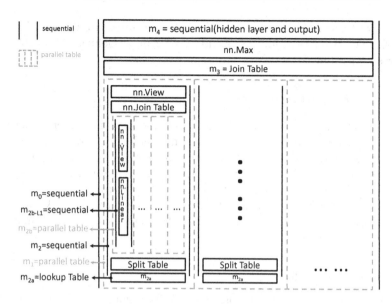

Fig. 3. The implementation of convolutional neural network model in torch.

3.1   Data Set and Tool Implementation

we choose 500 malicious APKs from Drebin's collection [6]. They spend two years to collect the malicious APKs from various sources, including the Google-Play Store, Chinese markets, Russian markets, and many others sources. The malicious data set is reliable and abundant. However, they do not disclose the benign data set. So we collect 500 benign APKs from GooglePlay. Together the data set contains 1000 APKs.

We use SOOT to decompile an APK to Jimple code, and then extract the call graph. Soot is a useful tool to get Jimple code, which is an easy language. After we get the call graph, we search the suspicious APIs on it. This step may take much time, especially for the benign apps. At first it takes more than 2 min, then we improve our algorithm for searching and recursion. Finally the average analysis time descends to 48.45 s. For the whole classification processing, which means to get the classification result from the very beginning, it takes about one minute. It is acceptable in malicious APK detection.

To construct convolutional neural networks, we use Torch, a common platform for deep neural networks. Torch is convenient and efficient when we need only regular models, for example the convolution model for picture classification. However, the size of the convolution window is changing all the time in our model. The size differs from different APKs and also from different locations on the call graph. Thus the architecture becomes complicated. Figure 3 shows the whole architecture of the Torch implementation. In Torch, we can use parallel table to handle many layers at the same time. Thus we use two parallel tables for uncertain number of convolution window and uncertain number of nodes in one window. Sequential is the normal feed forward structure in Torch. Pooling can be done by two layers: join table and max for max pooling, or join table and sum for sum pooling.

3.2 Detection Performance

To demonstrate the efficiency of local features, we carry the experiments using local features and features extracted from the whole-apk perspective. We also feed the whole-APK features to deep neural networks in order to control variable. Since the whole-APK feature doesn't have any structure, so we use a feed-forward neural network model. The result shows local features indeed help to detect malicious APKs. Following subsections will show the detect performance of whole-APK feature model first, and then the local feature model, finally the comparison and analysis.

3.2.1 Whole-APK Features

Whole-APK feature means the suspicious APIs invoked in the whole APK. Unlike local features, whole-APK features can not tell how many times an suspicious API is invoked or which APIs are invoked together. It can only tell the suspicious APIs that have been invoked by this APK.

To represent the API set, we try one hot model and API set model. In one hot model, the length of feature is fixed. The feature is a 01 sequence in which every digit represents an unique API. If this APK invokes the API, the corresponding digit is 1, otherwise is 0. In API set model, the feature is a set of API numbers. Every number represents an API and the size of the set differs from APKs. We feed the features to a deep neural network for both models.

The detect performance is evaluated in precision, recall and F1-value. Table 1 shows the experiments' result. One hot model is sensitive to find malicious APKs, which gives it a high recall but also low precision. The reason is possibly that fixed length and digits make it easy to mine patterns among suspicious APIs. API set model gets better F1-value because of its balanced performance in precision and recall.

3.2.2 Local Features

Local features can tell the APIs invoked together and the times they are invoked. Table 2 shows the detection performance of local features extracted by convolutional neural networks.

We change the dimension of embedding from 30 to 150. It comes out that long dimension contributes to precision but sometimes has a negative effect on recall. The balanced point is 80 on which the F1-value is 86.5%. We will compare this result with the whole-APK feature's performance in the next subsection. We also test some other parameter settings such as pooling, which will be discussed in detail in Sect. 3.3.

Table 1. Detection results using whole-APK features

Model	Precision(%)	Recall(%)	F1(%)
One hot	50.8	95.0	66.2
API set	81.1	78.2	79.6

3.2.3   Comparison of Detection Result

The best performance of whole-APK features and local features are displayed in Table 3. Model using local features detect more malicious APKs while making fewer mistakes. The F1-value of local feature model is 6.9% higher than the whole-APK feature model, which indicates the local feature can identify the malicious behaviors. The result also indicates that our convolutional neural network model is efficient in extracting local features.

3.3   Parameter Setting

During the cross validation, we try different parameters. For learning rate, we test 0.01, 0.03, 0.1, 0.3, 1.0. For batch size, we test 5, 10, 20, 50. We get best results when learning rate is 0.3 and batch size is 5. For pooling layer, we test sum pooling and 3-way pooling. Sum Pooling gets better performance. For the dimension of convolution layer and hidden layer, we set them to 512. To enlarge the capacity of the neural networks, the dimension can be changed, like the dimension of API embedding.

When we search for suspicious APIs in call graph, there are a huge amount of methods that only invoke one or two suspicious APIs. In such cases, the local feature is not strong and worth extracting. So we set a threshold to determine the minimum of suspicious API number in a convolution window, which means we do the convolution to a node only when it invokes suspicious APIs more than the threshold. With the limit to time and memory, the threshold is set to 5.

4   Related Work

Malicious APK detection has been a hot topic for many years. There are a lot of works about the different methods, models, or features used in the detection. We will focus on the static analysis and also mention some dynamic analysis works.

Many of the static analysis papers extract the feature out and then feed the feature to SVM [5,13,14]. Ma compares the description of an APK and its truly behaviours to identify the malicious APKs, using SVM as the final classcification [5]. Schmidt extracts function calls from binaries to detect milicous apps. One of his advantages is he can detect an installed app in the mobile [14]. There are many ways to detect malicious behaviours. Wang uses the context to infer the purpose of permission use in an APK. He also extracts the features from

Table 2. Detection results using local features

Embedding	Precision(%)	Recall(%)	F1(%)
30	85.6	80.1	83.2
80	83.2	90.0	86.5
100	76.6	89.1	82.4
150	77.4	87.3	82.1

Table 3. Detection results using different features

Features	Precision(%)	Recall(%)	F1(%)
Whole-APK	81.1	78.2	79.6
Local	83.2	90.0	86.5

decompiled code and then feed it to SVM [13]. To our best knowledge, our work is the first to use convolutional neural networks on the call graph.

There also many dynamic analysis for malicious APK detection [15,17]. Carter proposes a system which tests Android application user interfaces automatically and intelligently [16]. Enck tracks the information-flow to detect the misuse of users' private data [18]. Zhu does similar work but focus on tracking taint for real and interactive apps accurately and efficiently [19].

5   Conclusion

The increasing number of Android malwares makes it important to detect malicious applications. We propose a novel idea that use local features for malicious APK detection. Local features include the suspicious APIs invoked together and the times they are invoked. Then we design the convolution neural networks based on the call graph to extract the local features. We construct the networks in Torch and solve the problem of unfixed size of convolution window. Finally we carry experiments to compare the detection performance of local features and whole-APK features. Local feature model is 11.8% higher in recall and 6.9% higher in F1-score than whole-APK feature model, which indicates the efficiency of the local feature idea and our convolutional neural networks.

We can also improve our model by enlarge the convolution window or decrease the threshold. The local feature model needs to be tested in larger data set and various malicious APK families. Since the suspicious APIs remain nearly the same, our model may get good performance in detecting new malicious APK families.

References

1. Global cumulative shipments of smartphones using the Android operating system. https://www.statista.com/statistics/241943/forecast-of-global-cumulative-shipments-of-smartphones-using-android-os/ (2017)
2. Techcrunch: Android accounted For 79% of all mobile Malware In 2012, 96% In Q4 Alone. http://techcrunch.com/2013/03/07/fsecure-android-/accounted-for-79-of-all-mobile-malware-in-201296-in-q4-alone/ (2013)
3. Mirko Zorz: 4,900 new Android malware strains discovered every day. From www.helpnetsecurity.com, https://www.helpnetsecurity.com/2015/07/01/4900-new-android-malware-strains-discovered-every-day/ (2015)
4. The Register. Earn 8,000 a month with bogus apps from Russian malware factories. http://www.theregister.co.uk/2013/08/05/mobile_malware_lookout/ (2013)
5. Ma, S., Wang, S., Lo, D., Deng, R.H., Sun, C.: Active semi-supervised approach for checking app behavior against its description. In: 2015 IEEE 39th Annual Computer Software and Applications Conference (COMPSAC), vol. 2, pp. 179–184. IEEE (2015)
6. Arp, D., Spreitzenbarth, M., Hubner, M., Gascon, H., Rieck, K.: DREBIN: effective and explainable detection of android malware in your pocket. In: NDSS (2014)
7. Zhao, M., Ge, F., Zhang, T., Yuan, Z.: AntiMalDroid: an efficient SVM-based malware detection framework for Android. In: Liu, C., Chang, J., Yang, A. (eds.) ICICA 2011. CCIS, vol. 243, pp. 158–166. Springer, Heidelberg (2011). https://doi.org/10.1007/978-3-642-27503-6_22
8. Yang, W., Xiao, X., Andow, B., Li, S., Xie, T., Enck, W.: Appcontext: differentiating malicious and benign mobile app behaviors using context. In: 2015 IEEE/ACM 37th IEEE International Conference on Software Engineering, vol. 1, pp. 303–313. IEEE (2015)
9. Au, K.W.Y., Zhou, Y.F., Huang, Z., Lie, D.: Pscout: analyzing the Android permission specification. In: Proceedings of the 2012 ACM Conference on Computer and Communications Security, pp. 217–228. ACM (2012)
10. Rasthofer, S., Arzt, S., Bodden, E.: A Machine-learning approach for classifying and categorizing android sources and sinks. In: NDSS (2014)
11. Feizollah, A., Anuar, N.B., Salleh, R., Wahab, A.W.A.: A review on feature selection in mobile malware detection. Digital Invest. **13**, 22–37 (2015)
12. Ciresan, D.C., Meier, U., Masci, J., Maria Gambardella, L., Schmidhuber, J.: Flexible, high performance convolutional neural networks for image classification. In: IJCAI Proceedings-International Joint Conference on Artificial Intelligence, vol. 22(1), p. 1237 (2011)
13. Wang, H., Hong, J., Guo, Y.: Using text mining to infer the purpose of permission use in mobile apps. In: ACM International Joint Conference on Pervasive and Ubiquitous Computing, pp. 1107–1118. ACM (2015)
14. Schmidt, A.D., Clausen, J.H., Camtepe, A., Albayrak, S.: Detecting symbian OS malware through static function call analysis. In: International Conference on Malicious and Unwanted Software, vol. 23, pp. 15–22. IEEE (2010)
15. Zhao, M., Ge, F., Zhang, T., Yuan, Z.: AntiMalDroid: an efficient SVM-Based malware detection framework for Android. In: Liu, C., Chang, J., Yang, A. (eds.) ICICA 2011. CCIS, vol. 243, pp. 158–166. Springer, Heidelberg (2011). https://doi.org/10.1007/978-3-642-27503-6_22

16. Carter, P., Mulliner, C., Lindorfer, M., Robertson, W., Kirda, E.: CuriousDroid: automated user interface interaction for Android application analysis sandboxes. In: Grossklags, J., Preneel, B. (eds.) FC 2016. LNCS, vol. 9603, pp. 231–249. Springer, Heidelberg (2017). https://doi.org/10.1007/978-3-662-54970-4_13

17. Dash, S.K., Suarez-Tangil, G., Khan, S., Tam, K., Ahmadi, M., Kinder, J., et al.: DroidScribe: classifying Android malware based on runtime behavior. In: Security and Privacy Workshops, pp. 252–261. IEEE (2016)

18. Enck, W., Gilbert, P., Han, S., Tendulkar, V., Chun, B.G., Cox, L.P., et al.: Taintdroid:an information-flow tracking system for realtime privacy monitoring on smartphones. ACM Trans. Comput. Syst. 32(2), 1–29 (2014)

19. Zhu, D., Jung, J., Song, D., Kohno, T., Wetherall, D.: Tainteraser: protecting sensitive data leaks using application-level taint tracking. ACM Sigops Oper. Syst. Rev. 45(1), 142–154 (2011)

Software Requirements Elicitation Based on Ontology Learning

Jie Zhang[1], Min Yuan[1(✉)], and Zhiqiu Huang[2]

[1] College of Computer Science and Technology,
Nanjing Normal University, Nanjing, Jiangsu 210023, China
jzhnnu@gmail.com, yuanmn@gmail.com
[2] College of Computer Science and Technology, Nanjing University
of Aeronautics and Astronautics, Nanjing, Jiangsu 210016, China
zqhuang@nuaa.edu.cn

Abstract. User demand is the key to software development. The domain ontology established by artificial intelligence can be used to describe the relationship between concepts and concepts in a specific domain, which can enable users to agree on conceptual understanding with developers. This paper uses the ontology learning method to extract the concept, and the ontology is constructed semi-automatically or automatically. Because the traditional weight calculation method ignores the distribution of feature items, the concept of information entropy is introduced and the CCM method is further integrated. This method can improve the automation degree of ontology construction, and also make the user requirements of software more accurate and complete.

Keywords: Requirements engineering · Domain ontology ·
Ontology learning · Concept extraction

1 Introduction

1.1 Background

With the development of software engineering technology, the focus of software development has been changed from code writing to demand acquisition, and the understanding of requirements and software concepts by users and developers is also becoming more important even if it is difficult to maintain consistency. This bias may be overlooked in the early stages of software development, but when the software system design is completed, users will find that there is a difference in functionality, which can be costly for developers. Therefore, it is particularly important to identify the needs of users in software development. For users, they cannot provide accurate demand information at once, and do not know how to express their needs in terms. On the other hand, developers can only wait for users to provide information due to lack of domain knowledge, and the information provided by the user may be inconsistent with the terminology, which will make the developed software differently than the user expected. The main reason for this phenomenon is that the background knowledge of users and developers is inconsistent with the conceptual understanding. In semantics,

Z. Li et al. (Eds.): NASAC 2017/2018, CCIS 861, pp. 83–98, 2019.
https://doi.org/10.1007/978-981-15-0310-8_6

the meaning of ontology can be used to solve the inconsistency problem, and domain ontology [1] can describe domain knowledge to express the semantic relationships between concepts. Based on domain ontologies, it can enable users and developers to reach a conceptual understanding and communicate better, which can make the extraction of user requirements more accurate.

1.2   Related Work

At present, the ontology has been widely used in software requirements engineering. For instance, Yuan and Tripathi put forward a method that use ontology to deal with the problem of requirements elicitation [2]. Bhatia, Beniwal and Kumar used ontology to detect automatic and update of requirement specifications [3]. Karatas, Iyidir and Birtu proposed a method that ontology-based software requirements reuse and use this case in fire control software product line domain [4]. Also, Sitthithanasakul and Choosri used ontology to enhance requirement engineering in agile software process [5]. And in many literature, ontology plays an important role in software requirements. For example, Tatiana Avdeenko and Natalia Pustovalova used ontology to support the completeness and consistency of the requirements specification [6]. Saito, Iimura and Mikio Anyama proposed a requirements software ontology [7]. At the same time, Yang and Zhang used domain ontology as the basis of feature modeling [8]. Djilani, Khiat and Khouri explained ontology in requirements software through graph and ontology matching [9]. However, in ontology construction, the degree of automation of ontology acquisition is not high. It still rely on domain experts to extract. Therefore, this paper mainly focuses on the analysis of ontology construction, exploring the concept extraction method to make the software requirements more accurate. At present, the common concept acquisition methods are: rule-based methods, statistical methods and hybrid methods, among which the most important is based on statistics. Sometimes, the method based on rule is used to solve the problem of conceptual similarity.

Ontology can solve the semantic problems well and can be used to improve the ability of software requirements extraction, so the ontology construction becomes more important. There are two ways to build ontology: the manual construction of ontology and ontology learning. The main application is to use ontology learning methods to build ontology without the problems of domain experts to build ontology and updating in time. The purpose of ontology construction through automatic or semi-automatic way is to realize the sharing and reuse of information, spread the knowledge, and expand the field of influence.

However, the current ontology learning method still has many defects:

(1) Lack of a unified ontology learning method. Although it has been developed, the ontological learning methods provided by the system are difficult to be reused by other systems because of the different data sources, learning methods and learning objectives of each system.
(2) The semantic extraction is not accurate enough. Since all kinds of extraction algorithm have their own advantages and disadvantages, and no algorithm can be done in linear time, these algorithms are constantly optimized, which makes the ex-traction semantics can be further accurate.

(3) The current system lacks the processing of Chinese text. Most of the current popular systems are based on English. In the current system based on Chinese, the extraction algorithm is still not mature enough and the Chinese input has a variety, which makes it more difficult to deal with Chinese.

This paper presents a method to construct software requirement ontology [10] based on ontology learning. Through building ontology, it can create connections between users and developers, and also guide users to provide more accurate requirements [11].

2 Ontology Learning

2.1 Ontology Construction

Ontology [12] is the concept of philosophy category that can be used to express the subject or oneself of things. Since the development of computer science, it is defined as: "ontology is a clear specification of conceptualization." In a certain filed, ontology is only an indirect description of information. And the representation of information in the form of the model makes the domain concept more intuitive. Therefore, ontology has four characteristics [13], as shown in Table 1:

Table 1. Ontology feature

Features	Description
Conceptualization	An abstract representation of the objective world phenomenon
Explicit	Precisely define concepts and their relationships
Formal	Describe things accurately
Share	The knowledge defined in ontology can be used together

The modeling primitives commonly used in ontology construction are:

(1) Terminology: it is used to refer to concepts in a professional field. When used in a particular field, the representation of knowledge is conducive to the conceptualization of the text.
(2) Concept: it is used to reflect the unique properties of things.
(3) Axiom: it is used to model sentences that always true.
(4) Instance: represents the existing element.
(5) Relationships: it can be used to express a concept or to associate two concepts, representing the hidden connections between them.

The process of ontology construction is actually to obtain domain knowledge, and the main idea is to abstract the concepts and concepts in the domain to get the model of the field. There are several rules for constructing ontologies, as shown in Table 2:

These rules are just a simple abstract constraint. In practice, the rules are typically instances of these rules, so we do not necessarily follow it.

Table 2. Constructing ontology rules

Rules for construct ontology:
(1) Objectivity: the relationship between concepts and concepts defined in the ontology should exist objectively
(2) Completeness: the semantic description in ontology is as complete as possible
(3) Consistency: the concept of a predefined concept should be consistent with the concept of inference
(4) Extensibility: attributes can be added directly to the constructed ontology
(5) Minimum ontology commitment: the concept of ontology contained less is better, and the target should be given the smallest constraint modeling object

2.2 Ontology Learning

Ontology learning [14] is used to solve the problems created by the manual construction of ontology. It is mainly based on the different data of learning, which can implicitly reflect the general flow of ontology learning. At present, most of the ontology learning systems at home and abroad are based on this process, as shown in Fig. 1:

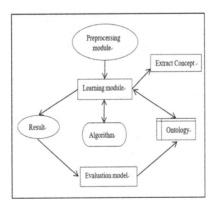

Fig. 1. Ontology learning flow chart

3 Acquisition of Ontology

Ontology acquisition is an important step in ontology construction, which is the core concept of domain extraction. Firstly, this section analyzes concept extraction methods, mainly introduces the CCM (Character Combine Method) and TFIDF (Term

Frequency Inverted Document Frequency) method. Then the concept of information entropy is introduced and the concept of information entropy is added to the TFIDF method. Finally, the algorithm of CCM and TFIDFE will be proposed.

3.1 Concept Extraction Method

(1) Rule-based methods: On the basis of linguistics, we analyze the text set, summarize the rules and establish a rule base, and then the concept of domain can be obtained by comparison. By comparing rules, it can be clear whether the concept is a domain concept.
(2) Statistical methods: the concept of domain concept is extracted from the difference in the information by using common concepts and domain concepts, which are mainly two kinds of domain relevance and domain consensus.
(3) Mixed methods: it generally can be divided into two kinds [15]. One is to summarize the rules, establish the rule base, and then to extract the domain concept by means of statistics; another is to extract conceptual by using statistics, and then establish rules for the concept of extraction.

3.2 The Common Approach

3.2.1 Domain Relevance and Domain Consensus

Domain consensus is used to represent the distribution of concepts in part of the realm, and the more evenly distributed, the more likely the concept is to be a domain concept. In the field of D_k, the calculation formula for calculating the degree of the concept t distribution is:

$$DC'(t, D_k) = H(p(t, d)) = \sum \left(p(t, d) \log \frac{1}{p(t, d)} \right) \tag{1}$$

Where d represents a randomly selected document in the domain, and p(t,d) can be used to estimate probability.

$$p(t, d) \approx \frac{f_{t,j}}{\sum_{d \in D_k} f_{t,j}} \tag{2}$$

Where $f_{t,j}$ represents the frequency that the concept t appears in the first j document, and use $H(p(t, d))$ to represents the information entropy.

Domain relevance is used to describe the relevance of the concepts and specific areas. And the closer the concept is to the field, the more likely the concept is to be a domain concept. In this field of D_k, the calculation formula of concept t is:

$$DR_{t,k} = \frac{p(t|D_k)}{p_{1 \leq j \leq n}(t|D_j)} \tag{3}$$

Where $f_{t,j}$ means the frequency of the concept t in the domain D_k and $p(t|D_k)$ can be calculated using formula 4:

$$E(p(t|D_k)) = \frac{f_{t,k}}{\sum f_{t,k}} \tag{4}$$

3.2.2   CCM+TFIDF

1. CCM

When preprocessing in the field, the problem of tool recognition or the meaning of the word itself may produce a single concept. So we can use the CCM method to deal with these individual concepts with practical significance. Specific steps can be performed in the following ways, as shown in Table 3:

Table 3. CCM processing steps

CCM processing steps:
(1) After a sentence is preprocessed, if there are adjacent words, you can combine these words into a single word
(2) If only it is produced in a sentence, the word is merged with the front word and the back word into a new word
(3) Filter the merged files to remove meaningless words. By calculating the frequency of all words, we can set a threshold to select all words with a frequency greater than the threshold

2. TFIDF
(1) TF

In general, the keyword is a simple expression of the views in the file, which can be displayed in many parts of the document, and so the frequency will be higher. Moreover, the number of words is also related to the length of the document. Though using the keyword or the number of the words cannot accurately express the word itself, the TF is presented, using the frequency of the word in the concentration to replace the word itself make more accurate. The formula in the concept set j is:

$$tf_{ij} = \frac{n_{ij}}{\sum\limits_{k} n_{kj}} \tag{5}$$

In this formula, $n_{i,j}$ represents the number of words that appear in the concept set j, and $\sum\limits_{k} n_{k,j}$ represents the sum of the occurrences of all the words in the concept set.

(2) IDF

This concept is mainly based on the frequency of words in the concept concentration to give the corresponding weight to the word, which can also be interpreted as the distribution of a word in a concept under certain conditions. So the frequency of a word in the concept is higher, the less information entropy is contained. When calculate the IDF value of a word, we use N to represent the number of the words that appear in the document, and use n to represent the total number of documents, so the formula is:

$$IDF = lbN - lb(n+1) \tag{6}$$

(3) TFIDF

TFIDF is formed by the concept of TF and IDF. It means that the frequency of a word appears in a document, making the TF value is high and having the stronger ability to express the content of the document, so it should be given a higher weighting. If a word appears in a set of documents and the calculated IDF value are smaller, we can know that the more ability to distinguish the content of a document and the higher weight should be given.

$$TFIDF = TF * IDF \tag{7}$$

The general steps of using the TFIDF algorithm to extract concepts are shown in Table 4:

Table 4. TFIDF processing step

TFIDF processing step:
(1)
Statistics the frequency of each word appearing in the field text;
(2)
Statistics the number of each word appears in the set of background corpus (a set of texts);
(3)
Calculate the TFIDF value of each word according to the formula;
(4)
Sorting according to the obtained TFIDF value;
(5)
Set the threshold value for TFIDF to be selected as a candidate set

3.2.3 Information Entropy

Entropy is used to indicate the degree of confusion in the system, it has its application in different fields; specifically, it can be used to describe the degree of uncertainty of the system in the domain of information technology. In other words, it is used to express certain states.

Information entropy [16] is a concrete application of the concept of entropy, which refers to the average amount of information after excluding from the information. In other words, because of the uncertainty of information, it is not clear what is going to be sent, and then we need to use an indicator to measure the probability of the occurrence of parameters. When the probability is greater, the uncertainty becomes smaller. Given an x, and use p(x) to represent the probability of x, and the uncertainty in space can be calculated using the following formula:

$$H(x) = -\sum_{i=1}^{n} p(x_i) \log_2 p(x_i) \tag{8}$$

3.3   CCM+TFIDFE

3.3.1   TFIDFE

There are some shortcomings when using the TFIDF method to extract the concept. For example, IDF is not the only criteria for the word in a text, only calculating this will produce a large errors; When determining the IDF parameters, we only calculate the number of words in the document but the distribution is not considered, which will lead to the calculation of the IDF parameters are not accurate. Because of the uncertainty of the information entropy in the whole space, this uncertainty can also be used to represent the distribution. When the uncertainty is higher, the distribution is more uniform in the whole space. In order to solve the problem of IDF parameters, the concept of information entropy can be introduced into TFIDF method to get TFIDFE method. At this time, the calculation formula of information entropy is changed to:

$$E(t) = -\sum_{1}^{n} p_t(d_i) \log_2 p_t(d_i) \tag{9}$$

Where $p_t(d)$ represents the probability that the concept t is in the document d_i, and use n to represent the total number of documents, and then the calculation method of $p_t(d)$ is shown in formula 10.

$$p_t(d) = \frac{f_{t,i}}{\sum_{j=1}^{n} f_{t,j}} \tag{10}$$

Where $f_{t,j}$ represents the number of times that the concept t appears in the document d_i, and $\sum_{j=1}^{n} f_{t,j}$ represents the total number of words that appear in all domain documents.

At this time, the calculation method of TFIDFE is:

$$TFIDFE = TFIDF(i) * E(i) \tag{11}$$

3.3.2   CCM+TFIDFE

When dealing with the document sets, we find some stop words in the document, and it only have the effect of connection and no practical significance. So we use the special characters to replace the stop words in this paper to reduce the complexity of the document.

First of all, preprocessing the acquired domain text sets. However, the retrieved data may be incomplete or dirty, so we need to clean up it, including deleting the text that contains the scrambled code, deleting duplicated documents, deleting a large number of duplicates in content and deleting documents containing a large number of tags. After the field text set is ready, the word segmentation and the word labeling should be carried out. And then using the special characters to replace the stop words, followed by the CCM method, however the candidate words cannot be directly used as the domain concept, mainly because the words that are written in a single word are not necessarily domain words. So in order to make the concept of capture more accurate, the result of the CCM method extraction is put into the user's dictionary, and then uses the TFIDFE method to handle it. Finally, the concept of domain is obtained through manual screening. At this point, the concept extraction process should be as shown in Fig. 2:

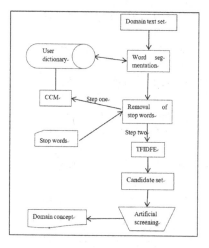

Fig. 2. Concept extraction process

3.4   A Sample for Computation Process

It is assumed that there are 10 sets of texts, which are described in the fields of automobile, finance, sports, computer and painting. Among the document 1,3,7 are described on automobile filed, the document 2,10 are described in painting field, the document 4 is described in financial field, the document 5 and 6 are described for sports field, and the document 8 and 9 are described in computer field. If the concept of "series" is calculated in the text, the probability of the occurrence of the text is counted firstly, and then calculates the total number of the concepts in the text. Lastly, we calculate the value of DC, DR and TFIDFE according to the formula.

The computational concept "series" focuses on the first text in the automotive field is:

$$p(t,j) = \frac{20}{20+23+21} = 0.3125$$

The concept "series" is in the automotive field:

$$p(t|D_k) = \frac{20+23+21}{120+235+560} = 0.069945$$

$$TF = \frac{20+23+21}{120+235+560} = 0.069945$$

$$IDF = \ln(120+235+560) - \ln(20+23+21+1) = 2.644537$$

The following text is resolved in this way, as shown in Tables 5 and 6.

Table 5. Training dataset

J	f_{tj}	Total	P(t, j)	−P(t, j)*log(t, j)
1	20	120	03125	0.157859
2	34	245	0.53125	0.145935
3	23	235	0.593	0.159725
4	45	123	1	0
5	62	452	0.446043	0.156393
6	77	178	0.553957	0.142103
7	21	560	0.328125	0.1588
8	12	450	0.66667	0.117394
9	6	348	0.33333	0.15904
10	30	569	0.46875	0.154246

Table 6. Calculating result dataset

Domain(K)	Number	Total	DC	DR	TF	IDF	E(K)	TFI-DFE
Automobile (1,3,7)	64	915	0.45	0.19	0.069	2.644	0.4763	0.088
Painting (2,10)	64	814	0.3	0.22	0.078	2.527	0.3001	0.059
Finance (4)	45	123	0	1	0.365	0.983	0	0
Sports (5,6)	139	630	0.29	0.60	0.220	1.504	0.2984	0.099
Computer (8,9)	12	798	0.12	0.06	0.022	3.737	0.2764	0.023

4   Examples of Requirements Elicitation

In order to better guide users to provide more accurate demands in the software development, this paper proposes a software requirements acquisition method based on ontology learning, which can be used to get the domain concept through the processing of relevant documents of user requirements in the domain. For example, employees at the company process impact presently spend an average of 65 min per day going to the cafeteria to select, purchase and eat lunch. Also, employees don't always get the selections they want because the cafeteria runs out of certain items, making the cafeteria wastes a significant quantity of food that is not purchased and must be thrown away. So many employees have requested a system that would permit a cafeteria user to order meals (defined as a set of one or more food items selected from the cafeteria menu) on line, to be picked up at the cafeteria or delivered to a company location at a specified time and date. The user requirements are obtained after the software designer's analysis of the system, but this may lead to extract less demand. Therefore, when using ontology learning method to extract the requirements, users will only need to deliver the requirements document to the system to get the user's demand without excessive human involvement. So the user demand will be more objective. In order to verify the feasibility of using the CCM+TFIDFE method to extract user requirements, this paper divides the Cafeteria Ordering System into several scenes based on the document 17, and then puts the description of each scene into the document. Then use this method to search the document to extract the user requirements.

4.1 Experimental Data

The acquisition of user requirements is to find out all possible concepts in the Cafeteria Ordering System [17]. According to the requirements of the system, it can be seen that the users include Patron, Cafeteria Staff, Menu Manager and Meal Deliverer, which will produce a series of relationships, and also lead to a lot of information and questions that need to be managed and answered. So we can answer and solve problems by creating ontology methods. We can separate the system into several scenarios depending on the user's differences, which can be searched in the scene, and the scenes described in the process including the place, deliver, menu, units, confirm, pay, and done. Last add a description of these types of scenes to the document. As shown in Table 7:

Table 7. The main description of the scene

Scene	Description
Place	Placing a meal order
Deliver	The patron shall specify whether the order is to be picked up or delivered
Menu	The COS shall display a menu for the date that the Patron specified
Units	The COS shall permit the user to order multiple meals and multiple food items
Confirm	The COS shall prompt the Patron to confirm the meal order
Pay	When the Patron indicates that he is done placing orders, the COS shall ask the user to select a payment method
Done	When the Patron has confirmed the order, it shall do the transaction as store, inventory, menu, times, patron, cafeteria and failure

4.2   CCM+TFIDFE

After preprocessing the documents, they are divided into words and its parts, and the words are removed from the list. Then use the CCM method to merge the documents and set the threshold to 4. After artificial screening, the concept of domain is gained and adds it to the user's dictionary. As shown in Table 8:

Table 8. Collection of concepts obtained by part of CCM

Concept	Word frequency	Concept	Word frequency
Deliver location	50	Employee ID	72
Food item price	59	Meal date	43
Meal order	42	Menu	24
Order date	10	Patron	79
Payment method	34	Transaction	20

Then, using the TFIDFE method to handle the words in the user dictionary, calculating the value of each words and setting the threshold to 0.35. After a manual test, you can get a collection of concepts. As shown in Table 9:

Table 9. Concept of part of domain

The concept of part of domain						
Deliver	Location	Time	Pay	Buy	Transaction	Employee
Food items	Price	Meal order	Menu	Order	Patron	Payment

4.3   Analysis of Results

The experimental results are analyzed, and the index [15] is precision and recall rate.

$$Recall = \frac{N}{A} \tag{12}$$

$$Pr\,ecision = \frac{N}{M} \tag{13}$$

Where N is the correct number of concepts obtained, and M is the number of concepts extracted while A is the number of concepts that exist in the document.

In order to verify the feasibility and validity of the CCM+TFIDFE method, we use three methods: TFIDF, CCM+TFIDF and CCM+TFIDFE to extract concepts. After artificial calculation, the correct concept number can be obtained, then compare it, and the method adopted in this paper can be obtained.

There are three methods to deal with any document, and using the X-axis to represent the number of the correct concepts, and the Y-axis is the way to extract the concepts, then the correct number of concepts is obtained as shown in Fig. 3:

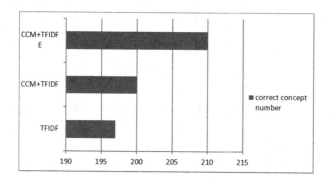

Fig. 3. The correct number of concepts extracted

It is easy to see that using CCM+TFIDFE method can improve the correct number of concepts extracted. Also the combination of CCM and TFIDF is higher than the correct concept number extracted by using any one method. When the number of documents to be selected is 1, 3, 5, 7, the number of concepts extracted by the above method are compared with the number of concepts extracted by the domain experts, and the comparison of the precision rate and the recall rate are shown in the figure below. In the figure, using the X-axis to show the number of different documents and the Y-axis is the difference in the concept of extraction, the precision rate and the recall rate (Figs. 4, 5 and 6).

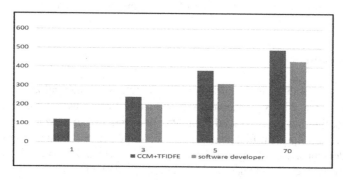

Fig. 4. The number of concepts extracted

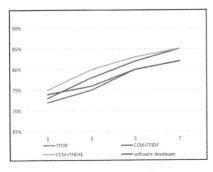
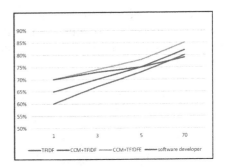

Fig. 5. Precision of concepts extracted   **Fig. 6.** Recalling of concepts extracted

The following conclusions can be drawn from the above diagram:

(1) The number of requirements extracted by CCM+TFIDFE method is more than the number of software developer, and the precision rate and recall rate are high. It is proved that CCM+TFIDFE method can improve the accuracy of extraction requirements.

(2) The method of CCM+TFIDF is more superior to the TFIDF method, which shows that the error caused by participle tool can be solved by the domain dictionary, and the method of using special characters to replace the stop words can also improve the accuracy of concept extraction. It is also possible to add more frequent concepts to the domain dictionary by manual checking, to increase the scope of the domain dictionary, and to improve the accuracy of the concept of TFIDF method extraction.

(3) It can be seen from the above chart that the method of CCM+TFIDFE is feasible regardless of the number of scenes chosen. And the accuracy of the number of experts extracted from the number of documents will decrease.

5   Conclusion

As a modeling tool that can describe the system at the semantic and knowledge level, ontology has been widely concerned and applied since it was put forward, and the ontology learning has also received great attention. In software development, demand acquisition is an important first step. Due to the difficulty of communication between users and developers, ontology can be used to solve semantic problems, so we proposed a software requirement acquisition method based on ontology learning. It mainly analyzes the concept extraction method, which can not only improve the automation degree of ontology construction, but also be more accurate and complete.

In the other aspects of ontology construction and application, ontology learning remains to be further studied. The extraction of concept relationship and the learning of axioms will also be the focus of future research in the domain of ontology learning, and the changing concept will also be a challenge for concept extraction.

Acknowledgement. This work is partially funded under The main of our work is supported by the National Key R&D Program of China (2018YFB1003902), the key Project of 13th Five-Year Plan of Education Science in Jiangsu Province (C-b/2016/01/24), the Postgraduate Research & Practice Innovation Program of Jiangsu Province (SJCX19_0201), the Key Project of Education Reform Research in 2018 and the Research Foundation for Advanced Talents at Nanjing Normal University.

References

1. Jin, Y., Zhang, P.: An approach to analyzing and verifying aspect-oriented requirements model. Chin. J. Comput. **36**(1), 63–72 (2013)
2. Yuan, X., Tripathi, S.: Combining ontologies for requirements elicitation. In: 5th International Proceedings on IEEE International Model-Driven Requirements Engineering (MoDRE), Ottawa, Canada (2015)
3. Bhatia, M.P.S., Beniwal, R., Kumar, A.: An ontology based framework for automatic detection and updation of requirement specifications. In: 1st International Proceedings on International Conference on Contemporary Computing and Informatics (IC3I), Mysore, India (2014)
4. Karatas, E.K., Iyidir, B., Birturk, A.: Ontology-based software requirements reuse: case study in fire control software product line domain. In: 14th International Proceedings on IEEE International Conference on Data Mining Workshop (ICDMW), Shenzhen, China (2014)
5. Sitthithanasakul, S., Choosri, N.: Using ontology to enhance requirement engineering in agile software process. In: 10th International Proceedings on International Conference on Software, Knowledge, Information Management & Application (SKIMA), Chengdu, China (2016)
6. Avdeenko, T., Pustovalova, N.: The ontology-based approach to support the completeness and consistency of the requirements specification. In: 11th International Proceedings on International Siberian Conference on Control and Communications (SIBCON), Omsk State Technical University Mira Ave, 11 Omsk, Russia (2015)
7. Saito, S., Iimura, Y., Anyama, M.: REO: requirements engineering ontology. In: 39th International Proceedings on IEEE Annual International Computers, Software & Applications Conference (COMPSAC), Taichung, Taiwan (2015)
8. Yang, G., Zhang, Y.: A feature-oriented modeling approach for embedded product line engineering. In: 12th International Proceedings on International Conference on Fuzzy Systems and Knowledge Discovery (FSKD), Zhangjiajie, China (2015)
9. Djilani, Z., Khiat, A., Khouri, S.: MURGROOM: multi-site requirement reuse through graph and ontology matching. In: 18th International Proceedings on International Conference on Information Integration and Web-based Applications and Services (iiWAS 2016), Singapore, Singapore (2016)
10. Baisong L.: A Study on Web-Based Domain Independent Ontology Learning. Zhejiang University, Hangzhou (2005)
11. Wang, C., Zhao, W., Wang, J., Chen, L.: Multidimensional customer requirements acquisition based on ontology. Comput. Integr. Manuf. Syst. **22**(4), 908–916 (2016)
12. Wang, X., Xu, J., Liu, M., Wei, Z., Bu, W., Hong, T.: An ontology-based approach for marine geochemical data interoperation. IEEE Access **5**(8), 13364–13370 (2017)
13. Ma, C.: Research on key technologies of ontology learning. Xi'an University of Posts and Telecommunications, Xian (2016)

14. Lu, R., Jin, Z., Chen, G.: Ontology-oriented requirements analysis. J. Softw. **11**(8), 1009–1017 (2000)
15. Jin, Z.: Ontology-based requirements elicitation. Chin. J. Comput. **23**(5), 192–486 (2000)
16. Qi, H., Guan, Y., Liu, Y.: Learning ontology of maize pets and diseases from Chinese text. Comput. Eng. Appl. **47**(20), 206–210 (2011)
17. Wiegers, K.E.: Software Requirements, 3rd edn. Microsoft Press, USA (2013)

Software Mining
(NASAC 2018 English Track)

An Empirical Study of Link Sharing in Review Comments

Jing Jiang, Jin Cao, and Li Zhang[✉]

State Key Laboratory of Software Development Environment, Beihang University,
Beijing, China
{jiangjing,CaoJin,lily}@buaa.edu.cn

Abstract. In the pull-based development, developers sometimes exchange review comments and share links, namely Uniform Resource Locators (URLs). Links are used to refer to related information from different websites, which may be beneficial to pull request evaluation. Nevertheless, little effort has been done on analyzing how links are shared and whether sharing links has any impacts on code review in GitHub. In this paper, we conduct a study of link sharing in review comments. We collect 114,810 pull requests and 251,487 review comments from 10 popular projects in GitHub. We find that 5.25% of pull requests have links in review comments on average. We divide links into two types: internal links which point to context in the same project, and external links which point to context outside of the project. We observe that 51.49% of links are internal, while 48.51% of links are external. The majority of internal links point to pull requests or blobs inside projects. We further study impacts of links. Results show that pull requests with links in review comments have more comments, more commenters and longer evaluation time than pull requests without links. These findings show that developers indeed share links and refer to related information in review comments. These results inspire future studies which enable more effective information sharing in the open source community, and improve information accessibility and navigability for software developers.

Keywords: Link sharing · Review comment · Pull request · Github

1 Introduction

Various open source software hosting sites, notably Github, provide support for pull-based development and allow developers to make contributions flexibly and efficiently [1,2]. In GitHub, contributors fork repositories and make changes without asking for permission. Contributors submit pull requests when they want to merge their changes into the repositories they fork from. Any developers can provide review comments and exchange opinions about pull requests [3–5]. Members of the project's core team (from here on, integrators) are responsible to inspect submitted code changes, identify issues (e.g., vulnerabilities), and decide whether to accept pull requests and merge these code changes into main repository [1].

© Springer Nature Singapore Pte Ltd. 2019
Z. Li et al. (Eds.): NASAC 2017/2018, CCIS 861, pp. 101–114, 2019.
https://doi.org/10.1007/978-981-15-0310-8_7

In the pull-based development, developers sometimes exchange review comments and share links, namely Uniform Resource Locators (URLs). Links are used to refer to related information from different websites, which may be beneficial to pull request evaluation. Link sharing is an important way of information diffusion [6,7]. Nevertheless, little effort has been done on analyzing how links are shared in a population of pull requests and on whether sharing links has any impacts on code review in GitHub. The understanding of link sharing in review comments can enable more effective information sharing in the open source community, and improve information accessibility and navigability for software developers.

In this paper, we conduct a study of link sharing in review comments. We collect 114,810 pull requests and 251,487 review comments from 10 popular projects in GitHub (Sect. 3). We first study the percentage of pull requests with links (Sect. 4). Then we divide links into two types: internal links which point to context in the same project, and external links which point to context outside of the project. We study the distribution of internal links and external links (Sect. 5). Finally, we explore impacts of links on pull request evaluation (Sect. 6).

The main findings of this paper are as follows:

- On average, 5.25% of pull requests have links in review comments.
- 51.49% of links are internal, while 48.51% of links are external. The majority of internal links point to pull requests or blobs inside projects.
- In comparison with pull requests without links, pull requests with links in review comments have more comments, more commenters and longer evaluation time.

2 Background and Research Questions

In this section, we first introduce background, and then introduce research questions.

2.1 Links in Pull Requests

Github provides support for pull-based development and allows developers to make contributions flexibly and efficiently [1,2]. In GitHub, contributors fork repositories, and make their code changes independent of one another. When a set of changes is ready, contributors create and submit pull requests to main repositories. Any developers can leave comments and exchange opinions about pull requests. Developers freely discuss whether code style meets the standard [8], whether repositories require modification, or whether submitted codes have good quality [3]. According to comments, contributors may modify codes. Integrators inspect submitted code changes, and decide whether to accept pull requests and integrate these code changes into main repositories or not [9,10].

Fig. 1. A link example in a review comment

Link sharing is an important way of information diffusion [6,7]. During discussion of code review, developers may share some links in comments, and refer to related information from different websites. In GitHub, pull requests have three types of comments [11]: First, review comments are comments on a portion of the unified diff[1]. Second, commit comments are applied directly to commits, outside of the pull request view. Third, issue comments are general comments posted in code review pages. Due to data collection, we mainly study review comments and describe detailed reasons in Sect. 3.

Figure 1 shows an example of the pull request ID 13638 in the project *symfony*[2]. In order to make the figure clear, we mainly show the review comment with a link. In this figure, a developer *hason* writes that "In require-dev section is symfony/security which replaces symfony/security-csrf. The symfony/security-csrf is optional dependency for Form component, see https://packagist.org/packages/symfony/form." In this review comment, the developer *hason* mentions a link which describes Symfony form component in PHP Package Repository. This link provides useful information in pull request evaluation.

---

[1] https://developer.github.com/v3/pulls/comments/.
[2] https://github.com/symfony/symfony/pull/13638.

2.2 Research Questions

The main motivation of this study is to make an empirical analysis on link sharing in GitHub. To achieve our goal, we would like to address the following research questions.

RQ1. What is the percentage of pull requests with links in GitHub?

In GitHub, no previous work has studied pull requests with links in comments. Based on our datasets, we compute the percentage of pull requests with links for each individual project. We explore to what extent are links used in pull requests of GitHub.

RQ2. What context does links point to?

In this question, we want to explore context of websites links point to. We divide links into two types: internal links which point to context in the same project, and external links which point to context outside of the project. Then we study categories of internal links.

RQ3. What kind of differences are between the pull requests with and without link? Does link sharing influence the evaluation of pull requests?

In order to answer this question, we mainly compare pull requests with links and without links on the basis of the following characteristics of pull requests: the number of comments, the number of commenters, evaluation time and acceptance. Then we use the statistical tests to verify the significance of these differences.

3   Data Collection

There are two ways to get data of open source projects in GitHub. First, GitHub provides access to its internal data through API[3]. Second, GHTorrent[4] creates a scalable, queriable, offline mirror of data offered through GitHub API. Considering the convenience and time cost, we use both methods to collect our datasets.

In data collection, we choose popular projects, because they receive many pull requests and provide enough information for experiments. We obtain a list of projects from previous work [12], which made their research projects public[5]. We sort their projects by the number of pull requests, and obtain 100 projects with the most number of pull requests. According to pull requests information, integrators assign tags to some pull requests from tag library. Tags are a simple and effective way to attach additional information (e.g., metadata) to pull requests [13]. According to our previous work[6], we select projects with more than 3,000 tagged pull requests and more than 30 tags in their tag libraries. Finally, we obtain 10 popular open source projects. Table 1 shows owner names and project names of these 10 projects.

---

[3] https://developer.github.com/.

[4] http://ghtorrent.org/.

[5] https://github.com/Yuyue/pullreq_ci/blob/master/all_projects.csv.

[6] Jing Jiang, Jin Cao, Xin Xia, Li Zhang. Exploring and Recommending Tags for Pull Requests in GitHub. In submission.

Table 1. Basic Statistics of projects.

Owner	Project	# Pull requests	# Review comments
angular	angular.js	7,722	10,909
bitcoin	bitcoin	8,852	24,216
ceph	ceph	20,554	34,097
owncloud	core	13,681	40,113
elasticsearch	elasticsearch	3,472	8,989
pydata	pandas	5,354	16,180
rails	rails	20,842	26,147
RIOT-OS	RIOT	7,009	29,779
symfony	symfony	16,492	41,716
tgstation	tgstation	10,832	19,341
	Total	114,810	251,487

Due to the large number of comments in 10 projects, comment collection through GitHub API is time-consuming. GHTorrent monitors the Github public event time line, and provides an offline mirror of datasets. We download the database dumps "mysql-2018-04-01" from GHTorrent, and extract review comments in above 10 projects. For each pull request, we collect its identifiers, the creation time, the close time, and code review decision. For each review comment, we collect its identifiers, commenter, context and the pull request identifier which this review comment belongs to. In order to extract links from review comment context, we extract strings which begin with http or https. We study link sharing in review comments in this paper. In future work, we will collect datasets though GitHub API, and study commit comments and general comments.

Table 1 presents statistics of 10 projects. The columns correspond to owner name (Owner), project name (Project), the number of pull requests (# Pull requests), and the number of review comments (# Review comments). In total, our datasets include 114,810 pull requests and 251,487 review comments.

4 Link Frequency

In this section, we want to investigate usage frequency of links, and know the proportion of pull requests which have links in review comments. Table 2 shows the number of pull requests, the number of links, the number of pull requests with links, and the percentage of pull requests with links. Since a pull request may have several links in review comments, the number of links is larger than the number of pull requests with links. The project *angular.js* has 7,722 pull requests, and 321 (4.16%) pull requests have links. On average, 5.25% of pull requests have links in review comments of 10 projects. When developers discuss pull requests on a portion of the unified diff, they indeed share links and refer to related information.

Table 2. Basic Statistics of link frequency in each projects.

Project	#Pull requests	#links	#/% Pull requests with links
angular.js	7,722	517	321/4.16 %
bitcoin	8,852	914	519/5.86 %
ceph	20,554	1,323	829/4.03 %
core	13,681	2,586	865/6.32 %
elasticsearch	3,472	114	94/2.71 %
pydata	5,354	486	305/5.7 %
rails	20,842	1,631	973/4.67 %
RIOT	7,009	1,202	702/10.02 %
symfony	16,492	2,175	1,227/7.44 %
tgstation	10,832	219	192/1.77 %
Total	114,810	11,167	6,027/5.25 %

RQ1: On average, 5.25% of pull requests have links in review comments.

5   Context of Links

In this section, we mainly explore context of websites links point to. We divide links into two types: internal links which point to context in the same project, and external links which point to context outside the project. We use string matching to decide whether a link is internal or external. For example, all context in project *symfony* has links with prefix "https://github.com/symfony/symfony/". Therefore, the link in review comment in Fig. 1 is considered as an external link. Note that we study project context in GitHub. Some projects may have websites outside GitHub, which are still considered as external links.

Table 3 shows the number of internal links and external links in each project. In all projects, the average percentages of internal links and external links are similar. On average, 51.49% of links are internal, while 48.51% of links are external. In review comments, developers use links pointing to context inside the project as well as outside the project.

We take a further step and study categories of internal links. We consider 6 categories, including pull request, issue, blob, commit, wiki and other. Developers submit pull requests when they want to merge code changes into main repositories [1]. In OSS projects, developers write issue reports to identify bugs, and document feature requests [14]. A Git blob (binary large object) is the object type used to store the contents of each file in a repository[7]. For example, a link[8] points to the line 81 in the code file 'config.sample.php'. Satisfactory codes are

---

[7] https://developer.github.com/v3/git/blobs/.
[8] https://github.com/owncloud/core/blob/master/config/config.sample.php#L81.

Table 3. Statistics of internal links and external links.

Project	#/% Internal links	#/% External links
angular.js	225/43.52 %	292/56.48 %
bitcoin	504/55.14 %	410/44.86 %
ceph	617/46.64 %	706/53.36 %
core	1,468/56.77 %	1,118/43.23 %
elasticsearch	59/51.75 %	55/48.25 %
pandas	253/52.06 %	233/47.94 %
rails	865/53.03 %	766/46.97 %
RIOT	671/55.82 %	531/44.18 %
symfony	988/45.43 %	1,187/54.57 %
tgstation	100/45.66 %	119/54.34 %
Total	5,750/51.49 %	5,417/48.51 %

Table 4. Percentage of internal links in different categories.

Project	Pull request	Issue	Blob	Commit	Wiki	Other
angular.js	51.11	8	28	9.33	0.89	2.67
bitcoin	65.67	0.99	27.98	1.59	0	3.77
ceph	57.7	0	38.74	2.59	0	0.97
core	41.83	12.67	39.1	5.52	0.27	0.61
elasticsearch	27.12	16.95	35.59	16.95	0	3.39
pandas	34.39	15.02	44.66	4.74	0.4	0.79
rails	38.5	3.01	43.93	11.79	0	2.77
RIOT	56.04	2.83	27.87	0.75	10.43	2.08
symfony	47.47	6.38	40.89	2.94	0	2.32
tgstation	51	1	42	2	0	4
Average	47.79	6.37	37.63	4.97	1.34	1.9

committed to repositories [12]. Some projects use wiki to write documentation which helps others use and extend projects[9]. If internal links do not belong to above categories, they are classified as other.

In GitHub, the four-level domain name in a link shows its category. For example, Fig. 1 shows an example of the pull request with link "https://github.com/symfony/symfony/pull/13638". In this link, the four-level domain name is "pull", which means that this link points to a pull request. We use the four-level domain name to classify internal links, and describe results in Table 4. Developers mainly use internal links which point to pull requests or blobs. In 7 projects, the majority of links point to the category 'pull request'. In review comments,

---

[9] https://help.github.com/articles/about-github-wikis/.

developers often mention some other related pull requests. In other 3 projects, the majority of links point to the category 'blob', and developers use internal links and refer to some specific locations of codes. Developers sometime write links pointing to issues or commits which are related to pull requests. In project *RIOT*, 10.43% of internal links point to documents in its wiki.

RQ2: 51.49% of links are internal, while 48.51% of links are external. The majority of internal links point to pull requests or blobs inside projects.

6   Impacts of Links

In order to answer RQ3, we mainly compare pull requests with links and without links, and explore impacts of links on pull request evaluation.

6.1   Review Comments and Commenters

We compute the number of review comments for each pull request. Then we calculate the average number of review comments for pull requests with links and without links. The Mann- Whitney-Wilcoxon (MWW) test is a non-parametric statistical test that assesses the statistical significance of the difference between two distributions [15]. Hence, we perform the MWW Test to test and confirm the significance of comment difference between pull requests with and without links.

Table 5. Average number of review comments in pull requests with links and without links.

Project	With links	Without links	P-value
angular.js	14.07	0.86	$<1.00e^{-05}$
bitcoin	19.62	1.68	$<1.00e^{-05}$
ceph	13.55	0.99	$<1.00e^{-05}$
core	11.81	0.89	$<1.00e^{-05}$
elasticsearch	23.3	1.94	$<1.00e^{-05}$
pandas	20.14	1.98	$<1.00e^{-05}$
rails	10.73	0.76	$<1.00e^{-05}$
RIOT	21.75	2.3	$<1.00e^{-05}$
symfony	15.93	1.44	$<1.00e^{-05}$
tgstation	12.99	1.58	$<1.00e^{-05}$
Average	16.389	1.442	

Table 5 presents average number of review comments for pull requests. We noticed that the average number of review comments for pull request with links are many more than these of pull requests without links. For example, in project *symfony*, the average number of review comments for pull request with links and without links are 15.93 and 1.44, respectively. The Mann-Wilcoxon-Whitney Test shows that the differences in review comments of pull requests with and without links are statistically significant at 0.05 significance level. For all the 10 projects, the $P-values$ are $<1.00e^{-05}$. This result indicates that pull requests with links are likely to have more review comments than pull requests without links. Links point to related information, and may promote code review discussion.

Table 6. Average number of commenters in pull requests with links and without links.

Project	With links	Without links	P-value
angular.js	2.68	0.34	$<1.00e^{-05}$
bitcoin	4.06	0.73	$<1.00e^{-05}$
ceph	2.56	0.38	$<1.00e^{-05}$
core	2.87	0.41	$<1.00e^{-05}$
elasticsearch	2.8	0.55	$<1.00e^{-05}$
pandas	2.74	0.59	$<1.00e^{-05}$
rails	3.09	0.37	$<1.00e^{-05}$
RIOT	3.08	0.74	$<1.00e^{-05}$
symfony	4.04	0.66	$<1.00e^{-05}$
tgstation	4.48	0.76	$<1.00e^{-05}$
Average	3.24	0.553	

We take a further step and study the number of commenters. Several review comments may belong to the same commenter. We compare the average number of commenters for pull requests with and without links, and describe results in Table 6. The average number of commenters is 0.553 for pull requests without links, while the value is raised to 3.24 for pull requests with links. Results on the number of commenters are similar as results on the number of review comments.

6.2   Evaluation Time

For each pull request, we compute evaluation time as time interval between the pull request's creation time and the pull request's close time. Then, we compute the average value of evaluation time for pull requests with links and without links, respectively. We also perform a Mann-Wilcoxon-Whitney Test to evaluate the difference significance of evaluation time between these two groups.

Table 7 presents the average evaluation time for pull requests with links and without links. Except project *elasticsearch*, the average evaluation time of pull requests with links is much longer than that of pull requests without links. The Mann-Wilcoxon-Whitney Test shows that the differences in evaluation time of

Table 7. Average evaluation time (days) of pull requests with links and without links.

Project	With links	Without links	P-value
angular.js	60.86	42.73	$<1.00e^{-05}$
bitcoin	60.19	23.08	$<1.00e^{-05}$
ceph	42.83	17.47	$<1.00e^{-05}$
core	40.98	13.63	$<1.00e^{-05}$
elasticsearch	23.77	24.98	$<1.00e^{-05}$
pandas	35.78	15.35	$<1.00e^{-05}$
rails	68.38	28.58	$<1.00e^{-05}$
RIOT	73.32	28.54	$<1.00e^{-05}$
symfony	60.31	17.2	$<1.00e^{-05}$
tgstation	9.27	5.97	$<1.00e^{-05}$
Average	47.569	21.753	

pull requests with links and without links are statistically significant at 0.05 significance level. Hence, we conclude that pull requests with links in review comments require more time to get closed than pull requests without links.

Table 8. The accept rate (%) of pull requests with links and without links.

Project	With links	Without links
angular.js	16.23	11.75
bitcoin	53.04	48.51
ceph	59.48	53.9
core	33.17	44.7
elasticsearch	7.59	11.18
pandas	18.25	37.09
rails	40.51	48.97
RIOT	42.41	46.93
symfony	31.46	45.79
tgstation	17.3	21.88
Average	31.944	37.07

6.3   Acceptance

In GitHub, integrators inspect submitted code changes, and decide whether to accept or reject pull requests [9,10]. The acceptance rate is defined as the number of accepted pull requests, divided by the total number of pull requests.

Table 8 shows acceptance rate of pull requests with links and without links. In the majority of projects, pull requests with links have lower acceptance rate than pull requests without links. In projects *angular.js*, *bitcoin* and *ceph*, pull requests with links have higher acceptance rate than pull requests without links. Since different projects have various results, impacts of links on acceptance are uncertain.

> RQ3: In comparison with pull requests without links, pull requests with links in review comments have more comments, more commenters and longer evaluation time.

7 Discussion

7.1 Implications

In this paper, we make an initial study of link sharing in review comments. Results show that developers indeed share some links which point to context inside and outside projects. Future works may further explore categories of external links, and understand why developers share links. Researchers may investigate methods for assisting developers discover related information and share links in review comments. Ye et al. understood the structure and dynamics of the knowledge network formed by URL sharing in Stack Overflow [7]. Future works may explore knowledge network formed by link sharing, and study knowledge diffusion process in GitHub.

7.2 Threats to Validity

In this subsection we introduce threats to the validity of our work and how we minimize their impacts.

Threats to conclusion validity relate to issues that affect the ability to draw the correct conclusion. In this paper, we study link sharing in review comments. Besides review comments, commit comments and general comments are also used in the discussion of pull requests. In future work, we will collect more datasets, and study commit comments and general comments.

Threats to external validity relate to the generalizability of our study. Our empirical results are based on projects in GitHub and it is unknown whether our results can be generalized to other open source software platforms such as Bitbucket. In future, we plan to use projects from other open source software platforms and compare the results with our findings in GitHub.

8 Related Work

Related work to this study could be divided into two main categories, including link sharing and pull requests evaluation.

Some previous works studied links in GitHub or Stack Overflow. Zhang et al. made a qualitative study of issue linking in GitHub [16]. Their results showed that developers tend to link more cross-project or cross-ecosystem issues over time. Ye et al. understood the structure and dynamics of the knowledge network formed by URL sharing in programming-specific Q&A sites [7]. Gomez et al. found that link sharing was a significant phenomenon in Stack Overflow [6]. Different from these works, we mainly study link sharing in pull requests of GitHub.

There have been several studies about pull request evaluation in GitHub [1–3,8,17–22]. Gousios et al. investigated the reasons for which some pull requests were rejected [1]. Dabbish et al. analyzed the association of various technical and social measures with the likelihood of contribution acceptance [2]. Dabbish et al. conducted a study of how developers in open work environments evaluated and discussed pull requests [3]. Hellendoorn et al. evaluated the existence and effects of code contributions in GitHub [8]. Yu et al. proposed a reviewer recommendation approach by mining each project's comment networks [23]. Jing et al. analyzed developers' activeness to recommend commenters for pull requests [5]. Li et al. designed automatic classification of review comments in pull-based development model [21]. In our work, we address a problem different from the above mentioned studies. In our study we mainly investigate link sharing in pull request evaluation.

9   Conclusion

In this paper, we study link sharing in review comments of GitHub. We find that 5.25% of pull requests have links in review comments on average. We divide links into two types: internal links which point to context in the same project, and external links which point to context outside the project. We observe that 51.49% of links are internal, while 48.51% of links are external. The majority of internal links point to pull requests or blobs inside projects. We further study impacts of links. Results show that pull requests with links in review comments have more comments, more commenters and longer evaluation time than pull requests without links. Our findings show that developers indeed share links and refer to related information in review comments. These results inspire future studies to build tools and services that help developers find related links in code review.

Acknowledgment. This work is supported by the National Key Research and Development Program of China No. 2018YFB1004202, National Natural Science Foundation of China under Grant No. 61732019 and the State Key Laboratory of Software Development Environment under Grant No. SKLSDE-2018ZX-12.

References

1. Gousios, G., Pinzger, M., van Deursen, A.: An exploratory study of the pull-based software development model. In: Proceedings of the 36th International Conference on Software Engineering, pp. 345–355. ACM (2014)

2. Tsay, J., Dabbish, L., Herbsleb, J.: Influence of social and technical factors for evaluating contribution in GitHub. In: Proceedings of the 36th International Conference on Software Engineering, pp. 356–366. ACM (2014)
3. Tsay, J., Dabbish, L., Herbsleb, J.: Let's talk about it: evaluating contributions through discussion in GitHub. In: Proceedings of the 22nd ACM SIGSOFT International Symposium on Foundations of Software Engineering - FSE 2014, pp. 144–154 (2014)
4. Rahman, M.M., Roy, C.K., Kula, R.G.: Predicting usefulness of code review comments using textual features and developer experience. In: Proceedings of MSR, Buenos Aires, Argentina, pp. 215–226, May 2017
5. Jiang, J., Yang, Y., He, J., Blanc, X., Zhang, L.: Who should comment on this pull request? Analyzing attributes for more accurate commenter recommendation in pull-based development. Inf. Softw. Technol. **84**, 48–62 (2017)
6. Gomez, C., Cleary, B., Singer, L.: A study of innovation diffusion through link sharing on stack overflow. In: Proceedings of MSR, San Francisco, USA, May 2013
7. Ye, D., Xing, Z., Kapre, N.: The structure and dynamics of knowledge network in domain-specific qa sites: a case study of stack overflow. Empir. Softw. Eng. **22**, 375–406 (2017)
8. Hellendoorn, V.J., Devanbu, P.T., Bacchelli, A.: Will they like this?: evaluating code contributions with language models. In: Proceedings of the 12th Working Conference on Mining Software Repositories, pp. 157–167. IEEE Press (2015)
9. Gousios, G., Zaidman, A., Storey, M.-A., Van Deursen, A.: Work practices and challenges in pull-based development: the integrator's perspective. In: Proceedings of the 37th International Conference on Software Engineering-Volume 1, pp. 358–368. IEEE Press (2015)
10. Bacchelli, A., Bird, C.: Expectations, outcomes, and challenges of modern code review. In: Proceedings of ICSE, San Francisco, USA, May 2013
11. Zhang, Y., Wang, H., Yin, G., Wang, T., Yue, Y.: Social media in github the role of @-mention in assisting software development. Sci. China Inf. Sci. **60**, 1–18 (2017)
12. Vasilescu, B., Yu, Y., Wang, H., Devanbu, P., Filkov, V.: Quality and productivity outcomes relating to continuous integration in GitHub. In: Proceedings of the 2015 10th Joint Meeting on Foundations of Software Engineering, pp. 805–816. ACM (2015)
13. Cabot, J., Izquierdo, J.L.C., Cosentino, V., Rolandi, B.: Exploring the use of labels to categorize issues in open-source software projects. In: 2015 IEEE 22nd International Conference on Software Analysis, Evolution and Reengineering (SANER), pp. 550–554. IEEE (2015)
14. Bissyande, T.F., Lo, D., Jiang, L., Reveillere, L., Klein, J., Le Traon, Y.: Got issues? Who cares about it? A large scale investigation of issue trackers from GitHub. In: Proceedings of ISSRE, Washington DC, USA, November 2013
15. Mann, H.B., Whitney, D.R.: On a test of whether one of two random variables is stochastically larger than the other. Ann. Math. Stat. **18**, 50–60 (1947)
16. Zhang, Y., Yu, Y., Wang, H., Vasilescu, B., Filkov, V.: Within-ecosystem issue linking: a large-scale study of rails. In: The 7th International Workshop on Mining Software Repositories, Montpellier, France, September 2018
17. Gousios, G., Storey, M.-A., Bacchelli, A.: Work practices and challenges in pull-based development: the contributor's perspective. In: Proceedings of ICSE, Austin, USA, pp. 285–296, May 2016
18. Coelho, J., Valente, M.T.: Why modern open source projects fail. In: Proceedings of FSE, Paderborn, Germany, pp. 186–196, September 2017

19. Zhu, J., Zhou, M., Mockus, A.: Effectiveness of code contribution: from patch-based to pull-request-based tools. In: Effectiveness of Code Contribution: From Patch-Based to Pull-Request-Based Tools, Seattle, USA, pp. 871–882, November 2016
20. Jiang, J., Lo, D., Ma, X., Feng, F., Zhang, L.: Understanding inactive yet available assignees in GitHub. Inf. Softw. Technol. **91**, 44–55 (2017)
21. Li, Z., Yue, Y., Yin, G., Wang, T., Fan, Q., Wang, H.: Automatic classification of review comments in pull-based development model. In: Proceedings of SEKE, Pittsburgh, USA, July 2017
22. Yue, Y., Yin, G., Wang, T., Yang, C., Wang, H.: Determinants of pull-based development in the context of continuous integration. Sci. China Inf. Sci. **59**(8), 1–14 (2016)
23. Yue, Y., Wang, H., Yin, G., Wang, T.: Reviewer recommendation for pull-requests in GitHub: what can we learn from code review and bug assignment? Inf. Softw. Technol. **74**, 204–218 (2016)

Changes Are Similar: Measuring Similarity of Pull Requests That Change the Same Code in GitHub

Ping Ma, Danni Xu, Xin Zhang, and Jifeng Xuan[✉]

School of Computer Science, Wuhan University, Wuhan 430072, China
jxuan@whu.edu.cn

Abstract. Pull-based development is widely used in globally collaborative platforms, such as GitHub and BitBucket. A pull request is a set of changes to existing source code in a project. A developer submits a pull request and tends to update the source code. Due to the parallel mechanism, several developers may submit multiple pull requests to change the same lines of code. This fact results in the conflict between changes, which makes the project manager difficult to decide which pull request should be merged. In this paper, we conducted a preliminary study on measuring the similarity of pull requests that aim to change the same code in GitHub. We proposed two methods, i.e., the *cosine* and the *doc2vec*, to quantify the structural similarity and the semantic similarity between pull requests and evaluated the similarity on four widely-studied open source Java projects. Our study shows that there indeed exists high similarity between competing pull requests and the similarity among projects diversifies. This complicates the merging decision by project managers.

Keywords: Pull requests · GitHub · Similarity · Empirical study · Code changes

1 Introduction

GitHub is widely-used in collaborative software development. A developer who is engaged in open-source projects tend to use GitHub to support their collaboration. According to the official website, up to June 2018, GitHub has over 28 million users and 57 million repositories, making it the largest host of source code in the world [2]. GitHub achieves collaborative development via the mechanism of pull requests. Once a developer wants to update a project, he can submit a pull request which consists of one or more code changes to the target project. A submitted pull request waits to be merged into the repository or discarded by the manager of the target project.

Due to the parallel mechanism of GitHub, it often happens that developers make different changes to the same lines of code during the same time period. This makes pull requests potentially compete with each other, i.e., competing pull requests [20]. Such pull requests may contain changes that have the same

© Springer Nature Singapore Pte Ltd. 2019
Z. Li et al. (Eds.): NASAC 2017/2018, CCIS 861, pp. 115–128, 2019.
https://doi.org/10.1007/978-981-15-0310-8_8

or different goals and may cause the conflicts on the structure or the semantics of code. It is complicated and time-consuming for a project manager to decide which pull request should be merged in high priority [7,8,23]. The existence of conflicts between changes by these pull requests exacerbates the difficulty for the merging decision. We speculate that the similarity between these pull requests may have a great impact on the difficulty that project managers have to face when they make decisions for merging pull requests.

In this paper, we conducted a preliminary study on measuring the similarity between pull requests that aim to change the same code in GitHub. We used the *cosine* and the *doc2vec* to measure the similarity of code structure and semantics, respectively. We evaluated the similarity on four open source Java projects with the most forks in GitHub. Our study contains 6,469 pairs of pull requests, each pair of which has two pull requests that contain changes on overlapped code. We explored the similarities between these pull requests via three research questions, including the similarities between pull requests, the similarity distribution, and the correlations between two measurement methods in use.

Our study shows that there indeed exists high similarity between pull requests that change the same code. In the four Java projects we studied, the average similarity between each pair of pull requests is over 0.9; the highest average similarity among these four projects is up to 0.9976. In the pull requests we measured, over 75% of the similarity between each pair of pull requests is above 0.8 and half of the similarity is 0.95 or higher. Our study shows that there is high correlation between the two measurement methods; this indicates that both the structural similarity and the semantic similarity exist between the pull requests that aim to change the same code.

This paper makes the following contributions:

- We conducted a study of measuring the similarity between pull requests that aim to change the same code. We proposed two methods to measure the similarity of code structure and semantics on four open source Java projects with the most forks in GitHub.
- We answered three research questions and found that there indeed exists high similarity between competing pull requests. This provides the foundational result for analyzing the conflicts between pull requests.

The remaining of this paper is organized as follows. Section 2 presents the background and the motivation. Section 3 describes two measurement methods of similarity. Section 4 presents the experimental setup, which includes data preparation, two measurement methods, and three research questions. Section 5 details the results of our experiment. Section 6 explains the threats to the validity. Section 7 lists the related work and Sect. 8 concludes this paper.

2   Background and Motivation

We introduce the background of merging pull requests and the motivation of exploring the similarity between pull requests.

2.1 Background

Collaborative platforms, such as GitHub and BitBucket, have provided high interaction between developers and code projects via pull requests. A project manager can deploy the codebase in GitHub and allows other developers to *fork* (i.e., clone) the project into their own account as a copy. Developers could freely make code changes to the project that has been forked in their account. Once several changes are made, a pull request that includes the changes can be submitted to the target project. A submitted pull request waits for the decision by the project manager, i.e., deciding merging this pull request into the project or discarding it.

Pull requests are the key artifacts that make developers accomplish collaborative development in GitHub. Technically, a pull request consists of one or more commits, each of which contains edits to the original source code at a particular time. Once these changes are accepted by the project manager, the pull request is merged into the original repository. Conversely, the pull request would be closed if the manager chooses not to accept these code changes. GitHub provides a free and flexible platform for developers to submit pull requests; hence, the project manager may receive multiple pull requests during a time period. In this case of multiple pull requests, it is time-consuming for the manager to decide which pull request should be merged.

2.2 Motivation

Due to the parallel mechanism of GitHub, several developers may submit different pull requests to change the same lines of code, which cause the competing pull requests [20]. This fact results in the conflict between changes because the code changes that competing pull requests have made focus on the same target. A project manager can choose one or zero among these competing pull requests and merge it into the original project.

As a manager of an open-source project, he/she has to manually check all competing pull requests to ensure the contribution of pull requests and to decide merging which pull request. The existence of competing pull requests makes the merging decision difficult. Do competing pull requests behave similar? – An intuitive speculation is that competing pull requests are similar since they aim to update the same lines of code. Supposing the similarity between competing pull requests is low, we can surmise that directly distinguish different competing pull requests is possible; supposing the similarity is high, a semantical or further detailed analysis could help for the merging decisions. Motivated by the exploration on the similarity of pull requests, we conducted a preliminary study on the similarity between pull requests that tend to change overlapped pieces of code.

3 Measurement Methods of Similarity

There is no reliable and effective way to measure the similarity of code. In this paper, we used two measurement methods to check the structural similarity and the semantic similarity between pull requests. For the structural similarity, we employ the *cosine* that is designed to measure the textual similarity between sentences; for the semantic similarity, we employ the *doc2vec* that is developed to extract the semantics of paragraphs.

3.1 The *cosine* Method

The *cosine* similarity is usually used to measure the textual similarity of sentences [21]. The key idea of the *cosine* is to count the number of co-appearance of words to reveal potential semantics [17].

We used the *cosine* method to measure the similarity between pull requests. The *cosine* similarity uses the *cosine* value of angles of two vectors in the vector space. Given two n-dimension vectors X and Y, the *cosine* similarity of two vectors is defined as follows,

$$Sim_{\cos}(X, Y) = \frac{\sum_{i=1}^{n}(x_i \times y_i)}{\sqrt{\sum_{i=1}^{n} x_i^2} \times \sqrt{\sum_{i=1}^{n} y_i^2}}$$

where x_i and y_i denote the element value of the ith dimension in X and Y, respectively. The closer the *cosine* is to 1, the more similar two vectors are.

Given two pull requests, we treat them as two pieces of code. To utilize the *cosine* to measure the similarity between pull requests, we convert the changed code into textual sentences based on the following two steps. First, we filter out the punctuation from the code and separate the code into tokens. For instance, giving the code `assertThat(processDefinitions.getBody().getContent().hasSize(4));`, we transfer the code into a sequence of `assertThat`, `processDefinition`, `getBody`, `getContent`, `hasSize`, and 4.

Second, we collect the frequency of tokens in two pull requests and obtain the word-frequency vectors. Then given two vectors, we leverage the *cosine* to calculate the similarity.

3.2 The *doc2vec* Method

In addition to measuring the structural similarity between pull requests with the *cosine*, we employ the *doc2vec* to reveal semantic similarity. The *doc2vec*, or the *paragraph2vec*, is an unsupervised algorithm that can extract the vector expression of sentences or documents [11]. This algorithm is an extension of a widely-used method *word2vec* [12].

In the *doc2vec*, a large corpus is used to train a model by maximizing the conditional likelihood between words and sentences with the hierarchical softmax and negative sampling. Different from the *cosine*, the *doc2vec* generates word vectors via an unsupervised learning process. Learned vector by the *doc2vec* can be used to calculate the similarity between sentences or documents. The implementation of the *doc2vec* directly outputs the distances between two sentences and can be converted into the similarity.

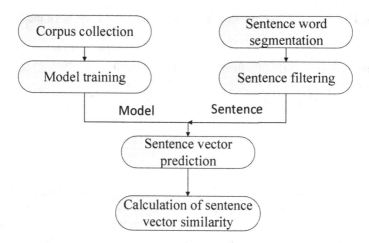

Fig. 1. Framework of using *doc2vec* to measure the similarity between pull requests.

Figure 1 presents the framework of using the *doc2vec* to obtain the similarity. To apply the *doc2vec* to calculate the semantic similarity of pull requests, we train the model to get the approximated likelihood of words and sentences. In each project, we extract the source code of a previous version before the submitted timestamps of pull requests. During the training, we filter out the punctuations in the source code and use all tokens in these processed source code as a training corpus. Then we employ the *doc2vec* to build the model with our training corpus. According to the implementation of the *doc2vec*, sentences that only contain tokens inside the corpus can be measured by the learned model. In each project, we use the learned model to infer the dependency of tokens in the input pull requests and use these learned vectors to calculate the similarity.

Note that the *doc2vec* is not the only way to measure the semantic similarity of two sentences or paragraphs. The Latent Semantic Analysis (LSA) by Deerwester et al. [6] and the Latent Dirichlet Allocation (LDA) by Blei et al. [5] are also widely used to detect the similarity in natural language processing. Our work does not aim to find out an optimal similarity measurement; instead, the goal of our work is to show the existence of similarity between pull requests.

4   Experimental Setup

We present the steps of data preparation and the design of three research questions.

4.1   Data Preparation

We conducted a preliminary study on four pairs of open-source Java projects with the most forks in GitHub. Table 1 presents the data of four projects in our study. There are 6,469 pairs of pull requests in total. We describe the data preparation as follows.

Table 1. Data collection of four Java projects with the most forks in GitHub

Project	# of forks	# of pairs of pull requests
spring-projects/spring-framework	14.7K	4799
spring-projects/spring-boot	20.0K	1178
apache/incubator-dubbo	14.4K	401
elastic/elasticsearch	11.5K	91
Total	60.6K	6469

First, we selected the top-5 Java projects with the most forks in GitHub. We followed Zhang et al. [20] to collect all pull requests that are submitted from January 1st to December 31st, 2017. Then we extracted all pairs of pull requests, which contain changes on overlapped code. Among the five projects, we found that one project iluwatar/java-design-patterns contains only four pairs of pull requests that change the same code, then we kept all other four projects in our study. These four are spring-projects/spring-framework,[1] spring-projects/spring-boot,[2] apache/incubator-dubbo,[3] and elastic/elasticsearch,[4] respectively.

Second, we identified the pull requests that change the same code as follows. We considered that a group of competing pull requests as all pull requests that change the same lines during an overlapping time period. For instance, if Pull request PrA and Pull request B PrB edit at-least one same line of code. We consider that PrA and PrB belong to one pair of pull requests. In this paper, we focus on the similarity between pull requests. Thus, we only identify all pairs of pull requests that change the same code, rather than groups of competing pull requests as shown in [20].

Third, we merged all changes in one pull request and collected the changed code from the original codebase. The changed code can be viewed as a combination of the added code and the deleted code. To evaluate the similarity of pull requests, we only reserved the added lines of code as the new code in a pull request. If a pull request has no added lines, we directly discarded this pull request. After data preparation, we collected 6,469 pairs of pull requests from four projects.

4.2 Research Questions

The aim of this paper is to explore the similarity between competing pull requests and to understand whether the high similarity between competing pull requests that complicates the merging decision by project managers. We designed three Research Questions (RQs) and conducted a preliminary study to find out the answers.

---

[1] Project spring-framework, http://github.com/spring-projects/spring-framework/.
[2] Project spring-boot, http://github.com/spring-projects/spring-boot/.
[3] Project incubator-dubbo, http://github.com/apache/incubator-dubbo/.
[4] Project elasticsearch, http://github.com/elastic/elasticsearch/.

RQ1. How does the similarity between competing pull requests perform?

In our work, we tend to understand the structural similarity based on the *cosine* and the semantical similarity based on the *doc2vec*. We give a numerical result on the similarity between each pair of pull requests via evaluating the two measurement methods in RQ1.

RQ2. What is the distribution of the similarity between competing pull requests?

Besides the statistical values, we further study the similarity distributions on each project. In RQ2, we show that the similarity between pull requests diversifies and we could obtain a distribution of the similarity between competing pull requests.

RQ3. Is there any correlation between the two measurement methods of similarity?

Our study showed the results of two measurement methods of similarity. Thus, in RQ3, we evaluate the Pearson correlation coefficient to detect the correlation between these methods. We also leveraged the Wilcoxon signed rank test to figure out whether the two measurement behave different.

5   Experimental Results

We empirically examined the results of three RQs and presented the existence of similarity between pull requests.

5.1   RQ1. How Does the Similarity Between Competing Pull Requests Perform?

In RQ1, we present the numerical result of the study that measures the similarity between pull requests that contain changes on overlapped code of four Java projects in GitHub.

Table 2 shows the results of similarity between pull requests by measuring the structural similarity with the *cosine*. The similarity between pull requests measured by the *cosine* is high with the maximum value of 1.0. In three out of four, the average similarity is over 0.9; the value of the exceptional project is 0.8963, which could be considered as 0.9.

Table 3 shows the results of similarity between pull requests by measuring the semantic similarity with the *doc2vec*. In four Java projects we studied, the average similarity between pull requests of each project exceeded 0.9. Project apache/incubator-dubbo has the highest similarity, whose average value is 0.9976.

As shown in Tables 2 and 3, the maximum value of the similarity is 1.0 regardless of any project or method. This shows that there indeed exists high similarity between pull requests that aim to change the same code. Meanwhile, the average value behave similar. For instance, the project with the maximum value of average similarity by the *cosine* and by the *doc2vec* is the same while

Table 2. Structural similarity between pull requests measured by the *cosine* on four projects

Project	Min	Median	Max	Average	Std
spring-projects/spring-framework	0.2887	0.9591	1.0000	0.8963	0.1552
spring-projects/spring-boot	0.3780	0.9881	1.0000	0.9251	0.1294
apache/incubator-dubbo	0.5164	1.0000	1.0000	0.9904	0.0370
elastic/elasticsearch	0.0000	1.0000	1.0000	0.9450	0.1190

Table 3. Semantic similarity between pull requests measured by the *doc2vec* on four projects

Project	Min	Median	Max	Average	Std
spring-projects/spring-framework	0.6893	0.9952	1.0000	0.9613	0.0735
spring-projects/spring-boot	0.7471	0.9989	1.0000	0.9744	0.0520
apache/incubator-dubbo	0.8855	1.0000	1.0000	0.9976	0.0091
elastic/elasticsearch	0.3899	1.0000	1.0000	0.9855	0.0472

the project with the minimum value is the same. This leads to the guess on the correlation between two measurement methods. We will further examine this correlation in Sect. 5.3.

We notice that among four projects, the minimum similarity between pull requests of several projects is relatively low, such as 0.0 in Project elastic/elasticsearch when measured with the *cosine* and 0.3899 when measured with the *doc2vec*.

Based on the above findings, we can conclude that the similarity between pull requests is generally high, but there is still low similarity between several pull requests. This results in the diversity of similarities. On the one hand, RQ1 shows the evidence that it is difficult for project managers to decide which pull request should be merged into the codebase because of the high degree of similarity between pull requests. On the other hand, project managers need to spend much time in figuring out the semantics of these pull requests because of the diversity of similarity. This exacerbates the difficulty of the merging decision.

5.2   RQ2. What Is the Distribution of the Similarity Between Competing Pull Requests?

In RQ2, we show the distribution of similarity between pull requests of four Java projects. The similarity values are calculated by the *cosine* and the *doc2vec*.

Figure 2 presents the box-plots of similarity measured with the *cosine* between pull requests from Table 2; Fig. 3 presents the box-plots of similarity measured with the *doc2vec* between pull requests from Table 3.

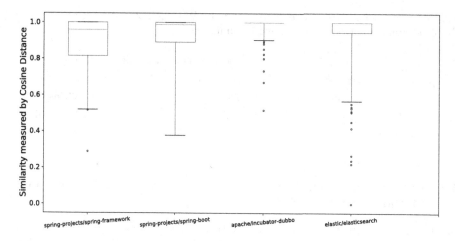

Fig. 2. Box-plots of similarity between pull requests measured by the *cosine* on four projects

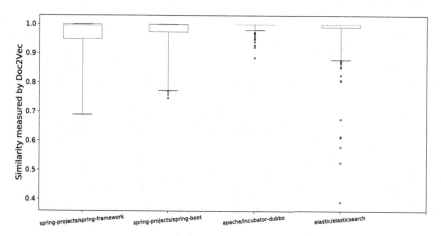

Fig. 3. Box-plots of similarity between pull requests measured by the *doc2vec* on four projects.

For each of the four projects, no matter which method is used for measurement, three-quarters of pairs of pull requests have a similarity of 0.8 or higher; half of pairs have a similarity of 0.95 or higher. These results indicate that between pull requests that contain changes on the overlapped code, both structural similarity and semantic similarity exist.

To sum up, we find that the similarity between the majority of pull requests is high. This fact undoubtedly adds the difficulty to project managers for the merging decision in GitHub.

Table 4. Pearson correlation coefficient and the Wilcoxon signed rank test between the structural similarity and the semantic similarity

Project	Pearson correlation coefficient	The p-value
spring-projects/spring-framework	0.8179	9.6490e−11
spring-projects/spring-boot	0.8626	3.1635e−29
apache/incubator-dubbo	0.8347	7.4276e−37
elastic/elasticsearch	0.7683	0.0000

5.3   RQ3. Is There Any Correlation Between the Two Measurement Methods of Similarity?

In RQ3, we show the correlation between the similarity by the two measurement methods. To conduct the evaluation, we used the Pearson correlation coefficient to detect the probability of correlation [14].

Table 4 shows the Pearson correlation coefficient and the p-value based on the Wilcoxon signed rank test. The absolute value of the Pearson correlation coefficient indicates the correlation. An absolute value over 0.7 could be considered as high correlation; We use the Wilcoxon signed rank test to explore how different are two measurement methods [14]. If the p-value is less than 0.05, we consider that there exists statistical significance between the similarities by the *cosine* and the *doc2vec*.

As shown in Table 4, the result explores the effect of two measurement methods on the similarity values. The values of Pearson correlation coefficient show that the two measurement methods reach high correlation with the maximum value of 0.86. This indicates that the structural similarity by the *cosine* and the semantic similarity by the *doc2vec* share many options on the similarity. Although the *cosine* and the *doc2vec* estimate the similarity in different ways, it is possible that many pieces of structural similarity are also contain the semantic similarity.

All the p-values are less than 0.05. This fact shows that the two measurement methods behave statistically significant differences on the pairs of pull requests in all the four projects.

We conclude the answers to RQ3 as follows. The two measurement methods, the *cosine* and the *doc2vec*, show statistically significant results. However, the result by these two methods is different but similar. This fact may indicate the overlap between the structural similarity and the semantic similarity.

6   Threats to Validity

We list the threats to the validity of our work in three categories.

Construct Validity. In our study, we only used pull requests of four open-source Java projects with the most forks in GitHub, which contains 6,469 pairs of pull requests. A large study on more pull requests may reveal more findings about the similarity between pull requests. Our experiment contains two measurement methods for the calculation of structural similarity and semantic similarity between pull requests; our result shows there exists diversity among the similarity. Our study has not covered many typical methods of measuring the similarity, such as the LDA method of topic models. The study in our work can be viewed as a preliminary result for counting the similarity between pull requests. The goal of our study is to motivate the exploration of solving merging conflicts.

Internal Validity. We used *doc2vec* to calculate the similarity between competing pull requests via learning a model from a corpus of previous source code. However, a learned model is usually limited by the scale of the corpus. In general, a corpus in natural language processing is much larger than the source code used in our work. Thus, it is possible that the corpus in use has already hurt the measurement in our work. A straightforward resolution is to involve more projects to form a corpus.

External Validity. Our study has only explored the similarity between pull requests in Java; meanwhile, the measurement of similarity is also conducted on Java source code. There exists a threat that the Java code is naturally more similar than code in other languages. In addition, is the detected similarity by the *cosine* or the *doc2vec* really similar? This is a bias between automatic measurement and program comprehension. A study on the opinions of developers could help understand the bias.

7   Related Work

We presented the related work in two parts, change merging and text similarity measurement.

7.1   Change Merging

In collaborative development, the modification of source code is implemented via merging changes. The main methods for change merging can be divided into three categories: unstructured merge, structured merge, and semi-structured merge.

The unstructured merge mixes different versions by using the largest common subsequences matching of textual lines. This method is fast, but can result in the disorder among changes [13]. The *diff* tool [1] is a typical technique using unstructured merge. The structured merge transfers the code into abstract syntax trees and combines the code among these trees. The process of combination is limited by the grammar of programming languages. A tool of structured merge is JDime, proposed by Apel et al. [3]. The semi-structured merge represents programs as program trees and uses an abstraction of the structure of the document to provide information on how the commits are merged, such as the tool FSTMerge by Apel et al. [4].

The process of merging changes into the codebase may be delayed by various factors. Yu et al. [18,19] have explored the factors of evaluation latency for pull requests and recommended reviewers for pull requests. Jiang et al. [10] have conducted a study on the inactive yet available assignees in GitHub. Xuan et al. [15] split test cases into small changes and refactored test cases to assist program repair. Zhu et al. [22] have studied the patterns of using folders to understand the project popularity. Xuan et al. [16] proposed a sampling strategy to learn the configuration from changes. Jiang et al. [9] studied the content and reasons of forking behaviors in GitHub.

7.2 Text Similarity Measurement

The measurement of text similarity has been widely studies. A typical approach is the vector-based similarity method. These methods, such as the *cosine* in this paper, transfer the original text objects that associates with a weight of importance into term vectors and then use a function to measure these vectors to calculate the final output similarity. The vector-based method is efficient, but cannot recognize the semantics of the text. Many methods are proposed to solve this problem. Blei et al. [5] proposed Latent Dirichlet Allocation (LDA), a typical method using generative topic models. This method samples words of two textual paragraphs and infers the similarity based on probability distributions of hidden topics. Latent Semantic Analysis (LSA) by Deerwester et al. [6] is a method based on linear projection, which identifies term-vectors from a low-dimensional space of a learned matrix.

A *word2vec* method is a family of modeling algorithms for generating word embeddings [12]. The word2vec model uses two-layer neural networks to train from linguistic contexts of words. The *doc2vec* [11] used in this paper is an extension version of word2vec and *doc2vec* supports the inference of document embeddings.

In this paper, we leverage both the structural similarity (i.e., the *cosine*), and the semantic similarity (i.e., the *doc2vec*) to identify the similarity between pull requests. We aim to examine the similarity and then understand the collaborative development behaviors.

8 Conclusion

In this paper, we conducted a study to find out whether there exist high similarity between pull requests that contain changes on the same code. We employed two measurement methods to calculate the similarity between pull requests and evaluated these methods on four Java projects with the most forks in GitHub. Our study has covered 6,469 of pull requests. We explored the similarity via answers to three research questions. Experimental results show that there indeed exist high similarity between pull requests, which may result in the difficulty of merging pull requests to project managers. The results also indicate that there exists shared opinions by two measurement methods, the *cosine* and the *doc2vec*.

Our future work is to conduct a large study on the similarity between code changes with the same target. We plan to examine and understand the reasons behind the similarity in this study.

Acknowledgments. The work is supported by the National Key R&D Program of China under Grant No. 2018YFB1003901, the National Natural Science Foundation of China under Grant Nos. 61502345 and 61872273, the Young Elite Scientists Sponsorship Program by CAST under Grant No. 2015QNRC001, and the Technological Innovation Projects of Hubei Province under Grant No. 2017AAA125.

References

1. Comparing and merging files (2016). http://www.gnu.org/software/diffutils/manual/
2. GitHub Repository Search (2018). https://github.com/search?q=+&type=
3. Apel, S., Leßenich, O., Lengauer, C.: Structured merge with auto-tuning: balancing precision and performance. In: IEEE/ACM International Conference on Automated Software Engineering, ASE 2012, Essen, Germany, 3–7 September 2012, pp. 120–129 (2012)
4. Apel, S., Liebig, J., Brandl, B., Lengauer, C., Kästner, C.: Semistructured merge: rethinking merge in revision control systems. In: 19th ACM SIGSOFT Symposium on the Foundations of Software Engineering (FSE) and 13th European Software Engineering Conference (ESEC), Szeged, Hungary, 5–9 September 2011, pp. 190–200 (2011)
5. Blei, D.M., Ng, A.Y., Jordan, M.I., Lafferty, J.: Latent Dirichlet allocation. J. Mach. Learn. Res. **3**, 993–1022 (2003)
6. Deerwester, S., Dumais, S., Furnas, G., Landauer, T., Harshman, R.: Indexing by latent semantic analysis. J. Am. Soc. Inf. Sci. **41**(6), 391–401 (1990)
7. Gousios, G., Pinzger, M., van Deursen, A.: An exploratory study of the pull-based software development model. In: 36th International Conference on Software Engineering, ICSE 2014, Hyderabad, India, 31 May–07 June 2014, pp. 345–355 (2014)
8. Gu, Y., et al.: Does the fault reside in a stack trace? Assisting crash localization by predicting crashing fault residence. J. Syst. Softw. **148**, 88–104 (2019)
9. Jiang, J., Lo, D., He, J., Xia, X., Kochhar, P.S., Zhang, L.: Why and how developers fork what from whom in GitHub. Empir. Softw. Eng. **22**(1), 547–578 (2017)
10. Jiang, J., Lo, D., Ma, X., Feng, F., Zhang, L.: Understanding inactive yet available assignees in GitHub. Inf. Softw. Technol. **91**, 44–55 (2017)
11. Le, Q.V., Mikolov, T.: Distributed representations of sentences and documents. In: Proceedings of the 31st International Conference on Machine Learning, ICML 2014, Beijing, China, 21–26 June 2014, pp. 1188–1196 (2014)
12. Mikolov, T., Chen, K., Corrado, G., Dean, J.: Efficient estimation of word representations in vector space. CoRR abs/1301.3781 (2013). http://arxiv.org/abs/1301.3781
13. Perry, D.E., Siy, H.P., Votta, L.G.: Parallel changes in large-scale software development: an observational case study. ACM Trans. Softw. Eng. Methodol. **10**(3), 308–337 (2001)
14. Ross, S.M.: Introduction to Probability and Statistics for Engineers and Scientists, 2nd edn. Academic Press, London (2000)

15. Xuan, J., Cornu, B., Martinez, M., Baudry, B., Seinturier, L., Monperrus, M.: B-refactoring: automatic test code refactoring to improve dynamic analysis. Inf. Softw. Technol. **76**, 65–80 (2016)
16. Xuan, J., Gu, Y., Ren, Z., Jia, X., Fan, Q.: Genetic configuration sampling: learning a sampling strategy for fault detection of configurable systems. In: Proceedings of the Genetic and Evolutionary Computation Conference Companion, GECCO 2018, Kyoto, Japan, 15–19 July 2018, pp. 1624–1631 (2018)
17. Xuan, J., et al.: Towards effective bug triage with software data reduction techniques. IEEE Trans. Knowl. Data Eng. **27**(1), 264–280 (2015)
18. Yu, Y., Wang, H., Filkov, V., Devanbu, P.T., Vasilescu, B.: Wait for it: determinants of pull request evaluation latency on github. In: 12th IEEE/ACM Working Conference on Mining Software Repositories, MSR 2015, Florence, Italy, 16–17 May 2015, pp. 367–371 (2015)
19. Yu, Y., Wang, H., Yin, G., Wang, T.: Reviewer recommendation for pull-requests in GitHub: what can we learn from code review and bug assignment? Inf. Soft. Technol. **74**, 204–218 (2016)
20. Zhang, X., et al.: How do multiple pull requests change the same code: a study of competing pull requests in GitHub. In: 2018 IEEE International Conference on Software Maintenance and Evolution, ICSME 2018, Madrid, Spain, 23–29 September 2018, pp. 228–239 (2018)
21. Zhou, J., Zhang, H., Lo, D.: Where should the bugs be fixed? More accurate information retrieval-based bug localization based on bug reports. In: 34th International Conference on Software Engineering, ICSE 2012, Zurich, Switzerland, 2–9 June 2012, pp. 14–24 (2012)
22. Zhu, J., Zhou, M., Mockus, A.: Patterns of folder use and project popularity: a case study of GitHub repositories. In: 2014 ACM-IEEE International Symposium on Empirical Software Engineering and Measurement, ESEM 2014, Torino, Italy, 18–19 September 2014, pp. 30:1–30:4 (2014)
23. Zhu, J., Zhou, M., Mockus, A.: Effectiveness of code contribution: from patch-based to pull-request-based tools. In: Proceedings of the 24th ACM SIGSOFT International Symposium on Foundations of Software Engineering, FSE 2016, Seattle, WA, USA, 13–18 November 2016, pp. 871–882 (2016)

Contiguous Sequence Mining Approach for Program Procedure Pattern

Jianbin Liu[1,2]($\boxtimes$), Jingjing Zhao[1,2]($\boxtimes$), and Liwei Zheng[1,2]

[1] School of Computer, Beijing Information Science and Technology University,
Beijing 100101, China
13126707629@163.com, struggle_jjz@mail.bistu.edu.cn
[2] Software Engineering Research Center, Beijing Information Science
& Technology University, Beijing 100101, China

Abstract. The program procedure patterns exist in the software development process. This paper gives a program procedure pattern mining approach based on MCSPAN (Maximal Contiguous Sequential pattern mining). First the program structure features are mined. Structure feature mining is transformed into a frequent sequence mining problem with contiguous constrains and maximal constrains and an algorithm: MCSPAN is given to obtain the program structure candidate patterns as follows. Then a filtering algorithm with the constraint of the data flow feature is given to filter the structure candidate patterns and then the program structure relationship candidate patterns are obtained which have the program procedure pattern form. For clarifying the function semantics, some heuristic rules are applied in the structure relation candidate patterns filtering and finally the program procedure patterns are obtained. Through mining more than 100,100 lines of java code, about 180 kinds of program procedure patterns are discovered. This mining approach is effective through analyzing the recall and precision rate in the experiment. And the availability of the mined program procedure patterns is analyzed.

Keywords: Code mining · Program procedure pattern ·
Sequential pattern mining

1 Introduction

In the software development process, software reuse technology is an important way to improve the efficiency of software production. Software reuse is based on code fragments which have the similar or identical functions from the existing code repositories to assist the development of new software systems. Software component is the carrier of the software reuse technology. It is the abstraction of the code fragment with independent function and reusable value. The program procedure pattern [1] is a description form of software components that abstracts reusable code fragments for data streams and control streams.

The extraction of program procedure pattern is the focus of the current research. Although the research has made some progress, the main extraction method still stays in the stage of manual induction and summary which has higher requirements for the

Z. Li et al. (Eds.): NASAC 2017/2018, CCIS 861, pp. 129–144, 2019.
https://doi.org/10.1007/978-981-15-0310-8_9

operator's knowledge reserve and lower expansion efficiency. And the increase in the amount of code will lead to the lack of the procedure pattern. How to achieve automatic mining of procedure patterns from source code is the key to solving the problem.

The program procedure pattern is summarized from the code source. The development of the open source movement has produced a wealth of code information, which contains many meaningful program procedure patterns. Based on legacy codes, data mining technology can be integrated into the program procedure pattern finding. For this reason, a program procedure pattern discovery method based on contiguous sequence mining is given. Firstly, define and extract the features of the program process pattern from source code. Then an improved contiguous sequence pattern mining algorithm and a filtering algorithm with the constraint of the data flow feature are given to obtain the candidate patterns. Then use heuristic rules to filter these patterns according to the semantic information. Finally, obtain and abstract the program process pattern instances as program procedure patterns and add them into the library. The mining method can reduce the cost of finding the procedure pattern from the source code.

This paper is organized as follows. Section 2 gives the related work. In Sect. 3, the contiguous sequence mining process model for program procedure pattern is given. In Sect. 3, we describe the structure candidate pattern mining phase in detail. An improved contiguous sequence pattern mining algorithm with maximal constraints is given and applied in structure feature mining. Section 4 describes the structure relation candidate pattern mining phase. Section 5 represents about 180 kinds of program process pattern mined from over 100,100 lines of code and shows the effectiveness of the proposed method. The last section is the summary and future work.

2 Related Work

The carrier of the program procedure pattern is the frequently occurring reusable code fragment with certain functions. The mining of the program procedure pattern depends on the mining of the reusable code fragments. Current researches on reusable code extraction are as follows. Allamanis [2] used nonparametric Bayesian probabilistic tree substitution grammars based on statistical natural language processing to mine the idioms which are code fragments that recurs frequently and have the single semantic role. Chen [3] proposed a method of automatic plan extraction based on suffix trees. Transform the source code into the token string then construct a suffix tree to get the candidates of software plans. Bian [4] analyzed the program structure and used the program dependency graph and the abstract syntax tree to preserve the relationship between the nodes, and then performed the amorphous transformation on the syntactic structure to extract the continuous cloned code fragments suitable for reconstruction. Zhao [5] used the informal information such as the demand document to establish the mapping relationship between the function and the code entity, and calculated the cluster of the recovered code entity in combination with the hierarchical structure of the function to extract the reusable code segments. Qiao [6] proposed a fast extraction method for similar modules based on key functions. The key function call graphs are constructed and then extract the common subgraphs between these call graphs. These similar modules are abstracted into reusable components. Li [7] proposed software knowledge entity extraction for software source code. The Visitor design pattern was used to traverse all nodes in the abstract syntax tree, and the method software knowledge entities were extracted and stored in the code entity pool. The above mining methods lack the analysis of the program procedure. And the tree and graph structure cannot describe the procedure well. Therefore, the continuous sequence pattern mining method [8] is used to make up for the lack of description of the program procedure in the abstract syntax tree and program dependency graph.

3   Contiguous Sequence Mining for Program Procedure Pattern

3.1   Prepared Knowledge

For the study of the program procedure pattern, Hu [1] proposed the program procedure pattern definition model based on the java process blueprint and elaborated the structure and content features of three-layer view of procedure pattern. The three-layer includes ACSD, ALSD, and AISD [9]. Some instances are given to describe the procedure pattern. For an example, the service obtain pattern are shown in Table 1.

Table 1. The service obtain pattern.

ACSD	@ obtain an service named <service: "\w + (\ [\ d \]) ?" >
ALSD	SEQ obtain an service named <service: "\w + (\ [\ d \]) ?" > ├─ IFT whether servicename <service: "\w + (\ [\ d \]) ?" > is in StringUtils │ └─ THR create an instance RuntimeException with <E: "\w + (\ [\ d \]) ?" > ├─ DCL an Object <obj: "\w + (\ [\ d \]) ?" > is null ├─ IFT whether the static ApplicationContext < ac: "\w + (\ [\ d \]) ?" > of the ServiceProvider Cord instance < spc: "\w + (\ [\ d \]) ?" > has the bean < service: "\w + (\ [\ d \]) │ └─ OPE get the bean < service: "\w + (\ [\ d \]) from the static ApplicationContext < ac: "\w + (\ [\ d \]) ?" > of the ServiceProviderCord instance < spc: "\w + (\ [\ d \]) ?" > and give it to the Object < obj: "\w + (\ [\ d \]) ?" > ├─ IFT the Object < obj: "\w + (\ [\ d \]) ?" > is null │ └─ THR create an instance RuntimeException with <E: "\w + (\ [\ d \]) ?" > └─ RET return the Object < obj: "\w + (\ [\ d \]) ?" >
AISD	SEQ getService(String <service: "\w + (\ [\ d \]) ?" >) ├─ IFT StringUtils.isBlank(<service: "\w + (\ [\ d \]) ?" >) │ └─ THR new RuntimeException(<E: "\w + (\ [\ d \]) ?" >) ├─ DCL Object <obj: "\w + (\ [\ d \]) ?" >=null ├─ IFT < spc: "\w + (\ [\ d \]) ?" >. < ac: "\w + (\ [\ d \]) ?" >.containsBean(<service: "\w + (\ [\ d \]) ?" >) │ └─ OPE <obj: "\w + (\ [\ d \]) ?" >= < spc: "\w + (\ [\ d \]) ?" >. < ac: "\w + (\ [\ d \]) ?" >.getBean(<service: "\w + (\ [\ d \]) ?" >) ├─ IFT <obj: "\w + (\ [\ d \]) ?" >==null │ └─ THR new RuntimeException(<E1: "\w + (\ [\ d \]) ?" >) └─ RET obj

According to the definition of the program procedure pattern, the control flow and data flow of a code fragment can describe its procedure features. The definition of the structure candidate pattern and the structure relation candidate pattern and the relationship between these two patterns and program procedure pattern (Prop) are given.

Definition 3.1 (Program Structure Candidate Pattern, PSCP). PSCP is a combination of program structures which are ordered and frequently occurring. And "ordered" means the sequential dependency of source code action execution.

Definition 3.2 (Program Structure Relation Candidate Pattern, PSRCP). PSRCP refers to the code fragments mapped when the program structure and data flow features are frequently appearing.

The relationship between these three patterns is as follows. The PSCP is the result of mining the program structure. The PSRCP is obtained by adding the data flow constraints to filter the PSCP. The PSRCP has the same formal characteristics as the program procedure pattern but still has uncertainty in the Functional semantics. These three patterns are gradually refined in the way of describing the process. Thus we can add constraints to reduce the scope of the target pattern. This paper gives a program procedure pattern mining method for legacy code, which is described in detail below.

3.2   Contiguous Sequence Mining Process Model for Program Procedure Pattern

The program procedure pattern is an abstraction of the reusable code fragment. It is the discovery of frequently occurring functional code sub-segments from a large number of legacy code fragments. This paper gives a contiguous sequence mining process model for program procedure pattern shown in Fig. 1 including four phase: preprocessing, structure candidate pattern mining, structure relation candidate pattern mining, and manual filtering.

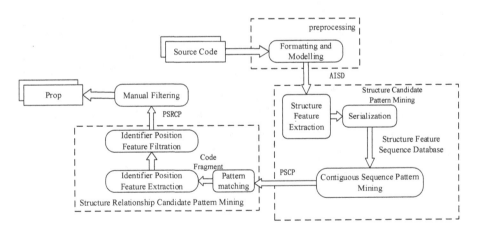

Fig. 1. Contiguous sequence mining process model for program procedure pattern

The preprocessing phase is to format the source code including slicing and deleting annotation and to model the source code to obtain the abstract implementation structure diagrams (AISD). By directly analyzing the node type and the expression with the data flow node, the program procedure pattern features can be obtained [10]. The detailed modeling process is given in the literature [11].

The structure candidate pattern mining phase is to mine the frequent program structure. Considering that the program procedure pattern mainly expresses the logic process of the code which emphasizes the order of the control flow and is frequently appearing in legacy codes, the mining of structure candidate patterns can be regarded as a frequent sequential pattern mining. Therefore, this paper presents a contiguous frequent sequential pattern mining method: the maximum contiguous frequent sequential pattern mining (MCSPAN). Firstly abstract the program structure feature from source code and then serialize them to form a program structure feature sequence database. Finally, execute the mining algorithm to obtain the structure candidate pattern.

In the structure relation candidate pattern mining phase, the structure relation candidate pattern is obtained by filtering structure candidate patterns with the constraints of the data flow. The program identifier location feature is selected as the constraint condition. Firstly obtain the code fragments that matches the structure candidate pattern from source code. Then abstract and compare the location features of different code segments with the same structure to obtain the structure relation candidate pattern.

The manual filtering phase further filters the structure relation candidate pattern according to the function semantic. Three heuristic rules are put forward as follows:

Heuristic Rule 1: Filter simple repeated basic operation statements, such as variable declarations, console output, etc. As shown in the Fig. 2(a).

Heuristic Rule 2: Filter the code fragments in which elements are independent of each other, as shown in Fig. 2(b).

Heuristic Rule 3: Filter the code fragments in which operand is unknown or the function name may from the different source, that is, the third-party or user-defined. For example, the method ".add" may be a user-defined method or a method in the List class provided in the JAVA API as shown in Fig. 2(c).

```
System.out.print("a");        setBounds(100,100,317,95);
System.out.print("b");        setDefaultCloseOperation(JFrame.EXIT_ON_CLOSE);    root.add(male);
System.out.print("c");        final JLable label=new JLabel();                   root.add(female);
       (a)                                    (b)                                       (c)
```

Fig. 2. The examples of heuristic rules

Through the above process, the obtained result can be regarded as the code fragment instances of the program procedure pattern. Abstract these instances into program procedure patterns. The following shows detailed descriptions of two main phases: the structure candidate pattern mining and the structure relation candidate pattern mining.

3.3 Structure Candidate Pattern Mining

The program procedure pattern structure features include control structure features and grammar structure features. The definitions of them are given below.

Definition 3.3 (Program Control Feature, PCF). The program control feature PCF is represented by a two-tuple:

$$PCF(program\ control\ feature) = (Layer = \{L_1, L_2, \ldots, L_n\}, A_c \\ = \{a_{c1}, a_{c2}, \ldots, a_{cn}\})\ (n \geq 2)$$

where *Layer* represents the ordered set of the hierarchical relationship of program actions. The hierarchical relationship is embodied in the nested structure of the program, and is reflected in the process blueprint tree structure as parent-child relationship and brother relationship, and A_c represents the ordered set of program logic control structure [9], and n represents the number of code line in a program procedure pattern.

The program logic control structure is mainly a description of the program control flow. The procedure blueprint uniquely abstracts the logic control structure of specific programming language. Taking JAVA language as an example, the control structure is shown as following:

$$a_{ci} \in \{SEQ, DCL, OPE, LAB, FOR, DOW, WHL, IFT, IFE, SWH, CAS, TRY, CAH, FNY, \\ BRK, RET, SYN, DFT, THR, UND, SYN\}$$

Definition 3.4 (Program Grammar Feature, PGF). The program grammar feature is a description of the type and order of program elements in a program statement. The program grammar feature is represented as:

$$PGF(program\ grammer\ feature) = \{pgf_1, pgf_2, \ldots, pgf_n\}\ (n \geq 2)$$

where pgf_i represents the grammar structure of a code line, and n represents the number of code lines.

The program elements mainly include identifiers and operators. One of the purposes of defining this structure is to eliminate the difference of identifier name and location due to different habits of developers. In order to facilitate the extraction of various identifiers, identifiers are classified into variables and constants. Variables represented by "VAR" include the package name, parameter name, method name, interface name, local variable names, class names, enumeration names, and attribute names. Constants contain string constants and numeric constants, which are represented by "CHS" and "NUM" respectively. Take the java program as an example: System.out.println(student.getAge(10+"a")). The process pattern grammar feature is described as: $PGF = \{pgf_1\}$, $pgf_1 = $ VAR.VAR.VAR(VAR.VAR(NUM + CHS)).

Generating program procedure pattern structure feature sequence database includes features extraction and serialization.

Step 1: Establish the variable dictionary IdeDic to storage the variables.
Step 2: Model the source code to obtain the AISD and perform depth-first traversal in AISD to avoid losing the hierarchical relationships of source code.
Step 3: Get the control features and grammar features from AISD.

Step 4: Use a limited-length digital mapping method to encode the control features and use the ELFhash algorithm to encode grammar features and add them into database.

The generation algorithm is shown in Algorithm 1.

Algorithm 1. Structure Feature Sequence Database Generation Algorithm	
Input: $C = \{m_1, m_2, ..., m_n\}$:The source code	8: **if** ele_k in IdeDic **then**
Output: $PS = \{ps_1, ps_2, ..., ps_n\}$:The database of program structure feature sequence	9: $code_j$ .replace(ele_k ,VAR)
1: IdeDic=GetAllIDE(C)	10: **if** ele_k is CHA **then**
2: **for all** m_i in C **do**	11: $code_j$ .replace(ele_k ,CHA)
3: $AISD_i$ =create(m_i)	12: **if** ele_k is NUM **then**
4: **for all** $node_j$ in $AISD_i$ **do**	13: $code_j$ .replace(ele_k ,NUM)
5: a_{cj} =getAc($node_j$)	14: ps_i .add(mapCode(a_{cj}),ELFHash($code_j$))
6: $code_j$ =getData($node_j$)	15: PS .add(ps_i)
7: **for all** ele_k in $node_j$ **do**	

The program procedure pattern is a description of the program process logic, which reflects a certain continuity. Therefore, the mining of the structure candidate pattern should focus on the continuity of frequent sequences before the procedure feature of the program procedure pattern can be preserved. CCSPAN [12] adds continuity constraint into frequent sequence mining and the closed test is used to simplify the mining result set to obtain closed contiguous sequence pattern. This paper adopts CCSPAN to mine structure candidate patterns. After the closed check, the candidate set may still contain redundant sequences, of which the support degree is different from super sequence, but the code fragment represented by the super sequence is more complete. We need to filter these sequences. Therefore, this paper enhances the closed test in CCSPAN to the maximum test and gives Maximal Contiguous Sequential pattern mining (MCSPAN).

Definition 3.5. Item is the smallest unit in sequential pattern mining. In the feature sequence, an item represents the control and grammar feature of a program statement.

Definition 3.6. A sequence is a set of items. K-sequence is a sequence with k items. A program process pattern structure feature sequence sa represents the structure features of all the code lines in a fragment.

Definition 3.7. A sequence database SDB is a list of sequences $SDB = \langle sa_1, sa_2, ..., sa_n \rangle$, where n represents the number of sequences. The structure feature sequences of all function units in the source code build up the procedure pattern feature sequence database.

Definition 3.8. The maximum sequential pattern is a sequence that does not have frequent super sequences, that is $MS = \{s_j | s_j \in FS \wedge \forall s_k \in FS, s_j \not\subset s_k\}$, where FS represents all frequent sequences. It ensures the functional integrity of frequent sequences and reduces the size of the candidate set without the loss of frequent sequences.

Definition 3.9. Given sequence $s = \langle a_1 a_2 \ldots a_i \rangle$ and $s' = \langle b_1 b_2 \ldots b_j \rangle$, $s \sqcup s'$ means s concatenates s', i.e., $s \sqcup s' = \langle a_1 a_2 \ldots a_i b_1 b_2 \ldots b_j \rangle$. The pre-subsequence s_{pre} and post-subsequence s_{post} of sequence s are given by

$$s_{pre} = f_{\sqsubset_{pre}(s)} = \bigsqcup_{i=0}^{l(s)-2} s_i \qquad s_{post} = f_{\sqsubset_{post}(s)} = \bigsqcup_{i=1}^{l(s)-1} s_i$$

Where i is the index of an item in s.

Algorithm 2. MCSPAN	
Input: $PS = \{ps_1, ps_2, \ldots, ps_m\}$:The database of program structure feature sequences . n is the number of sequence in PS . Output: $PSCP$: The program structure candidate patterns. $PSCP_k$:The patterns with k-sequence. P_k :The patterns checked 1: $PSCP \leftarrow \phi$; $PSCP_k \leftarrow \phi$; $P_k \leftarrow \phi$ 2: **for all** ps_i in PS **do** 3: **for all** 1-sequence s in ps_i **do** 4: **if** s in P_i **then** 5: continue; 6: **else** 7: s .count=calculate(s) 8: **if** $s.count / n \geq \delta$ **then** 9: $PSCP_1 \leftarrow \cup_1 s$ 10: $P_1 \leftarrow \cup_1 s$ 11: **for**($k = 2$; $PSCP_{k-1} \neq \phi$; $k++$) 12: **for all** ps_i in PS **do** 13: **for all** $s \subseteq ps_j$ and $l(s) = k$ **do**	14: **if**(s not in P_k && $s_{pre} \in PSCP_{k-1}$ && $s_{post} \in PSCP_{k-1}$) 15: s .count=calculate(s) 16: **if** $s.count / n \geq \delta$ **then** 17: $PSCP_k \leftarrow \cup_k s$ 18: $P_k \leftarrow \cup_k s$ 19: $PSCP_{k-1}$ .remove(s_{pre}) 20: $PSCP_{k-1}$ .remove(s_{post}) 21: **else** 22: $P_k \leftarrow \cup_k s$ 23: **else** 24: $P_k \leftarrow \cup_k s$ 25: $PSCP \leftarrow \cup_{k-1} PSCP_{k-1}$ 26: $PSCP \leftarrow \cup_k PSCP_k$

To avoid the generation of candidate sets that do not exist in the source database, MCSPAN uses the fragment growth strategy to generate candidate sets, each of which is obtained by splitting the sequence in the source database according to the sequence length increasing order. The three pruning strategies for the candidate set are as follows:

Strategy 1: Prune the split snippet which already exists and add the new snippets into traversed snippet set P_k.

Strategy 2: Prune the snippet whose pre-subsequence or post-subsequence is infrequent.

Strategy 3: Prune the sequences whose support is less than the minimum support.

The candidate sets obtained need to be examined for maximum. According to the theorem 2 proposed in [12], two single-length candidate subsets with a length difference of 1 are examined. The complexity is reduced to some extent relative to comparing each sequence to all sequences in the candidate set. The maximal contiguous sequential pattern mining algorithm is shown in Algorithm 2.

The structure candidate patterns obtained reflects the frequentness of the program structure features. However, the program structure is still not sufficient to fully describe the program procedure pattern as is shown in Fig. 3

```
int a,b,temp,c;          int a,b,temp,c;          int a,b,temp,c;
temp = a;                a = b;                   a = temp;
a = b;                   a = temp;                a = b;
b = temp;                b = temp;                b = c;
    (a)                      (b)                      (c)
```

Fig. 3. The code fragments with same structure

The control structure and grammar structure of the three code fragments are the same. The program shown in Fig. 3(a) represents the two-digit exchange process which is used frequently by developers in actual software projects while the other two programs in Fig. 3(b) and (c) have no functional significance. Therefore, only the program in Fig. 3(a) can be regarded as a program procedure pattern. The data flow feature can distinguish these programs with the same structure but different meanings. So we select program identifier location feature to filter the structure candidate patterns.

3.4   Structure Relation Candidate Pattern Mining

Definition 3.10. The program procedure pattern identifier location feature is expressed as:

$$PIL(program\ identifier\ location) = \{LOC_1, LOC_2, \cdots, LOC_n\}$$

where LOC represents a collection of location in which the identifier appears in the code fragment, n indicates the number of different operand identifiers.

The identifier location feature extraction algorithm is shown in Algorithm 3. First, the identifier dictionary *IDESet* is established; then all the identifiers appearing in the code fragment are written into an array *IDEArray* in the order of appearance, including duplicate identifiers. Then traverse *IDESet* and determine whether the same identifier pair exists in *IDEArray*, if it exists, add the array subscript of the identifier pair to the location set LOC_i. Finally, determine whether the size of LOC_i is greater than 1. If yes, it indicates that there exists an identifier dependency, the LOC_i is meaningful to the filtration, and add LOC_i into *PIL*.

Algorithm 3. getPIL(CodeFragment)	
Input: *CF* :The fragment of code	4: **for all** *ide_array* in *IDEArray* **do**
Output: $PIL = \{LOC_1, LOC_2, L, LOC_n\}$	5: if(ide_i == *ide_array*) **then**
1: *IDESet* =getIDE(*CF*)	6: LOC_i .add(*ide array.subscript*)
2: *IDEArray* =getIDEArray(*CF*)	7: if(LOC_i .length ≥ 2) **then**
3: **for all** ide_i in *IDESet* **do**	8: *PIL* .add(LOC_i)

The program procedure pattern not only requires specific structure features to appear frequently but also the specific identifier location features. Therefore, the filtering condition is that the program identifier location feature appears more frequently than a threshold. The threshold is defined as follow:

Definition 3.11. The identifier location support *sup_l* indicates the number of code fragments with the same identifier location and program structure feature. The minimum identifier location support *min_sup_l* is the minimum threshold for determining the structural relation candidate pattern. If the *sup_l* of a structure candidate pattern is greater than or equal to *min_sup_l*, then it is a structure relation candidate pattern.

Algorithm 4 describes the filtration process. Firstly match each structure candidate pattern with AISD to obtain a code fragment set *CFList*. Then traverse each code fragment and perform getPIL (CodeFragment) to get the code-location set. Compare the identifier location features of the code fragments with the same structure feature to find the fragments whose appearance frequency is greater than or equal to *min_sup_l*. Finally, add these fragments to structure relation candidate pattern set *PSRCP*.

Algorithm 4. Program Identifier Position Feature Filtration Algorithm	
Input: *PSCP* , *AISDs* ; θ: *min _ sup _l* Output: *PSRCP* 1: $CF\_PIL \leftarrow \phi$ 2: **for all** $pscp_i$ in *PSCP* **do** 3: *CFList* =PatternMatch($pscp_i$, *AISDs*) 4: **for all** CF_i in *CFList* **do** 5: PIL_i =getPIL(CF_i)	6: CF_PIL_i .add(CF_i , PIL_i) 7: CF_PIL .add(CF_PIL_i) 8: **for all** CF_PIL_i in CF_PIL **do** 9: $CF\_PIL_i . PIL_i$ .count = Count($CF\_PIL_i . PIL_i$) 10: **if**($CF\_PIL_i.PIL_i.count \geq \theta$) **then** 11: *PSRCP* .add($CF\_PIL_i . CF_i$)

4   Experiment and Result Analysis

4.1   Experiment Design

In order to verify the effectiveness of the mining method, a program procedure pattern mining system is realized. The experimental object is derived from the source code in books on Java, ranging from basic teaching code to large-scale development projects. The details are shown in Table 2.

Table 2. The experiment projects codes.

Book name	Java files	Lines of code	Methods
The 150 cases of Java [14]	166	7061	705
Java example [15]	230	15405	1368
Java programming practical tutorial [17]	385	11359	1564
One hundred cases of Java utility design [18]	116	4306	423
Computer programming (Java) [19]	121	2580	358
JDKDemo (java.sun.com)	297	27135	2796
Java development combat [16]	1190	9610	1069
Course design case [20–22]	760	36083	2884
Total	3265	113539	11167

4.2 Experiment Process

- Procedure blueprint conversion
  Split the source program by method and remove the comment line and convert it into a procedure blueprint through the blueprint conversion tool. The abstract implementation structure diagram of the procedure blueprint is shown in Fig. 4.

Fig. 4. The AISD of getService

- Structural features extraction
  Perform deep traversal of the procedure blueprint, and extract the control structure of each node, and obtain the implementation layer code of each node. Then replace the different types of identifiers in the code with different characters (M, N, K), and delete unnecessary spaces to get the syntax structure. Finally, retain the source code to get an ordered collection of structural features for each method. The result of processing the abstract structure diagram of Fig. 4 is as follows:

$$< SEQ\,[M(M\,M)]\,IFT\,[M(M\,M)]\,THR\,[M\,M\,(N)]\,DCL\,[M\,M = M]$$
$$IFT\,[M.M.M(M)]\,IFT\,[M == M]\,THR\,[M\,M\,(N)]\,RET\,[M] >$$

- Coding structural features
- The structure control construct of each code statement is encoded using a number in a custom canonical format. The syntax structure is encoded using the ELFhash algorithm and normalized to the spmf format [13]. Then the process pattern structure feature sequence is obtained. The result of coding the above structural features is as follows:

<-130 -1 83686649 -1 -150 -1 83686649 -1 -330 -1 83164425 -1 -240 -1 5198109 -1 -150 -1 50526713 -1 -150 -1 332061 -1 -330 -1 83164425 -340 77 -2>

- Contiguous sequence pattern mining
  Obtain all the procedure pattern structure feature sequences to construct the sequence database to be used as the input of the MCSPAN algorithm to obtain the structure candidate pattern. An example pattern is as follows:

-200 128536269 -360 84081913

- Source code matching
  Traverse the structure candidate patterns and source code to get the corresponding code fragments. An example is obtained in Fig. 5 according to the pattern: *-200 128536269 -360 84081913*.

> [-200 -1 128536269 -1 (c=in.read())!=-1 -1 -360 -1 84081913 -1 out.write(c) -1 ,
> -200 -1 128536269 -1 (a=b.judge())!=-1 -1 -360 -1 84081913 -1 out.write(1) -1 ,
> -200 -1 128536269 -1 (c=bin.read())!=-1 -1 -360 -1 84081913 -1 bout.write(c) -1 ,
> -200 -1 128536269 -1 (a=user.getAge())!=10 -1 -360 -1 84081913 -1 user.setAge(age) -1]

Fig. 5. The code fragments with the program structure candidate pattern

- Identifier location feature filtering
  Get the identifier location for each code with the same structural feature, and calculate its identifier location support. If the support is less than *min_sup_l*, the corresponding code fragment is filtered. The result after filtering the example in Fig. 5 is shown in Fig. 6.

> [-200 -1 128536269 -1 (c=in.read())!=-1 -1 -360 -1 84081913 -1 out.write(c) -1 ,
> -200 -1 128536269 -1 (c=bin.read())!=-1 -1 -360 -1 84081913 -1 bout.write(c) -1 ,

Fig. 6. The program structure relation candidate pattern

- Manual Filtering
  The code fragments filtered by the identifier location feature are manually filtered according to heuristic rules, and the result is shown in Fig. 7.

> [-200 -1 128536269 -1 (c=in.read())!=-1 -1 -360 -1 84081913 -1 out.write(c) -1]

Fig. 7. An example of program process pattern

The code fragments processed by the above steps are examples of possible program process pattern, which satisfy the characteristics of the program procedure pattern and have a certain functional significance.

4.3 Analysis of Mining Results

The parameter of contiguous sequence pattern mining in this paper is $sup_l = 0.0004$, and the parameter of identifier location feature filtering is $min\_sup\_l = 3$. Through the abstract analysis of the program procedure pattern instances obtained by mining, there are 179 kinds of available program process patterns.

Table 3 gives the statistical results of the program procedure pattern function and granularity. By classifying the functional meaning of the program process patterns, six categories are obtained. The code line number of the program process pattern instance is greater than or equal to 5, which can be regarded as a large granularity pattern, and less than 5 is regarded as a small granularity pattern.

Table 3. List of program process patterns.

Function type	Program process patterns	Small granularity pattern	Large granularity pattern	Instances
Java based method	53	51	2	Thread sleeps for a few seconds;
				Instantiate the timer and start
Graphical user interface design	64	49	15	Customize component size and join panels;
				Draw a login form
File and stream process	25	21	4	Read files by line using BufferedReader;
				Close the file input and output streams and handle exceptions
Network communication	15	15	0	Socket disconnects from the server;
				Send data using DatagramPacket and socket
Database operation	20	14	6	JDBC connection database;
				Get the number of columns from the database metadata
Java security model	2	2	0	Generate a key using the RSA algorithm

As can be seen from the Table 3, the number of graphical user interface design process patterns is the largest, because the graphical user interface design functions are varied and the combination of components is flexible. The smallest procedure pattern is the Java security model pattern which has less application in project development or basic teaching. The number of database operation process patterns is small, mainly because the corresponding APIs are used in a single way and have fewer types of functions. On the other hand, the size of the large-grain pattern is much smaller than that of the small- grain pattern. With the increase of the code lines, the user's coding habits have an increased influence on the code style, and the frequency of the program structure features is greatly reduced.

Table 4 presents the number of the phase product. Using the identifier location feature, about 1000 redundant and wrong pattern candidates were filtered to obtain the PSRCPs. By manual filtration using the heuristic rules, about 600 candidates are filtered to obtain the Props. Therefore, the program identifier location feature plays an important role in filtering the program procedure patterns with saving time and effort.

Table 4. The number of the PSCP, PSRCP and Prop.

PSCP	PSRCP	Prop
1822	828	179

4.4   Evaluation of Experiment Results

In this paper, the recall and precision of the mining method and the availability of the program process pattern are evaluated to verify the effectiveness of the method. This paper defines the precision P and recall R as follows:

$$P = \frac{PropR}{PropM} \times 100\% \quad R = \frac{PropR}{Prop} \times 100\%$$

where *Prop* represents the total number of program procedure patterns actually presenting in the training set, *PropM* represents the total number of program procedure patterns obtained by mining the training set, *PropR* represents the number of correct patterns in the obtained program procedure patterns.

The 20 cases were selected as the training set from the source code in Table 2. By the recall manual induction and summary, we found the 12 kinds of *Prop*. Then use the method this paper proposed to mine the experiment cases. The recall and precision results are shown in Table 5.

Table 5. The recall and precision.

Prop	PropM	PropR	P	R
12	16	10	62.50%	83.33%

The program procedure pattern has certain functional semantics. But the patterns obtained by mining the code structure features and identifier location features and the heuristic rules are functionally semantically redundant and fuzzy, and the functional meaning of some program procedure patterns is incomplete. Moreover, there are highly targeted patterns due to the repeated requirements of specific functions in one project but not involved in other projects, which are not in the scope of the program procedure pattern. Moreover, due to the different development styles of developers, the code of the same function is implemented in various ways, and some patterns cannot be directly represented. Based on the above reasons, the precision is low in Table 5, but the design idea of this paper is to rich the program procedure pattern library, which greatly saves the time and effort consumed by the manual to summarize the program procedure pattern according to experience, so the lower precision is acceptable.

The factors affecting the recall rate mainly include the following points: First, the distance between the variable declaration definition statement and the variable use statement is relatively uncertain, resulting in the lack of functional meaning. Second, the implementation of some functions is flexible in code execution order resulting in the lack of hierarchical structure frequency. Third, there is a functional equivalence method in the Java language, that is, the same function can be realized by using different method names. In the manual analysis, such methods can be summarized in the same program procedure pattern. For these reasons, in the future research, it is necessary to focus on the improvement of the recall rate.

5   Summary and Future Work

In this paper, a contiguous sequence mining approach for program procedure pattern algorithm is presented. The algorithm uses the frequent sequence pattern mining method to mine the program structure candidate pattern, and the candidate pattern of the structure relationship is obtained according to the constraint of the location characteristics of the program identifier, and the heuristic rules are used to filter to get the program procedure pattern instance. Finally, the instance is abstractly defined to get the program procedure pattern.

The contributions of this paper mainly include:

- an effective method of mining program procedure patterns is presented;
- define the control structure feature, the grammar structure feature, the identifier location feature and the formal representation, and propose a program procedure pattern feature extraction method based on process blueprint;
- give an improved closed contiguous sequence mining algorithm called MCSPAN with maximum checking, and apply it to source code mining.

The program procedure pattern can be applied to the fields of program modeling, program understanding, program automatic generation, etc. And the corresponding code instances can be used as materials for code recommendation, code completion, code defect detection and other fields to accelerate the program development procedure. In this paper, the contiguous frequent sequence mining algorithm ignores the relationship between variable definition declarations and calls, and the operand variables in most program process patterns lack definitions and declarations. Therefore, it is a direction for improvement in the future to establish parameter definition declaration dependency in the mining process. An incremental procedure pattern discovery algorithm should also be developed to adapt to the need of code database to expand and update contiguously.

Acknowledgment. This research is sponsored by the Science Research Level Improvement Project (5211823406) and the Information+ Discipline Construction Project of Beijing Information Science & Technology University.

References

1. Hu, W.Q., Liu, J.B.: Formalised definition framework of procedure pattern based on java blueprint. Comput. Appl. Softw. **32**(5), 24–29 (2015)
2. Allamanis M., Sutton C.: Mining idioms from source code. In: Proceedings of the 22nd ACM SIGSOFT International Symposium on Foundations of Software Engineering, pp. 472–483. ACM (2014)
3. Chen, H., Chen, C., Tang, W.B., Qian, J.F., Liu, K.M.: Automatic extraction of software plans for program comprehension based on suffix trees. Zhejiang Daxue Xuebao (Gongxue Ban)/J. Zhejiang Univ. **42**(8), 1340–1344 (2008)
4. Bian, Y.X., Wang, T.T., Su, X.H.: A semantics preserving amorphous procedure extraction method code. J. Comput. Res. Dev. **50**(7), 1534–1541 (2013)

5. Zhao, W., Zhang, L., Mei, H., Sun, J.S.: A functional requirement based hierarchical agglomerative approach to program clustering. J. Softw. **17**(8), 1661–1668 (2006)
6. Qiao, Y.C., Jiang, Q.S., Gu, L.: A fast similar module extraction method based on API sequence (2017)
7. Li, W.P., Zhao, J.F., Xie, B.: Summary extraction method for code topic based on LDA, **44**(4), 35–38 (2017)
8. Fournier-Viger, P., Lin, J.C.-W., Kiran, R., Koh, Y., Thomas, R.: A survey of sequential pattern mining. Data Sci. Pattern Recognit. **1**(1), 54–77 (2017)
9. Liu, J.B.: Procedure Blueprint Design Methodology. Science Press, Beijing (2005)
10. Liu, J.B., Li, J.Z., Yu, C.Y.: A software cyclomatic complexity metrics method based on procedure blueprint. Comput. Sci. **33**(6), 267–269 (2006)
11. Liu, J.B.: Program representation model and view derivation approach for procedure blueprint. Comput. Eng. **31**(13), 3017–3021 (2010)
12. Zhang, J., Wang, Y., Yang, D.: CCSpan: mining closed contiguous sequential patterns. Knowl.-Based Syst. **89**, 1–13 (2015)
13. Fournier-Viger, P., Gomariz, Gueniche, T., Soltani, A., Wu, C., Tseng, V.S.: SPMF: a Java open-source pattern mining library. J. Mach. Learn. Res. (JMLR) **15**, 3389–3393 (2014)
14. Zhang, H.Q.: The 150 Cases of Java. Metallurgical Industry Press, Beijing (2005)
15. Yin, J.P., Zhang, F.: Java Example. China Machine Press, Beijing (2009)
16. Java development combat: Tsinghua University Press, Beijing (2013)
17. Ye, H.Y.: Java Programming Practical Tutorial. Tsinghua University Press, Beijing (2010)
18. Yuan, H.Y.: One Hundred Cases of Java Utility Design. Posts and Telecom Press, Beijing (2005)
19. Wang, X.P.: Computer Programming (Java). Publishing House of Electronics Industry, Beijing (2016)
20. Zhang, G.B.: Java Course Design Case Editing. Tsinghua University Press, Beijing (2011)
21. Zheng, L.: Java Course Design. Tsinghua University Press, Beijing (2007)
22. Li, Z.X.: Java Programming Experiment and Course Design Tutorial. Tsinghua University Press, Beijing (2011)

Mining the Contributions Along the Lifecycles of Open-Source Projects

Hang Zhou[1,2], Lei Xu[1,2(✉)], and Yanhui Li[1,2]

[1] State Key Laboratory for Novel Software Technology, Nanjing, China
[2] Department of Computer Science and Technology,
Nanjing University, Nanjing, China
xlei@nju.edu.cn

Abstract. Recently the impact of developers' behavior on the evolution of open-source software (OSS) has become a hot topic. When does the developer commit his/her code? Is there any regularity of the time distribution of commit along the lifecycles of open-source project? Will the change of the core member in a development team has an impact on software evolution process? We are quite interested in these above questions so we conducted an empirical study in this paper. We collect more than 50,000 commits from 6 open-source software in Github and design a formula to measure the contributor's contribution value. We then take four major experiments to analyze some issues about inert intervals and the impact of the change of main contributors on software evolution. To make the result visible, we also design an automatic mining tool which can automatically mine the metadata from specified repository and make it graphically presented. Through the experiments we gained some interesting findings such as there is no inevitable statistical connection between a contributor's inert interval and his contribution value, and main contributors' change has a huge impact on the software evolution. We believe that these findings will have deeper research significance in the future.

Keywords: Code repository mining · Open source software · Github

1 Introduction

Software has become a major part of the economic and civilized life of mankind. Over the past decades, the software development environment has gradually been open sourced and cooperated, and the distributed version control system Git borned at the same time. A software process is a collection of activities that are implemented during the software lifecycle. Activities are collections of tasks, and tasks act to process inputs into outputs. The software evolution process, as a branch of the software process, is also a software process that attempts to establish a unified process framework for the software evolution process by managing some of the more difficult activities in the software evolution process.

© Springer Nature Singapore Pte Ltd. 2019
Z. Li et al. (Eds.): NASAC 2017/2018, CCIS 861, pp. 145–160, 2019.
https://doi.org/10.1007/978-981-15-0310-8_10

The goal of the software evolution process is to manage the evolution process of the software system without violating the constraints of the system [10], so that the evolved software system can meet the user's needs in function, and at the same time, the quality attributes it shows are maintained at a satisfactory level. So how to guide software to evolve in a positive and correct direction has always been a major issue for researchers nowadays [2].

We are quite interested about the behavioral characteristics that developers shows when they contribute in an open-source software. We believe that this feature will directly affect the software development process. So specifically, what is the behavioral characteristics of contributors? For instance, the commit time distribution of contributors in the open-source software life cycle is not completely continuous. We define a inert interval as the max time period for each contributor to be inactive during the life cycle of open-source software. And we designed a measure of a contributor's contribution value which will be detailed in Sect. 2.4. Does the contribution value of contributors has a certain relationship with the time gap of leaving the project? From an intuitive point of view, the inert interval and the contributor's contribution value may have a certain relationship, that is, we can easily think that contributors with large contribution values seem to be more diligent, which make the inert interval smaller than the contributor who get a lower contribution value. On the other hand, we define the main contributors as contributors who have contributed more than half of the time to participate in project development for a certain period of time. What will happen in the open-source software project evolution when the main contributors have changed? With these questions above we conduct an empirical study on the impact of contributors' behavioral characteristics on open-source software and the experimental result will benefit future research in this filed:

Benefit 1. The experimental results analyze the contribution characteristics of contributors from the time distribution of contributor contribution, the inert interval and the changes of the main contributors for the first time, so as to analyze its influence on the software evolution process. The results will play an important role in future software maintenance, improving development efficiency, and planning evolution routes.

Benefit 2. The experimental results will provide insights on the software development team configuration. We can get the contributor's basic contribution information such as the number of commits, the commit time, the number of lines of additions and deletions, etc. Then we can draw some chart to analyze the commit trend and calculate the contribution value of every contributor, so that we can get some insights on the main contributors of the project.

Despite the previous benefits, conducting such an empirical study perfectly is difficult, because it is challenging to implement the automatic tool. Checking thousands of commits and carrying out some statistical work manually is infeasible and time- consuming, so it is desirable to implement a support tool for mining the code repository automatically. To address the challenge, we implement a tool, called MCSV (Mining Contribution's Statistic information and Visualizing), which can automatically mine commits in an open-source project and preprocess it to get some statistical data and finally visualize it as the form of chart. With the support of MCSV, we conduct the empirical study to investigate the behavioral characteristics of the contributor.

The remainder of this paper is organized as follows. In Sect. 2 we describe our experimental methodology. Section 3 presents the results of our empirical study, including some key findings and implications. In Sect. 4 we discuss the threats to validity. We review the related work in Sect. 5 and finalize with our conclusions in Sect. 6.

2   Research Methodology

In this section, we first highlight our four research questions in Sect. 2.1. Then the automatic mining tool MCSV is introduced in Sect. 2.2. In Sect. 2.3 and Sect. 2.4, we describe the dataset and analysis methods used in our study respectively.

2.1   Research Questions

The development habits of contributors in different domains are different [22] and we believe that the inert intervals of contributors in a project can reflect the health of the project in some ways, in addition, we are interested in the emergence of inert intervals and the impact of changes in major contributors on project evolution. So we summarize four research questions as follows:

RQ1. What is the distribution of the inert intervals of contributors for different software development teams?

RQ2. What is the relationship between a contributor's inert interval and his contribution value?

RQ3. Are there any other factors that may affect inert interval besides the contribution value of contributor?

RQ4. What is the impact of changes in the main contributors in the first half and the second half of the project's lifecycle on project evolution?

2.2   MCSV

To reduce the manual effort for mining commit and collection of statistical data, and at the same time in order to accurately locate the distribution and length of inert intervals of contributors in a given period of time, and to rank contributors directly according to our definition of contribution degree, we implement an automatic mining and visualizing tool called MCSV based on a Java web framework called Wicket [6].

The framework of MCSV is shown in Fig. 1. For each project under Git control, we mine all commits from the source code repository by using the Java library function called JGit, which is the java implementation of the version control software Git. Faced with massive commit data, the server system performs data sorting and composing, what's more, we use some Java serialization techniques to maintain data persistence. Note that we choose Xodus database,

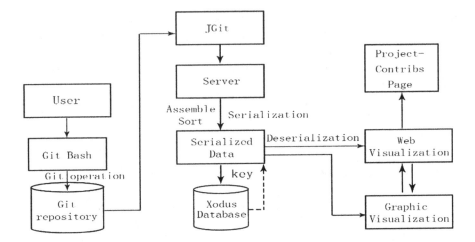

Fig. 1. Framework oF MCSV.

a pure Java-written, modeless embedded high-performance database to store the data. We chooses the Xodus database not only because its modeless can avoid the trouble of mode reconstruction, but also its zero deployment features are easy to manage. Then MCSV abstracts the data into components defined in Wicket, combining some JavaScript libraries and Ajax operations to draw a variable-precision contribution graph in a webpage. And the user interface of MCSV is shown in Fig. 2.

When the Git project is pushed in our system, the MCSV will catch the every single commit information including the commit time, commit author, commit content, the number of lines of additions and deletions automatically and rapidly, then it will draw a contribution overview graph and a contribution trend graph for each contributor respectively. We have added a lot of practical and operable functions. In the ten boxes in the Fig. 2, Box A is the name of the project, Box B is a navigation bar, notice that we implemented a drop-down selection box in Box C to draw three different contribution graphs ordered by commits, additions and deletions, Box D shows the commit information, we implement a slidable time interval which can be shown in Box E and Box J, users can choose the specific period and the variable-precision contribution trend graph are shown the next seconds after choosing the interval. Besides, the interval chosen in overview graph will have a direct impact on every contributor contribution graph, which is very convenient to examine the contributions of all contributors over a certain period of time. In addition, the time interval text, contributor's name, the numbers of commits, additions and deleitions, and the rank of the contributors are shown in Box F, G, H, I.

Table 1. Descriptive information of the studied projects

Project	LOC	Years	Commits	Contributors	Files	Language
RxJava	405804	6.2	5346	200	1626	Java
Guava	770706	8.9	4698	141	3239	Java
Caffe	100556	4.3	4128	267	697	C++, Python
tensorflow	2547749	2.7	32625	1453	11131	C++, Python
D3	53982	7.3	4138	122	43	JavaScript
Leaflet	164847	7.3	6553	567	449	JavaScript

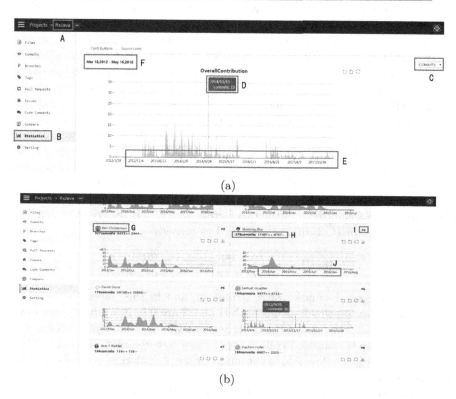

Fig. 2. User interface of MCSV

2.3   Dataset

To mining the code repository and investigate the behavioral characteristics of contributor, we selects 6 of the top 10 on Github's 2017 popularity projects in different domains including RxJava and Guava (Java project), Caffe and tensorflow (deep learning project), D3 and Leaflet (data visualization project). The selection of data sets is mainly selected from three different fields: integrated Java library, Deep Learning framework and data visualization library, and the main programming languages used are also different, mainly considering eliminating the impact of some extent the particularity of the results and of different fields and different programming languages on software evolution. Besides, the years and domains of these projects make a big difference in their evolutionary trends. We collect the lines of code, project time, the number of commits, contributors and files, which are shown in Table 1.

2.4 Research Methods

Before answering 4 research questions listed before, we first need to specify a unified measure of contribution value of each contributor. The contributor's contribution value measure mainly uses the project's commit data, which refers to the information submitted by the project from the beginning of the evolution so far, that is, from the first commit of the project to the time of the experiment. Each commit that is fetched includes the submitted version number, submitter information, submission time, modified file and content, and modified file line count (addition and deletè). Gousios et al. [7] combined the research of code and non-code contribution and proposed a complex measurement system, which is different from the traditional simplest and most intuitive contribution measure value of the contributor that only use the LOC (Lines Of Code). Combined with the actual research situation of this paper, we mainly consider the measure of the number of commits and the number of modified lines of code. Note that the number of modified lines is the accumulation of addition lines and deletion lines. Considering the weight α, β of the two factors above, and the contribution from the i-th contributor (C_value) we designed as follows:

$$C\_value(i) = \alpha \frac{LOC(i)}{\sum LOC(n)} + \beta \frac{Commit(i)}{\sum Commit(n)} \qquad (1)$$

Where n is the total number of contributors, and in this paper the weight is considered the same, which means both α and β are 0.5. It is worth mentioning that for a project, the sum of the contributions values of all contributor is 1.

To answer RQ1, we need collect every contributor's inert interval in the 6 open-source projects. We add some appropriate calculation code to the tool implementation to calculate the contribution value for each contributor and record the longest time they left the project. Although we can get the lazy range for each contributor in different projects, it is still not feasible to get some objective laws from such a pair of data manually. Since the contributors in each project are inconsistent, considering the universality and credibility of the results, we use the a random sample method to calculate the sample capacity [13]. And then we randomly select samples of size calculated from the 6 projects. To observe the distribution of these samples carefully, we plot boxplot and scatter plots in the same rectangular coordinate system and the results will be shown in Sect. 3.

In RQ2, we want to study the relationship between contributors' contribution values and their inertia intervals, so a very intuitive way is to count each contributor's contribution value and inertia interval in each project and draw them in the same coordinate system, then observe the direction of the two curves. It is well known that there are a large number of one time contributors(OTC) in each project, so our approach is to select the top 100 contributors in each project, if there is an OTC, then filter it out. And the graph and the result will be shown in Sect. 3.

In RQ3, we want to study what factors are possible for the occurrence of inertia intervals besides the contribution values of contributors. First of all, we want to know the relationship between the rest period of the whole project and the inert interval distribution of the contributors. The rest period is the time when the project does not receive any contributor's commit. This problem is very easy to solve, just counting the number of contributors who get an inert interval in the project's rest period. At the same time, we are more interested in the way each contributor returns to the project after the end of the inert interval. For this, we have designed a semi-automated approach. We counted the commit log information when each contributor returned to the project, then partitioned the every words and counted the frequency of each word. Finally, we conducted a manual review to find some key words to infer the reasons for the occurrence of inert intervals. Our results and findings will be shown in Sect. 3.

To investigate the impact of change of the main contributors on software evolution in RQ4, we use a new graphical form [21] in which we equally divide the time, and draw a vertical line in the time of receiving a commit in the project. The vertical line in the graph represents the contribution in the project, and the blank area between the lines is the period in which the project receive no commits from any contributors at the same time. We can represent different contributors's contribution at a certain time with dots in different colors in the graph at the same time, the advantage of which is that we can use the density of these dots to explore changes in the main contributors of the project. Since we investigate the main contributors, contributors with lower contribution values are almost impossible to be main contributors to the project, and OTCs who even doesn't have a inert interval, is common in every project, so we can just draw the top 10 contributors' commit dot on their project commit graph so that we can judge the main contributors and their changes according to the intensity of the points and time distribution of the points. The new graph and the result will be shown in Sect. 3.

3 Experimental Results

In this section, we present the experimental results in detail for each research question. For each of the four research questions, we decompose the results through a series of findings and implications.

3.1 RQ1

To investigate the similarities that distribution of contributors' inert intervals shows across different software development teams, we randomly sample from thousands of contributor inert intervals and plot the box plots and scatter plots of the six samples in the same coordinate system and the result is shown in Fig. 3. Observing and analyzing distributions of the points in Fig. 3, we can get some interesting findings:

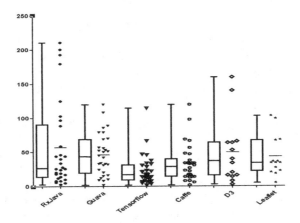

Fig. 3. Inert interval box-plot graph.

Finding 1: There are some contributors who have left the project for more than 100 days in each project may return to the project again.

Finding 2: There are short-term development contributors for each project, making the inert interval very small.

Finding 3: The median of the inertia of the project is basically concentrated in the region of 20–40 days.

Finding 4: The inert interval distribution is related to the field of the project.

3.2 RQ2

To investigate the issues about the distribution of inert intervals and the relationship between the inert intervals and contribution value, We calculated the contribution value and inert intervals of top 100 contributors ranked by contribution value from studied projects, and screened out OTCs of every project. And the graph is shown in Fig. 4.

Observing from the trend of the two curves of the studied projects in the above graph, we can get the followings findings in common:

Different from our previous speculation that the greater the contributor's contribution value, the smaller the lazy range. Of course, for the core members of the team, the Top 3 contributors of the project have a relatively small inert interval, but unexpectedly, there are some contributors with lower contribution value also have smaller inert intervals, which proves our incorrect inference talked in Sect. 2. Besides, we also take the contribution values of the contributor and

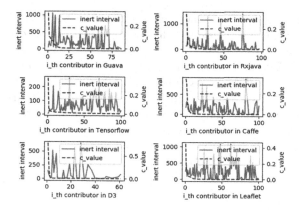

Fig. 4. Inert interval and C-Value graph.

their inert intervals into calculation of Spearman's correlation coefficient [14], the result of which turn out very low generally. What's more, we find that the trends of the c-value curve are very similar among the 6 projects and satisfy the long tail effect. So we can conclude the following findings to answer the RQ2.

Finding 5: There is no necessary connection between the contribution value and the inert interval of a specific contributor.

Finding 6: The c-value curve of each project shows a long tail effect. The contribution value of the main contributors and other contributors differs significantly, while it of other contributors is not significant.

Implication 1: The contribution value of the contributor is not necessarily related to his inert interval. For a contributor who get high contribution value, he may have been diligent in his contribution cycle so he may get a smaller inert interval, or he may get a larger inert interval resting for a period of time after the end of an engineering cycle. For a contributor with a small contribution value, he may be a less diligent person leading to a larger inert interval, or he may get a small interval for his hardworking in a very small commit period.

3.3 RQ3

We first study the relationship between the distribution of contributors' inert intervals and project inert intervals by simply count the times they overlap. And we found that most top 10 contributors' inert interval lie in the longest project's inert interval. Then we extracted the commit submission information from each contributor which is just after their inert interval and we then performed a semi-automatic detection. We have an automated word frequency count for each word in the commit information, and then manually review the commit and word frequency. We found a high frequency of words like "ADD", "FIX" and "REMOVE" in the commits information of contributors returning to projects in each project. So we conclude the following findings to answer the RQ3.

Finding 7: The project's inert interval is often the inert interval of the contributor, and the contribution of the core members of the team is important to the project.

Finding 8: A large proportion of contributors return to the project with Bug Fix operation, and ADD and REMOVE act second.

Implication 2: We speculate that there may be two reasons for this team member and project's inert interval overlap: one is that the current branch task is completed and the next branch task has not been developed, causing the current project to appear stagnant; the second is that the current branch bug has not been found yet which cause that there is currently no work to be done, and once a certain point in time is discovered, each member is required to participate in the modification of multiple codes.

3.4   RQ4

To investigate the impact of the main contributor's change on software evolution we designed a graph on which we draw contributor' commits. Like we have discussed in Sect. 2, we draw 6 graphs to analyze the change of the main contributor. Take RxJava as an example, we first collect the top 10 contributors ranked by the contribution value and the basic information of them are shown in Table 2 And the barcode graph are drawn for these 10 contributors which is shown in Fig. 5.

Table 2. Information of the contributors in RxJava

Contributor	Total commits	Earliest commit	C-value
benjchristensen	1046	2013/1/9	0.19566
akarnokd	815	2013/11/19	0.15245
zsxwing	275	2013/9/16	0.05144
DavidMGross	170	2013/5/29	0.031799
samuelgruetter	154	2013/9/6	0.028807
jmhofer	130	2013/3/26	0.024317
AppliedDuality	107	2013/11/20	0.020015
davidmoten	102	2014/2/14	0.01908
JakeWharton	73	2015/10/16	0.013655
mairbek	72	2013/2/7	0.013468

Observing Fig. 5, we can see that the project is divided into two phases based on the inert interval of the project. According to the intensity and distribution of the observation points, we can judge that the main contributors in the first half of the project are mainly Benjchristensen (#1), akarnokd (#2), zsxwing (#3), DavidMGross (#4) these four contributors. It is worth mentioning

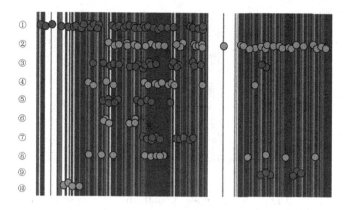

Fig. 5. Top 10 contributors's commit in Rxjava.

that these four are also the top four contributors of the entire project. Subsequently, the project experienced a period of almost half a year of contribution to the cold period, during which only akarnokd (#2) contributed a small amount. Since then, in the second half of the project, main contributors have undergone important changes, from the original four to akarnokd (#2) only, and the main contributors who contributed the most in the first half did not even participate in the development of second half of the project. Caffe and Leaflet is similar to RxJava that the main contributors have also changed. We found that the contribution values of several main contributors to RxJava and Caffe are very close, which indicates that the relationship between them may be a collaborative relationship rather than a management relationship. In Leaflet there is only a main contributor in the first phrase and another one in the latter phrase.

Unlike RxJava, the main contributors to the Guava project and the D3 project didn't change in the whole lifecycle. The three main contributors of the Guava contribution developed throughout the entire project development process, while the D3 project has only one main contributor from start to the end. It is worth mentioning that the Top 1 contributor of the Guava project not only participated in the whole process development, but also had a small inert interval and contributed more than the sum of the other two main contributors, which is a "leading phenomenon". In addition, from the contribution trend of the project, we found three different types of contribution evolution trends, which are stable type, increasing type and decline type. The three evolution trends are shown in Fig. 6.

The project with stable evolution characteristics is Guava. And the contribution trends in the whole period are basically the same. We speculate it may result from the fact that the main contributors of Guava's remain unchanged and no significant changes happen in configuration of the team. While Tensorflow is a typical increasing type mainly because the current stage is the hot period of deep learning, and the commit numbers has been on the rise. The remaining 4 projects' contribution trends show some decline characteristics. Among Caffe

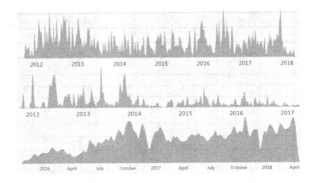

Fig. 6. Three types of contribution trends.

and RxJava, most contributors are only involved in the first half of the development. We speculate that the result of this phenomenon may due to significant changes in the internal structure of the team. However, this phenomenon in D3 and Leaflet can be related to the project background, since the age of the projects is relatively long, and most basic development is completed in the first half of the period, which cause the latter half tends to be stable. So we finally got the finding and implication as follows:

Finding 9: Changes in the main contributors of the team will change the evolution of the entire project

Implication 3: The change of core member configuration and the age of the project as well as the domain of the project will play an important role in software evolution together. A positive change may lead the software to evolve in a healthier direction.

4   Threats to Validity

In this section, we discuss the main threats to the construct, internal, and external validity of our study.

4.1   Threats to Construct Validity

The most important threat to construct validity in our experiments is the accuracy of the calculation of the inert interval. We choose the longest time that the contributor leave the project as his inert interval, however, for that contributors who commit just once in the project lifecycle, the length of the interval we get is 0. So we just eliminate all one time contributor in the 6 projects in our experiments.

4.2   Threats to Internal Validity

The internal threat mainly comes from that we did not select the data of each project in the same time period considering the impact of different eras on the experimental results, but we just select the data of their entire life cycle. This may affect the conclusions of the experiment in some respects but since we are studying some behavioral characteristics of contributors during the life cycle of each project, we just ignore this factor. Besides, in the measurement of contributor's contribution value, without considering the subjective factors such as contributors' impact on the project, we only consider the number of commit and the number of modified lines of code of them, which may also have a certain influence on the experimental results. We use the longest commit-free time interval to represent the inert interval and to study the behavioral characteristics of contributors, which in some respects exists some certain randomness.

4.3   Threats to External Validity

Threats to external validity mainly concern the possibility to generalize our findings. In this study, we studied six widely used projects and exhausted our ability to cover various domains. Although we believe our results can reveal the characteristics of contributor's behavioral characteristics in many projects, we do not intend to draw general conclusions on all software, because of all the projects we studied are open source. Consequently, our findings may not be generalized to commercial software. More comprehensive and general results still require further case studies and a more wide variety of projects in the future works.

5   Related Work

5.1   Data Mining && Visualization Technology

As the size and amount of information of software projects continue to increase, complex data structures and multi-level algorithm design make the complexity of information increase, the intermediate results and final result data generated by software also increase exponentially. There comes a new problem: how do we get useful data quickly and correctly from massive data? And visualization technology is a very effective solution to this type of problem. Jonardo R, who have found a hidden model that can be used as a preventive measure by mining, analyzing and visualizing road traffic accident data: there is no significant correlation between the location of the accident and the mortality of the victim. On the other hand, the researchers also found that time and date play a crucial role in the fatality or severity of road traffic accidents, especially car crashes [1]. Yiran Shan et al. proposed a visualization method, which based on tree-layered interactive user interface when faced with the increasing number of biomedical data and how to use this large-scale data set to achieve the query of the relationship among goals, compounds and diseases. Basing on the correlation between them, the path width between the two biological entities is shown. So biomedical scientists can further study the potential relationship between the extended results [17].

5.2 Mining Software Repository

The mining software repositories (MSR) field analyzes and cross-links the rich data available in repositories to uncover interesting and actionable information about software systems. We can guide decision processes in modern software projects by transforming these repositories from static record-keeping ones into active repositories [9]. Leibzon et al. visualized the collaboration between core members into a more intuitive graph through the mining of the Github open source code repository, and combined with social network analysis methods to find core members of the team [12]. Williams et al. use the source code change history of a software project to drive and help to refine the search for bugs [20]. Ralph Peters et al. evaluate the lifespan of code smells using software repository mining [15]. Ariel Rodriguez analyzes the working habits of software developers and the effects these habits have on efficiency based on a large amount of data extracted from the actions of developers in the IDE [16]. Vladimir Kovalenko et al. who analyze over 1,400 Git repositories, evaluate the importance of proper handling of branches when calculating file modification histories, and they find that considering full file histories leads to an increase in the techniques' performance that is rather modest [11].

5.3 Software Evolution

Godfrey et al. explore the evolution of the Linux kernel both at the system level and within the major subsystems, and they discuss why they think Linux continues to exhibit such strong growth [19]. Emitza et al. used machine learning methods to automatically classify and rank 68,108 tweets on Twitter social networks, finding tweets related to software evolution, and combining short-term informal user feedback with social components into software evolution process [8]. Sneed et al. designed a tool for measuring software evolution, which is based on data analysis, and analyzed a series of data such as error report, defect location and bug repair report to describe the trend of software evolution [18].

For contributors, their abilities, willingness, and opportunities are considered to be three dimensions of interaction [3]. Curtis claims that individual differences between project personnel are the largest source of change in project performance [5]. Couger and Zawacki determined how the differences between programmers' motivational structures interacted with the types of work they assigned [4]. They found that programmers' demand for personal growth and personal development was higher than any other job category. Minghui Zhou et al. conducted a statistical analysis of the positive degree and community-oriented attitude of the team contributors in the first month of the project, and found that whether the team contributors can become long-term contributors (LTCs) relates to their wishes and surroundings [23]. It has been found that contributors who start participating in development with comments rather than reporting problems are more than twice as likely to become LTCs. These findings may provide the basis for empirical methods for designing better community architectures and improving the experience of contributors.

6 Conclusion

The impact of contributor's behavioral characteristics on software evolution is an innovative study. In this paper, we implement an automatic mining tool called MCSV, with the help of which we conduct an empirical study mainly on the issues about inert intervals and the change of main contributors. And finally we gained some valuable findings. We believe our observations will improve the understanding of the contributor's behavioral characteristics and software evolution and hence improve the efficiency and maintenance of software. In addition, the tool we introduced in this paper can be used as an aid to deeper research in the future.

Acknowledgement. This work is partially supported by the Natural Science Foundation of Jiangsu Province of China (Grant No. BK20140611), the Natural Science Foundation of China (Grant Nos. 61272080,61403187). All support is gratefully acknowledged.

References

1. Asor, J.R., Catedrilla, G.M.B., Estrada, J.E.: A study on the road accidents using data investigation and visualization in los baños, laguna, philippines
2. Bird, C., Rigby, P.C., Barr, E.T., Hamilton, D.J., German, D.M., Devanbu, P.: The promises and perils of mining Git. In: 6th IEEE International Working Conference on Mining Software Repositories, MSR 2009, pp. 1–10. IEEE (2009)
3. Blumberg, M., Pringle, C.D.: The missing opportunity in organizational research: some implications for a theory of work performance. Acad. Manag. Rev. **7**(4), 560–569 (1982)
4. Couger, J.D., Zawacki, R.A.: Motivating and Managing Computer Personnel. Wiley, New York (1980)
5. Curtis, B.: Fifteen years of psychology in software engineering: individual differences and cognitive science. In: Proceedings of the 7th International Conference on Software Engineering, pp. 97–106. IEEE Press (1984)
6. Dashorst, M., Hillenius, E.: Wicket in Action. Dreamtech Press (2008)
7. Gousios, G., Kalliamvakou, E., Spinellis, D.: Measuring developer contribution from software repository data. In: Proceedings of the 2008 International Working Conference on Mining Software Repositories, pp. 129–132. ACM (2008)
8. Guzman, E., Ibrahim, M., Glinz, M.: Mining twitter messages for software evolution. In: Proceedings of the 39th International Conference on Software Engineering Companion, pp. 283–284. IEEE Press (2017)
9. Hassan, A.E.: The road ahead for mining software repositories. In: Frontiers of Software Maintenance, FoSM 2008, pp. 48–57. IEEE (2008)
10. Honsel, V.: Statistical learning and software mining for agent based simulation of software evolution. In: Proceedings of the 37th International Conference on Software Engineering-Volume 2, pp. 863–866. IEEE Press (2015)
11. Kovalenko, V., Palomba, F., Bacchelli, A.: Mining file histories: should we consider branches? In: Proceedings of the 33rd ACM/IEEE International Conference on Automated Software Engineering, pp. 202–213. ACM (2018)

12. Leibzon, W.: Social network of software development at GitHub. In: Proceedings of the 2016 IEEE/ACM International Conference on Advances in Social Networks Analysis and Mining, pp. 1374–1376. IEEE Press (2016)

13. McIntyre, G.: A method for unbiased selective sampling, using ranked sets. Aust. J. Agric. Res. **3**(4), 385–390 (1952)

14. Mukaka, M.M.: A guide to appropriate use of correlation coefficient in medical research. Malawi Med. J. **24**(3), 69–71 (2012)

15. Peters, R., Zaidman, A.: Evaluating the lifespan of code smells using software repository mining. In: 2012 16th European Conference on Software Maintenance and Reengineering (CSMR), pp. 411–416. IEEE (2012)

16. Rodriguez, A., Tanaka, F., Kamei, Y.: Empirical study on the relationship between developer' s working habits and efficiency (2018)

17. Shan, Y., Wang, X.: Visualization of linked biomedical data using cluster chart. In: 2017 14th Web Information Systems and Applications Conference (WISA), pp. 293–296. IEEE (2017)

18. Sneed, H.M., Prentner, W.: Analyzing data on software evolution processes. In: 2016 Joint Conference of the International Workshop on Software Measurement and the International Conference on Software Process and Product Measurement (IWSM-MENSURA), pp. 1–10. IEEE (2016)

19. Tu, Q., et al.: Evolution in open source software: a case study. In: Proceedings of the International Conference on Software Maintenance, 2000, pp. 131–142. IEEE (2000)

20. Williams, C.C., Hollingsworth, J.K.: Automatic mining of source code repositories to improve bug finding techniques. IEEE Trans. Softw. Eng. **31**(6), 466–480 (2005)

21. Xu, B.: Visual mining of behavior characteristics of open source software developers. Ph.D. thesis, Shanghai Jiao Tong University (2013)

22. Ying, A.T., Wright, J.L., Abrams, S.: Source code that talks: an exploration of eclipse task comments and their implication to repository mining. ACM SIGSOFT Softw. Eng. Notes **30**, 1–5 (2005)

23. Zhou, M., Mockus, A.: What make long term contributors: willingness and opportunity in OSS community. In: Proceedings of the 34th International Conference on Software Engineering, pp. 518–528. IEEE Press (2012)

Issue Workflow Explorer

Jiaxin Zhu[1,2], Zhen Zhong[3,4], and Minghui Zhou[3,4(✉)]

[1] State Key Lab of Computer Science, Institute of Software,
Chinese Academy of Sciences, Beijing, China
`zhujiaxin@otcaix.iscas.ac.cn`
[2] University of Chinese Academy of Sciences, Beijing, China
[3] School of Electronics Engineering and Computer Science,
Peking University, Beijing, China
`{johnzz,zhmh}@pku.edu.cn`
[4] Key Laboratory of High Confidence Software Technologies,
Ministry of Education, Beijing, China

Abstract. Resolving issues is an essential part of Free/Libre and Open Source Software (FLOSS) development. For large and active projects, there could be hundreds of new issues reported every month, which have mixed quality. To deal with this complexity, the projects developed different protocols of resolving issues (i.e., issue workflows). To help understand existing practice and develop best practice, it's important to explore how the workflow evolves in the history, e.g., under what circumstances a particular workflow emerges, how efficient and effective it is and whether it can be improved. We build Issue Workflow Explorer (*IWE*) to help practitioners seek answers. Based on ubiquitous records in issue tracking system, *IWE* provides functionalities of discovering workflows, quantifying, visualizing and comparing their efficiency and effectiveness. We demonstrate *IWE*'s effectiveness with two large OSS projects, Mozilla and GNOME. We explore what workflows there are for issue triaging and handling of incomplete issues. We obtain helpful insights for future development, e.g., triage conducted by reporters themselves should be restricted and it is not cost-effective to keep incomplete issue reports open.

The source code of *IWE* is available at https://github.com/johnarseal/IWE.

Keywords: Issue tracking · Issue workflow ·
Mining software repositories

1 Introduction

To maintain high product quality, participants in Free/Libre and Open Source Software (FLOSS) projects constantly report and resolve issues of bugs, feature requests, etc. [12]. A number of facts make issue resolution a sophisticated task. In large and active projects, e.g., Gnome[1] and Mozilla[2], there are more

---

[1] https://www.gnome.org/.
[2] https://www.mozilla.org/en-US/.

© Springer Nature Singapore Pte Ltd. 2019
Z. Li et al. (Eds.): NASAC 2017/2018, CCIS 861, pp. 161–171, 2019.
https://doi.org/10.1007/978-981-15-0310-8_11

than one thousand new issue reports per month filed by various participants, including users and developers with diverse experience and skills, which lead to mixed report quality. Meanwhile, many of the reporters and developers in FLOSS projects voluntarily and some even occasionally participate, which brings more difficulties like unstable communications, lack of time and effort [12,13]. To address the complexities and difficulties and get issues properly resolved in time, projects develop issue workflow, i.e., the sequence of issue resolution steps, that allows participants to communicate with each other and to coordinate the tasks. The workflow has to evolve to stay efficient. For example, the Mozilla bugmaster meeting discussed how to adjust the strategy of issue triage to scale as more Mozilla teams and community members were engaging in triage[3]. This suggests the importance of understanding issue workflow.

However, the knowledge of issue workflow in practice is typically tacit. It is often neither known explicitly nor is accurately reflected in the meager documentation even when such documentation exists. For example, in Mozilla, the issue workflow easily confused a junior developer[4] even though it was posted on-line. While GNOME also defines standard triage steps on its website[5], they are not consistent with how triage is done in practice as illustrated in this paper.

Issue tracking systems such as Bugzilla[6], record history of how issue reports were resolved [5]. These data can be used by practitioners to review actual workflow they practiced in the past or to learn from others. It's always complicated to conduct such exploration with raw issue repositories. Effort of data collection, cleaning, sorting, aggregation, measurement and visualization is required [8]. To facilitate the investigations, we propose Issue Workflow Explorer (*IWE*). Based on issue tracking data, *IWE* offers functionalities of discovering, measuring and visualizing the issue workflows, and it quantifies how various workflows affect the lead time, complexity and output of the resolution process. By applying *IWE* to GNOME and Mozilla, we study two major concerns about issue workflow, issue triaging and handling of incomplete issue reports. Workflows with private triage vs. public triage, and leaving incomplete issue open vs. closing them, are discovered and evaluated. We obtain insights that triage conducted by reporters themselves should be restricted and it is not cost-effective to keep incomplete issue reports open. These studies demonstrate the ability of *IWE* to discover and evaluate different types of issue workflows.

The paper is organized as follows: Sect. 2 introduces the concept of issue workflow, Sect. 3 describes the design of *IWE*, Sect. 4 presents the empirical evaluation, and Sect. 5 demonstrates the detailed operations of *IWE*.

---

[3] https://old.etherpad-mozilla.org/bugmasters-meeting-20121220.

[4] https://groups.google.com/forum/?hl=de#!topic/mozilla.dev.platform/3DAYBckD2C4.

[5] http://live.gnome.org/Bugsquad/TriageGuide.

[6] https://www.bugzilla.org/.

2   Issue Workflow

In an issue workflow, issue reports transfer through a sequence of steps, e.g., submission, triaging, fixing, etc. Results of these steps are shown with status label in issue tracking systems. For example, in the standard workflow defined by GNOME (see Footnote 1), new filed issues should be labelled as *UNCON-FIRMED*. When a triager confirms it is a valid issue, its status changes to *NEW*. Alternatively, if it is, for example, a duplicate report, it may be immediately closed and its status changes to *RESOLVED*. When the report does not contain sufficient information for developers to reproduce and fix, the status would change to *NEEDINFO* waiting for the reporter or others to complete it. Issue reports in status *NEW* are to be assigned and resolved. The assignee may accept the report (status *ASSIGNED*), or pass it to someone else (remains in the status *NEW*), or resolve it (status *RESOLVED*). Finally, each *RESOLVED* report results in a resolution of *FIXED*, *DUPLICATE*, *INCOMPLETE*, or *INVALID*. In *IWE*, the issue workflows are described through transitions of these status.

3   Design of IWE

The basic goal of *IWE* is to simplify query and evaluation of issue workflows with the power of visualization [1,6] assisting practitioners to analyse previous issue resolution practices. We introduce four types of measures to evaluate issue workflows and design selectors and interactive views to conduct and visualize the measurements. The overview of the tool is shown in Fig. 1.

3.1   Measurements

Based on literature and our experience on investigating issue workflow (e.g., [16,17]), we introduce five measures to characterize issue workflows and quantify their efficiency and effectiveness.

The number of issue reports within a defined scope, e.g, modules, time span, is a basic metric to indicate the project workload, software quality [2,7], etc. We use it to measure the population trend of investigated issues, i.e., the number of reports with properties P_s, submitted or resolved during time span T (M1).

Status transitions tells what workflow practitioners follow to resolve the reports, and a number of studies have tried to model and present the transitions [2,14,16]. We measure the occurrence of a workflow through the number of selected issue reports that were transferred through status sequence S_s (M2).

People have shown great interest on the efficiency of time spent to resolve issue reports [7]. To address this concern, we calculate time spent on transition from the beginning to status S_e (M3).

Finally, the results and complexity of issue resolution process, e.g., whether they are fixed, determine the effectiveness of effort cost, which have also been paid attention to [3]. To address this concern, we calculate the fraction of reports with resolution result R (M4) and number of transitions a report experienced (M5).

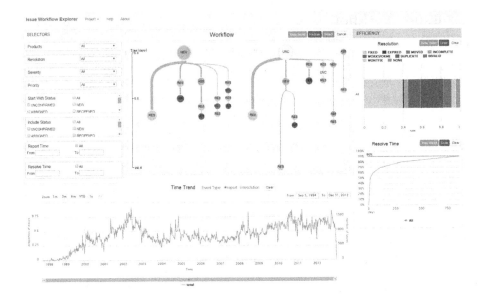

Fig. 1. Overview of *IWE*.

3.2 Selectors

We propose eight selectors for querying workflows. Users can customize the input of the views (introduced in Sect. 3.3) to direct or narrow down their exploration. Issue tracking systems, e.g., Bugzilla, define a number of fields[7] to describe the issue properties. We focus on the commonly used fields [11,15] and build the **products, severity and priority selector** to specify issue reports in which product with which severity and priority to investigate. The **transition selectors**, i.e., *starts with* and *includes*, pick out issue reports starting with or including the selected status for further investigation. Since workflow effectiveness is related to the issue resolution result, we make **resolution selector** to screen out issue reports ending with a specific result. The other two **time span selector**, i.e., *report time* and *resolve time*, are built to set the time span for choosing issue reports submitted or resolved within it.

3.3 Views

We design three views, which receive the input from selectors, for users to conduct the measurements and observe the results.

The **Workflow View** visualizes the measurements of issue population (M1), status transitions (M2), efficiency (M3) and effectiveness (M4). We present issue workflows, i.e., status transitions, in forms of trees. Thickness and length of the edges visually indicates the number of issue reports experiencing the transitions

---

[7] https://bugzilla.mozilla.org/page.cgi?id=fields.html.

and time cost respectively. The level of a leaf means the number of transitions that reports in this workflow experienced. Quantitative measures are shown in tips where time spent of each workflow is given by the first quartile, median and third quantile in addition to the mean in consideration of distribution bias. To support investigation of single workflow or part of it, we add selectors to pick it out as the input for the *Investigation View* and *Time Trend View*.

The **Investigation View** is built for studying the efficiency and effectiveness of selected workflows. It has two parts, *Resolution View* and *Resolve Time View*, to present measures of efficiency (M3) and effectiveness (M4) respectively. The *Resolution View* is a bar chart showing the fraction of issue reports with each result. The *Resolve Time View* is a line chart describing the fraction of reports resolved within the time indicated by X axis.

We design the **Time Trend View** to adjust measurements in *Workflow View* and *Investigation View* by time slots (e.g., days, weeks or months) on time line for investigating trends of those measures. The report time or resolution time option is used to decide which time slot a issue report belongs to, e.g., for a report which was submitted in day $d1$ and resolved in day $d2$, if report time is selected and time slot is day, the number of issue reports in day $d1$ plus one, otherwise, the number of reports in day $d2$ plus one. The indication of y axis differs when triggered by different views. It is number of reports of the selected workflow for *Workflow View*, fraction of fixed issued for *Resolution View* and number of days spent within 90% reports for *Resolve Time View*.

For comparing the efficiency, effectiveness and trend of different workflows, we remain recent measurement results in *Investigation* and *Time Trend* views.

4   Emprical Evaluation

To demonstrate *IWE*'s value of helping practitioners understand issue workflows, we study the following research questions.

RQ0: Can *IWE* help users discover and evaluate previous workflows in practice and get insights for future development? This is the over all question about effectiveness of the tool. We answer it by studying two major concerns of issue workflow, issue triaging and handling of incomplete issues.

RQ1: What manners are there for issue triage and what are their strength and weakness on efficiency and effectiveness? Issue triage has got wide attention from both practitioners (see Footnote 1) and researchers [9,17]. We expect to discover and evaluate workflows with different triage manners and get implications.

RQ2: What strategies are there for handling incomplete issue reports and what are their advantages and disadvantages? It is well known that many reporters voluntarily or occasionally participate in FLOSS projects. Therefore, the issue resolution process often stops and waits for responses from reporters or developers for a long time [16]. Similar with **RQ1**, we want to discover and evaluate workflows with different strategies for incomplete reports and obtain insights for improvement.

We use the issue tracking data of GNOME and Mozilla, two famous large scale FLOSS projects, from our previous study [18]. Both of them uses Bugzilla, and the issue repositories have 432K and 679K reports submitted in over 10 years. In the following, we study the above questions through *IWE*.

4.1   Issue Triage

Since issue tracking systems of FLOSS projects are open to everyone, a reporter may be the one who has little experience to properly file issues. As mentioned in Sect. 2, an inspection process is conducted by the community to filter the irrelevant reports, screen out reports needing additional information and assign remained ones to right product. Usually, projects set the status of *UNCON-FIRMED* for new reports, and after public triage, valid reports are transferred to *NEW* waiting for developers to fix the issues.

Workflow Discovery: Among the workflows of Mozilla and GNOME (Fig. 2(a) and (b)) presented by *IWE*, we find that not all the reports began with *UNCON-FIRMED*. It implies that trusted reporters were granted privilege to directly file a *NEW* or *ASSIGNED* report. Different from public triage, such triage is self-conducted by the reporters (private triage) who may be skilled developers. In the *Time Trend View*, we can see that private triage was periodically popular, which means these two projects have attempted and adjusted this manner for a long time. We speculate that **Hypothesis 1:** workflows with private triage could shorten the lead time of the resolution process when the triages are correct but increase the time and effort cost on the contrary.

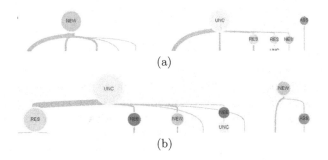

(a)

(b)

Fig. 2. Workflows of Mozilla and GNOME.

Efficiency and Effectiveness Exploring: To test Hypothesis 1, first, we study the Mozilla project. Selecting issue reports that started with *NEW* or *ASSIGNED* and those began with *UNCONFIRMED*, we evaluate these two types of workflows respectively through *Investigation View*. Figure 3 (a) shows the results, and we can see that reports through private triage were processed faster than those through public triage. However, when we restrict selection to reports that are judged as duplicated, i.e., we only include incorrect pri-vate triages, the results (see Fig. 3(b)) become opposite. Through looking at the

Workflow View, we find the reason that when the private triage was incorrect and the reports were assigned to developers, the resolution was delayed. This may also waste effort of those assigned developers. When we apply the same investigation on GNOME project[8], we get similar results. All the evidences support Hypothesis 1.

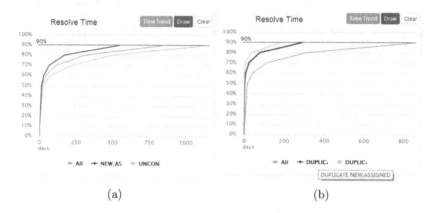

(a)   (b)

Fig. 3. Efficiency of different triage manners.

Insights: Through investigating the workflows and testing H1, we have answered RQ1. When properly applied, private issue triage could help community save effort and time in resolving issues, but it will bring side effect when the triage is wrong. Therefore, the privilege to conduct private triage should be strictly restrict to experienced developers. Meanwhile, developers should carefully do that.

4.2 Handling of Incomplete Reports

Less experienced reporters may file issue reports without enough information for developers to understand or reproduce the bug. Therefore, the resolution process must stop and wait for the reporters to come back and complete it. Too many stuck reports may overwhelm other reports, and projects need strategies to address this problem.

Workflow Discovery: In the workflows of GNOME presented by *IWE*, we find a status, *NEEDINFO*, which is used to label incomplete issue reports. However, workflows of Mozilla does not have this status. In Mozilla, incomplete reports are directly closed with the resolution of *INCOMPLETE*. If reporters come back and find the resolution, they may reopen it and provide additional information.

---

[8] GNOME has workflows with the specific status *NEEDINFO*, and they are not considered here because of the different strategies discussed in Sect. 4.2, which strongly impact the resolution time and may introduce bias.

In the *Time Trend View* of GNOME (Fig. 4), we observe that from October 2006 to November 2007, there were a great deal of reports resolved as *INCOMPLETE*, in particular, majority of the reports submitted before April 2007 experienced *NEEDINFO* while most of reports filed after that time did not. This suggests that the GNOME community decreased their use of *NEEDINFO* when there were too many incomplete reports. We searched the mailing list of GNOME and found an email which confirms this observation[9]. We propose **Hypothesis 2:** skipping *NEEDINFO* status and closing incomplete issues directly would reduce the resolve time and avoid retention of too many unresolved issues, while using *NEEDINFO* would make incomplete issues get sufficient information later.

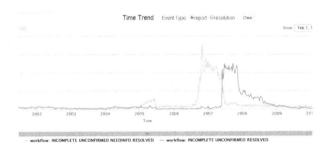

Fig. 4. Trend of incomplete issue reports.

Efficiency and Effectiveness Exploring: To inspect Hypothesis 2, we study the GNOME project which applied both of the strategies for incomplete reports. Targeting at reports resolved as incomplete, we select those went through *NEED-INFO* and those did not in *Workflow View*. Conducting measurement in *Investigation View*, we get the result that issue reports processed with the latter strategy were resolved much faster than the former (Fig. 5(a)). It offers evidence for the first half of **H2**. When no criteria are given, in *Investigation View* we can see that 14.3% of all the 432k issue reports, i.e., 62k reports, were finally incomplete (Fig. 5(b)). When we select issue reports that experienced *NEEDINFO*, we can see that 45.7% of the 71k reports were finally incomplete (Fig. 5(b)), i.e., only 54.3% of them got enough information. This evidence does not strongly support the second half of H2.

Insights: By exploring the workflows and testing H2, we have got answers for RQ2. To avoid blocking the resolution process and overwhelming other issues, skipping the *NEEDINFO* status would be the first choice. Using the *NEED-INFO* status cannot ensure that majority of the incomplete issues get sufficient information.

Through studying RQ1 and RQ2, the answer for RQ0 is clear, i.e., *IWE* can help users discover previous workflows in practice, evaluate their efficiency and effectiveness and get insights for future development.

---

[9] https://mail.gnome.org/archives/gnome-bugsquad/2007-April/thread.html.

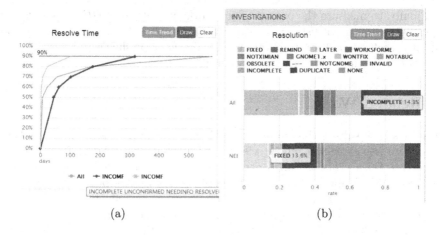

(a)   (b)

Fig. 5. Efficiency and effectiveness of strategies for incomplete reports.

5 Operations of IWE

We walk through the detailed operations of *IWE* to show its usability. We take the analysis conducted in Sect. 4.2 as an example.

First, we select the GNOME project through the drop-down list of *Project*.

Second, to measure the resolve time, we start from *Selectors* to specify the issue reports resolved as *INCOMPLETE* in the drop-down lists of *Resolution*. Through clicking the "Redraw" button in the *Workflow View*, *IWE* draws a workflow tree shown in Fig. 6 where there are two workflows, one has the *NEED-INFO* status, and the other one does not. On the workflow tree, we pick out the workflow with *NEEDINFO* status using the *Select* button. In the bottom half of *investigation View*, we click the *Draw* button to see time spent within this workflow. We measure resolve time using workflow without *NEEDINFO* status through similar steps. These results are presented in Fig. 5(a).

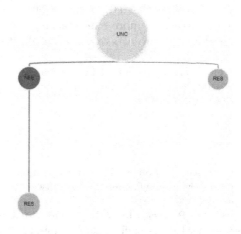

Fig. 6. Workflows end with *INCOMPLETE*.

Finally, to measure the output of the workflow with *NEEDINFO* status, we select with drop-down lists of *Include Status* and click *Draw* button in the top half of *Investigation View* to obtain the result, which is shown in Fig. 5(b).

Analysis of the result has been elaborated in Sect. 4.2.

6   Related Work

There has been substantial amount of work on developing approaches or tools to investigate issue tracking repositories in order to understand bug life-cycle and properties. Data visualization is a popular topic in this field and the approach proposed by D'Ambros et al. [2] was one of the early attempts. They proposed system level view which visualizes the distribution of open bugs in the components over time and bug level view for the status changing of a single bug. Similarly, Knab et al. visualized the effort measures, the sequence of issue resolving steps and the duration of each step [10]. Hora et al. proposed a tool to present the bugs in each class/package of a software system [7]. Different from [2], they detailed the change of number of bugs with version iteration and bug lifetime in each class. Gong and Zhang visualized the location of bugs in the system in a topographic map, where contour lines depict the number of bugs in each component/file [4]. Besides the visualization, Ripoche et al. proposed a generalized probabilistic network model in form of Markov model and probabilistic finite state automata (FSA) as a statistical and computational foundation for understanding bug fix process [14].

In this paper, we focus on issue workflow discovery and evaluation in a quantitative and visualized way to help practitioners make their decisions.

7   Conclusions

We build *IWE* to support exploring issue workflow. Providing practitioners with visualized measurements, *IWE* makes it easy to find out unsatisfactory workflows to improve. Empirical studies show that *IWE* achieves our goal. In future, we are going to make *IWE* compatible with more issue tracking systems and introduce it to both commercial and FLOSS projects to collect feedbacks for improvement.

Acknowledgements. This work is supported by the National Key R&D Program of China Grant 2018YFB1004201, the National Natural Science Foundation of China Grants 61802378, 61432001 and 61825201.

References

1. Ciani, A., Minelli, R., Mocci, A., Lanza, M.: Urbanit: visualizing repositories everywhere. In: 2015 IEEE International Conference on Software Maintenance and Evolution (ICSME), pp. 324–326 (2015)
2. D'Ambros, M., Lanza, M., Pinzger, M.: "A bug's life" visualizing a bug database. In: Visualizing Software for Understanding and Analysis, pp. 113–120. IEEE (2007)

3. Davies, S., Roper, M.: What's in a bug report? In: ESEM, p. 26. ACM (2014)

4. Gong, J., Zhang, H.: BugMap: a topographic map of bugs. In: FSE, pp. 647–650. ACM (2013)

5. Herzig, K., Zeller, A.: Mining bug data. In: Robillard, M.P., Maalej, W., Walker, R.J., Zimmermann, T. (eds.) Recommendation Systems in Software Engineering, pp. 131–171. Springer, Heidelberg (2014). https://doi.org/10.1007/978-3-642-45135-5_6

6. Hollan, J., Hutchins, E., Kirsh, D.: Distributed cognition: toward a new foundation for human-computer interaction research. ACM Trans. Comput. Human Interact. **7**(2), 174–196 (2000)

7. Hora, A., et al.: Bug maps: a tool for the visual exploration and analysis of bugs. In: Software Maintenance and Reengineering, pp. 523–526. IEEE (2012)

8. Howison, J., Conklin, M., Crowston, K.: FLOSSmole: a collaborative repository for floss research data and analyses. Int. J. Inf. Technol. Web. Eng. **1**(3), 17–26 (2008)

9. Jeong, G., Kim, S., Zimmermann, T.: Improving bug triage with bug tossing graphs. In: Proceedings of the the 7th Joint Meeting of the European Software Engineering Conference and the ACM SIGSOFT Symposium on the Foundations of Software Engineering, pp. 111–120. ACM (2009)

10. Knab, P., Pinzger, M., Gall, H.C.: Visual patterns in issue tracking data. In: Münch, J., Yang, Y., Schäfer, W. (eds.) ICSP 2010. LNCS, vol. 6195, pp. 222–233. Springer, Heidelberg (2010). https://doi.org/10.1007/978-3-642-14347-2_20

11. Lamkanfi, A., Demeyer, S., Giger, E., Goethals, B.: Predicting the severity of a reported bug. In: 2010 7th IEEE Working Conference on Mining Software Repositories (MSR), pp. 1–10. IEEE (2010)

12. Mockus, A., Fielding, R.T., Herbsleb, J.D.: Two case studies of open source software development: Apache and mozilla. ACM Trans. Soft. Eng. Methodol. **11**(3), 309–346 (2002)

13. Rigby, P.C., Storey, M.A.: Understanding broadcast based peer review in OSS. In: International Conference on Software Engineering (2011)

14. Ripoche, G., Gasser, L.: Scalable automatic extraction of process models for understanding F/OSS bug repair. In: ICSSEA (2003)

15. Tian, Y., Lo, D., Xia, X., Sun, C.: Automated prediction of bug report priority using multi-factor analysis. Empirical Soft. Eng. **20**(5), 1354–1383 (2015)

16. Xie, J., Zheng, Q., Zhou, M., Mockus, A.: Product assignment recommender. In: ICSE Formal Demonstrations. pp. 556–559. ACM, New York, NY, USA (2014). https://doi.org/10.1145/2591062.2591073, http://doi.acm.org/10.1145/2591062.2591073

17. Xie, J., Zhou, M., Mockus, A.: Impact of triage: a study of Mozilla and gnome. In: ESEM, Baltimore, Maryland, USA, pp. 247–250, 10–11 October 2013

18. Zhou, M., Mockus, A.: Who will stay in the FLOSS community? Modeling participant's initial behavior. IEEE Trans. Softw. Eng. **41**(1), 82–99 (2015)

Author Index

Printed in the United States
By Bookmasters